J. Ewing (James Ewing) Ritchie

British Senators: Or, Political Sketches, Past and Present

J. Ewing (James Ewing) Ritchie

British Senators: Or, Political Sketches, Past and Present

ISBN/EAN: 9783337156107

Printed in Europe, USA, Canada, Australia, Japan

Cover: Foto ©Suzi / pixelio.de

More available books at **www.hansebooks.com**

BRITISH SENATORS:

OR,

POLITICAL SKETCHES,

PAST AND PRESENT.

BY

J. EWING RITCHIE.

" For these are the men that when they have played their parts, and had their exits, must step out and give the moral of their scenes, and deliver unto posterity an inventory of their virtues and vices."—Sir Thomas Browne.

LONDON:
TINSLEY BROTHERS, 18, CATHERINE STREET, STRAND.
1869.

TO

EBENEZER HOMAN, Esq.,

THIS BOOK IS GRATEFULLY,

AND WITH MUCH ESTEEM,

Dedicated.

PREFACE.

THE writer has a few words of explanation to offer.

This book consists of sketches, some of which appeared some years ago, and which have been by many subsequent writers so widely adapted—one gentleman in particular taking page after page without the slightest acknowledgment or sign of quotation; others, merely terming the writer "an intelligent auditor," that to assure himself of his own identity he has reproduced them, with others written and published at a later date—of Members of Parliament, who, if they do not come under the denomination of "Modern Statesmen," may yet be described as British Senators. Of many here delineated, some have ceased to be M.P.'s, others have become Peers, others are deceased,—on the whole, however, the writer has thought it best to let the sketches remain, with some slight alterations, as they were originally written.

One word more. This book is not intended for clever critics, but for country people who like to know a little about Members of Parliament and the way in which they transact business. The reader will also please to remember that when these sheets were passing through the press a change occurred—the effect of which has been to place on one side of the Speaker's chair those whom the author in his want of political foresight had seated on the other.

IVY COTTAGE, BALLARD'S LANE, FINCHLEY.
Dec. 21, 1868.

CONTENTS.

CHAPTER I.

CHAPTER II.

CHAPTER III.

CHAPTER IV.

CHAPTER V.

CHAPTER VI.

CHAPTER VII.

CHAPTER VIII.

CHAPTER IX.

BRITISH SENATORS.

CHAPTER I.

INSIDE THE HOUSE.

PARLIAMENT has met; and it is scarcely necessary to observe that its proceedings have seldom been regarded with greater curiosity or interest. The people have unmistakeably declared themselves in favour of Mr. Gladstone and his measures. I propose, then, gentle and intelligent reader, to get you into the House of Commons, not by means of bribery, or corruption, or intimidation; and to give you an idea of what it is like, and how its proceedings are carried on.

Let us assume, then, we have made our way, with a Member's order, as far as Westminster Palace. The House commences at four, but if the business of the evening promises to be of interest you had better be there some hours previously, as each Member has the right to give an order, and the chances are that five or six times more tickets have been given than the Strangers' Gallery can hold. You will then be stowed away in a cellar under the care of the police, and as it is too dark to read, and in summer time too sultry to talk, your chief amusement will consist in sucking oranges, of which I beg you to have enough. Happily there is an end to all things, even to the dreary waiting for a place in Parliament. A little before four you will hear the tinkling of a bell, which indicates the Speaker, preceded by the mace and followed by the train-bearer and chaplain (the latter looking as if the place agreed with him), has marched through the lobby, greatly to the astonishment of the vulgar, has entered the House, and is now at prayers. That operation over, the Strangers' Gallery is opened, in small detachments you are marched up to it, and you are inside the House.

Let us look about us. It is certainly an elegant and spacious chamber, not gorgeously ornamented, but looking what an Englishman always likes to see, thoroughly respectable. Just before you is the Speaker's Gallery, the occupants of which have comfortable cushioned seats,—here in the Strangers Gallery we have only the bare boards to sit on; before them is another gallery, devoted to ambassadors and peers, and on each side are galleries, generally empty, where members come and have a quiet nap, or a little gossip, and which are crowded only when a great crisis is at hand, and the House is thronged and expectant. Exactly opposite the gallery in which we are seated is that devoted to reporters. It has two rows: in the front sit the reporters actually engaged; behind are those who are waiting to take their places. Each reporter in the front row has a cosy little box to himself. Altogether there may be about thirty present. They are taking it easy now; they will have to work hard enough by-and-by. Above the reporters there is a lattice-work partition, behind which we can see faintly the dim outline of female forms; and if you chance to be in the Reporters' Gallery under, you will occasionally hear the murmur of melodious voices. Before the new House was built, ladies had to resort to odd stratagems to get inside. An old lady of my acquaintance, when a girl, often attended parliamentary debates, but then she adopted male attire, and did not wear a chignon! And now let us look a little higher, and glance at the ceiling. It is formed of beautifully stained glass, and when the shades of evening draw nigh it is lighted up as if by enchantment, and sends down upon all a flood of mellowed light, clearer and brighter than what may, by a stretch of courtesy and imagination, be denominated as that of day.

But it is time we look at the Commons themselves. There they are before us, the real rulers of England, and of that world-wide realm which owns an English Queen and speaks the English tongue. Most of them are gentlemen and men of honour, and have little to fear from an enlarged constituency, or from the rapid growth of democratic power. Old families and territorial traditions will always have weight in this land of ours. During the Regency, who was the champion of the people? Sir Francis Burdett. Was not Charles James Fox the son of a peer? Who rejected Burke? The tradesmen of Bristol. When the battle of Reform was fought under William IV., by whom did the nation swear but by the aristocrat Lord John Russell, and that still greater aristocrat Earl Grey? In our time, who fought the battle of the factory children better than Lord Ashley, now the Earl of Shaftesbury? Under any measure of Reform, we believe that the House of Commons will be as truly national an assembly as ever.

Seated in his chair of state, wearing wig and gown, is the Speaker—a gentleman of commanding presence and of good voice, and whose power of endurance must be far greater than yours or mine, as he has to sit out the long weary debates, and has to maintain order all the while. Nearly a hundred years ago a wit in the Rolliad wrote of the Speaker:—

> "There Cornwall sits, and oh, unhappy fate!
> Must sit for ever through the long debate.
> Painful pre-eminence! he hears, 'tis true,
> Fox, North, and Burke—but hears Sir Joseph, too.
> Like sad Prometheus fastened to his rock,
> In vain he looks for pity to the clock;
> In vain the effect of strengthening porter tries,
> And sends to Bellamy for fresh supplies."

And the language is applicable now. In front and beneath the Speaker are two or three clerks, who keep the records of the House, and store the petitions and other papers members bring them, in large bags provided for the purpose. In front of the clerks is a massive table, at the end of which lies the mace, and on which are the mysterious-looking boxes on which Ministers are so fond of thumping when an oratorical climax has been achieved. On each side are ranges of gradually ascending benches for the Ministerial and Opposition Members. The front row is occupied by the respective leaders, Mr. Disraeli sitting in the middle, on the right-hand side of the Speaker; and on the left, exactly opposite, Mr. Gladstone. Mr. Goschen generally sits near the latter, while Sir J. Pakington and Sir S. Northcote support the former. Just underneath the Strangers' Gallery is the bar of the House, and the seat where is placed in full evening dress, with a sword by his side, the Sergeant-at-Arms ready to protect the mace and Speaker at the peril of his life, or take into custody refractory, chiefly Irish, M.P.'s. At the further end, but excluded from the stranger's view, are a few rows of benches set aside for the accommodation of peers or the sons of peers; and where, if you are lucky enough ever to find your way, you can hear and see better than you can anywhere else. Almost on a line with the mace is a division of the benches on which the members are seated. Those of them on the seats nearest us in the Strangers' Gallery are said to sit below the gangway. Their occupants are chiefly on the Ministerial side—Irish M.P.'s—and on the Opposition side the more advanced Liberals, such as John Bright, his brother Jacob, Mr. Bazley, James White, Peter Taylor, and many of the Dissenting M.P.'s, who, if not seated below the gangway, generally sit as near to it as possible, as if for the purpose of reminding the Liberals they had better mind how they deal with Church questions. Mr. Horsman complained last year that he and his friends had not a place to themselves. This was true, but generally the Cave Adullamites were seated below the gangway just in front. All eyes turn anxiously in this direction. All strangers ask at once for Mr. Bright; next to him, I think, as objects of attraction, are the chiefs of parties—pre-eminently, of course, Mr. Gladstone and Mr. Disraeli. The latter has an imperturbable face. It is rarely it gives any signs of feeling. Nothing seems to excite his interest or attention, except when he darts upon his legs. The former is far more eager and excitable; his vitality is almost irrepressible. Leaning forward—with pen and paper in hand—he seems to watch and take note of everything. Last session strangers saw Mr. Mill, Mr. Roebuck, and Mr. Bernal Osborne—now banished—thanks to the fickleness of the democracies of Westminster, and Nottingham, and Sheffield.

And now let us see how they manage their business in St. Stephen's. As we have entered early, petitions are being presented. The Speaker names a gentleman; he rises, reads the name of the petition he has to present; the Speaker then, unless opposition be manifested, orders that "it do lie upon the table,"—in reality it is, as we have already said, popped into the bag. The petitions over, then comes the time for asking Ministers questions, more or less unpleasant, and to give notices of motion. The House then begins its discussions on the various Bills before it, and while little men are speaking, the House thins off and goes to dine. Later in the evening it gets better filled again, and if the leading members speak they are listened to with all the attention they deserve. At other times the buzz of conversation often overpowers the voice of the orator; and especially during the time allotted to private Bills or presenting petitions is the inattention of the House to what is going on very manifest. As a rule, the debates are orderly enough, and there is something grand in the cheers which greet the orator as he makes a hit in debate or resumes his seat after an eloquent harangue. As a rule also it may be added that it is only easy to get into the House when there is scarcely anything worth hearing, and that when you are there, as soon as you have satisfied your curiosity, and had a good look at the M.P.'s and the reporters, you are not sorry to find the House adjourning, and to hear the well-known accents of the respected doorkeeper, "Who goes home?"

The Cabinet is the Government, and while some of the members are in the House of Commons, others adorn the House of Lords. As a rule the Cabinet does not constitute more than a fourth part of those whom a change of Ministry deprives of office. The members of it are more immediately responsible for the conduct of public affairs, their deliberations are always confidential and kept secret even from their colleagues who are less exalted in office; newspaper correspondents belonging to second-rate provincial journals alone, and by a process which would be wonderful if true, are the possessors of Cabinet secrets. They know what Under Secretaries do not. The distinguished, let us add the talented individual (for the age of mediocrities is gone by for ever,—we can have no more Goderichs or Liverpools at the head of affairs), who fills the situation of the First Lord of the Treasury, is the chief of the Ministry, and therefore of the Cabinet. It is at his immediate recommendation that his colleagues are appointed, and with scarcely any exception he dispenses the patronage of the Crown. Every Cabinet includes the following officers: the First Lord of the Treasury, the Lord Chancellor, the Lord President of the Council, the Lord Privy Seal, the Chancellor of the Exchequer, and the principal Secretaries of State. When Parliament is sitting, all eyes of course are turned to the Premier. "He fills," said Canning, "that station in the House of Commons which points out him who holds it as the representative of the Government in that House, the possessor of the chief confidence of the Crown and of the Ministers. His prerogative is, that in all doubtful questions—in all questions which have not previously been settled in the Cabinet, and which may require instant decision, he is to decide—upon instant communication with his colleagues sitting by him, if he be courteously inclined, but he is to decide—with or without communication with them, and with or against their consent." Not of the Cabinet are the remainder of the gentlemen seated very often in very ungraceful postures on the Treasury Bench. Sneer at them as you will, they are indispensable to that form of Parliamentary Government, which at any rate suits the people amongst whom it has grown.

Before us are the nation's chiefs—the heads of parties—the leaders of the people. I know not a more illustrious assembly, nor one which should be more honoured by Englishmen. I claim for it that it is eminently fair and many sided, and that not an idea flashes across the nation's brain but is represented here. If a man fails in the House it is his own fault alone. If he achieve a position it is because he has the requisite capacity. Not all the blood of all the Howards can save the fool from being laughed at for his folly. It recognises the true man at once.

In days such as ours—when all things are being changed, when our ancient universities are ceasing to be sectarian, when our best and truest churchmen would fain make our State Church, in spite of evangelical narrowness and ritualistic folly, the Church of the nation,—when we hear of the rights of industry as well as of property, when the penny paper has quickened the intellectual life of the masses, the House of Commons, representing the living, not the dead, is a Liberal assembly. It was clear when Mr. Disraeli educated his party into giving the nation household suffrage and the lodger franchise, Conservatism was gone. The old Conservatives, men of unsullied honour and of unflinching faith, such as General Peel, have either retired from political life, or like the Marquis of Salisbury have been removed into the lotus-land of the Upper House. Their successors, with the worn-out cries of No Popery and the Church in Danger, stand powerless and ashamed, repudiated by the national vote. The following table shows in the most unmistakeable manner to what side of politics the electors of the great constituencies incline:—

Name of Constituency.	No. of Electors.	L.	C.
Glasgow	47,500	3	
Manchester	45,000	2	1
Birmingham	42,306	3	
Hackney	40,613	2	
Liverpool	36,538	1	2
Marylebone	35,575	2	
Leeds	35,460	2	1
Lambeth	33,373	2	
Tower Hamlets	32,000	2	
Finsbury	31,759	2	
Sheffield	29,995	2	
Bristol	21,153	2	
Edinburgh	20,779	2	
Bradford	20,561	2	

Name of Constituency.	No. of Electors.	L.	C.
Westminster	18,879	1	1
London	18,136	3	1
Southwark	17,701	2	
Chelsea	17,400	2	
Wolverhampton	16,000	2	
Wednesbury	15,612	1	
Greenwich	15,588	2	
Salford	14,859		2
Dundee	14,798	2	
Merthyr Tydvil	14,577	2	
Hull	13,046	2	
Oldham	13,000	2	
Nottingham	12,991		2
Bolton	12,650		2
Norwich	12,000	1	1
Sunderland	11,464	2	
		53	13

No success in the counties, where the voters are more under clerical and landlord influence, can deprive these figures of significance and power.

CHAPTER II.

THE CONSERVATIVES.

THE RIGHT HON. BENJAMIN DISRAELI.

(Buckinghamshire—unopposed.)

TOWARDS the close of the year 1837, a young man of somewhat singular appearance and gesticulation, broke down in his maiden speech in the House of Commons. Great things had been expected from him. In most circles he had contrived to get talked about—in some to be admired. Years before, with all the confidence of genius and youth, he had told the Irish O'Connell that he would meet him at Philippi, and the hour of that meeting had at length arrived. Already the young *débutant* had become remarkable for the facility with which he had learned to repeat the most contrary doctrines, and to champion interests and prejudices seemingly the most opposed. Marylebone had heard his declaration that unless the ballot and triennial parliaments were conceded, he could not conceive how the Legislature could ever be in harmony with the people. At High Wycombe he had told the electors that in all financial changes the agricultural interest ought especially to be considered; and at Taunton, he who had appeared at Marylebone as the friend of Joseph Hume became the representative of the Duke of Buckingham and the Carlton Club. At Maidstone, by the defeat of a liberal almost as incomprehensible as himself, he at length succeeded in gaining a seat in St. Stephen's. With pride he took his stand in the presence of the Whig dignitaries of whom he had spoken evil, and of the puzzled country gentlemen who could not understand how their Toryism was more democratic than the politics of the Whigs who were wont to drink to civil and religious liberty all over the world, and to toast the people as the only source of legitimate power. Not merely also in the troubled walk of politics, or as the paradoxical commentator on the English constitution, or, as in "Runnymede," the most keen dissector of the *matériel* of the Whig cabinet, was the aspirant for parliamentary laurels known to fame. In the world of fashion and of literature he had already become notorious for the piquancy and satire of his novels. The speaker also was a dandy—there were dandies in 1837—and therefore was to be regarded with curiosity. The Conservatives mustered in considerable numbers to back their new man. On the Whig benches there was awe and expectation. Sir Robert Peel cheered the youthful orator with most stentorian tones. Alas! in vain was the cheer; the *début* was a failure. The exaggerated attitude and diction of the speaker excited universal ridicule. At length, losing his temper and pausing in the midst of his harangue, Disraeli—for it is he of whom we write—at the top of his voice exclaimed, as he resumed his seat, baffled, beaten, derided, but not despairing, "Though I sit down now, the time will come when you will hear me." It is not always such predictions are realized. In this case, however, it was no empty boast. The man thus ridiculed and coughed at, thus rejected and despised, was he who lived to hurl at Sir Robert Peel the fiercest philippics known in modern parliamentary annals, and who, by his mere strength of brain, lifted himself up to be the leader of the renowned historic party which had been illustrated by the splendid eloquence of a Bolingbroke and the administrative skill of a Pitt.

Seated on the Opposition benches, half-way down, with some small-brained son of a duke by his side, night after night may be seen the leader of Her Majesty's Opposition. Generally, his eyes are cast down, his hands are crossed in front, and he has all the appearance of a statue. Cold, passionless, he seems of an alien race—a stranger to the hopes, and fears, and interests of a British House of Commons. You wonder how he got there, and how the Tyrrels, and Spooners, and Newdegates, and the rosy-cheeked country gentlemen could have borne banners under such as he. However fierce the debate, or heated the House, or pressing the crisis, there sits Disraeli, occasionally looking at his hands or the clock—otherwise silent, unmoved, and still. Yet an Indian scout could not keep a more vigilant watch—and immediately an opportunity occurs, he is on his legs, boiling with real or affected indignation. I say real or affected, because Disraeli has so much of the artist about him that you never know whether he is in earnest or not.

As an illustration, let me refer to the debate which ensued on Lord John Russell's diplomatic proceedings at Vienna. It was amusing to see how, at such times, with an elaborate deference all the bitterer for its transparent hollowness, Disraeli would turn to Lord John, and leaning confidentially against the table, pour out against the miserable little man, now looking very angry, all the invective which his folly justified and required. Such a situation can only be shadowed forth by simile. Lord John seemed as you can imagine the traveller in the desert overtaken and whirled along by the fierce simoom; or as the hapless voyager caught in his frail bark in the Mediterranean in a white squall, and entombed for ever beneath its unpitying waves; or, if you are not a traveller, and have ever seen him in such a plight, as some poor Cockney with his Easter Monday garments on, in a heavy storm of rain and hail on Primrose Hill or Hampstead Heath. Disraeli used no sugared phrases, no mincing terms, no artifice, to veil his contempt; and the noble scion of the House of Bedford was compelled for a couple of hours to sit through a hell such as only a Dante could describe, or a Fuseli or a Martin paint. You thought of the Indian dancing on the dead body of his prostrate foe; of yourself at a respectable dinner-party, in tight boots and with aching corns, seated between two strong-minded females, with a purple-faced London alderman opposite; of the boa-constrictor drinking the last drop of his victim's blood, and crushing his last bone; of the sufferers of Greek tragedy, with its stern, unrelenting fate;—and you were not sorry when the task was over, and his mauled and mangled foe released.

For savage sarcasm Disraeli stands unrivalled. His self-possession—his intellèctual versatility—his clear and cold voice—his plucky appearance, all aid him in a wonderful manner. In his own peculiar line it is dangerous to attempt to cope with him. Roebuck on one occasion did so, and signally failed. Somehow or other, one does not speak of Disraeli as an orator, or as a philosopher—like Burke or Mackintosh—uttering sentences that will form the wisdom of after-ages; or even as a rhetorician, as Macaulay and Sheil. We do not read that he was eloquent, argumentative, pathetic, or patriotic. You speak of him as you would of Tom Sayers. His admirers tell you that he was "in good condition"—that he "showed fight"—that he was "plucky as usual"—that he "hit right and left"—that he was "up to the mark"—and there is a similar isolation and singularity in his parliamentary conduct. Though the leader of a party, he is not its slave; and on occasions he fails even to do the proper thing.

Thus at the close of the Crimean war, on the vote of the address on peace—an opportunity which only comes once in a generation—when, according to conventional rules, Disraeli should have made a grand oration, he was actually dumb, and jumped up immediately and left the House after Palmerston's two hours' speech—as if he were one of the silent members who ingloriously sleep on back benches during the very hottest of a parliamentary debate. Historians tell us how Prince Rupert was more than a match for the old-fashioned commanders of the Commonwealth. From his lair at Kinsale—from his lair in the Scilly Isles—from his lair in Jersey, he would pounce upon his enemy, and was irresistible—till a new system was inaugurated, and Blake, a man of greater genius and daring, raised the red cross of the Commonwealth. Lord Derby has been called the Prince Rupert of debate, but the term is more applicable to Disraeli. When you expect him to speak, he has nothing to say; when you do not expect him, he is on his legs; when you think he will go on for another hour, he sits down as rapidly and unexpectedly as he gets up. He delights in surprises, and you cannot tell which is the studied effort and which the impromptu retort. Herein especially is manifest his superiority over conventional speakers—a superiority especially apparent when he came to be the leader not merely of a party, but England's Premier.

In his own peculiar style of personal attack,

Disraeli has the field entirely—too entirely—to himself, and no wonder is it that personality is his favourite weapon, and the one the best appreciated by the young lordlings behind him, who cheer infinitely better than speak. At the same time, it must be confessed that Toryism is always more ungentlemanly and personal than that sublime intellectual abortion, the pure old Whig. The only personal paper attempted in our day was the *Press*, and that soon gave up personalities; the *Satirist* was a Conservative paper; so was the *John Bull;* so was *Blackwood,* when it charged Hazlitt with having pimples on his face; so was the *Anti-Jacobin,* when it called Charles James Fox

"The Catiline of modern times."

If we go back to the days of Swift, L'Estrange, and Mrs. Manley, we shall find the same personality characteristic of the High Church and Tory party. Dr. Arnold, somewhere in his letters, makes a similar remark.

It is wonderful—the power of oratory. The speaker, whether from the platform or the pulpit, is the only worker who gets his reward at once. You may invent what shall enrich a nation, and die a beggar; you may write, but your hair will be grey before the world is familiar with your name; you may be a poet, and fame may not own your genius till the turf on your grave is green; but, possess the magic power with the living voice to reach the living heart of multitudes, and immediately you are a king amongst men. Not merely amongst a rude, untutored peasantry, or inflammable youth, or a middle-class public particularly prone to clap-trap, or an Exeter Hall audience, rather feminine than select; but amongst educated gentlemen and polished scholars, amongst men who have long mastered emotion, and to whom most oratory is as "sounding brass or as a tinkling cymbal." On a grand field night you feel this as you see Disraeli, perfectly aware that victory is beyond his grasp, standing on the floor of the House, his eyes flashing defiance, his lip curled with sarcasm, his arm pointed to the object of attack, and his voice alternately expressing indignation and contempt. As I have already hinted, as an orator Disraeli stands by himself. It is not English—that elaborately-dressed form; that pale Hebrew face, shaded with curling hair, once luxuriant and dark; that style, so melo-dramatic, yet so effective; that power of individuality which makes you hate the object of his hate; that passion which you scarce know whether to call malignant or sublime. When he rises, it is needless for the Speaker to announce his name. A glance at the orator, with his glistening vest, tells you that the great advocate of the pure Semitic race is on his legs. You have seen that face in *Punch*. You have imagined Coningsby just as attentively listened to, or Vivian Grey looking just as cool. It is not every man that can play a losing game. To speak from the Treasury benches with a whipper-in to make a House and secure you a cordial welcome, to feel that a triumphant speech will be succeeded by a triumphant vote, are privileges granted but to few—to Disraeli seldom indeed. So far as the Opposition are concerned, the debate generally languishes till the Speaker announces the name of the member for Buckinghamshire. Immediately you lean forward. In his face there is a dazzling, saucy look which at once excites your interest. You see that if not a great man, he is an intensely clever one, and though on reflection you see more display than reality in his performance, and are not sure that he is in earnest, or that he means what he says, or that he is sustained and prompted by any great principle, you feel that as an orator he has few rivals. When he soars, as he occasionally does, you tremble lest he should break down, but Disraeli never attempts more than he can achieve, and when nearest to bathos he saves himself by a happy flight. But even in his highest efforts he aims at a doggedly cool and unconcerned appearance, and will stop to suck an orange, or actually, as he did in his great Budget speech, to cut his nails. It is true there are times when he looks more emotional. On that memorable December morning when he was ousted from his chancellorship, when his party were ingloriously driven from the Eden in which they had hoped long

"To live and lie reclined
On the hills like gods together, careless of mankind,"—

back into the bleak and desert world, the ex-Chancellor of the Exchequer came out of the House at half-past five A.M., gay and fresh as if the majority had been with him, not against him. There was an unwonted buoyancy in his walk and sparkle in his eye; but the excitement of the contest was hardly over—the swell of the storm was there still—still rang in his ears the thunders of applause, audible in the lobby, which greeted his daring retorts and audacious personalities. Even when, as occasionally, he leads his party into a *cul de sac,* and listens to their murmurs and hears their threats, you cannot perceive any feeling of disappointment or regret on his impassive face. No stone could display more indifference.

But Disraeli, I am told, has no principles. In the House of Commons men deal not with principles, but with facts. The best statesman in modern times is he who is least hampered by principles, and is free to follow the leading of public opinion, and yet it is not difficult to perceive a certain amount of consistency in Mr. Disraeli's political opinions, whether you study his novels or his speeches. It may be a grave fault—granting, for the sake of argument, that the charge be true—but, if other statesmen are equally remiss, why is Disraeli alone to be singled out for censure? Was Lord Palmerston so consistent that the British public are to fire with indignation at the licentiousness of Disraeli's political career? Lord John Russell's earlier speeches were against reform. The great Whig idol entered the

House of Commons under Tory auspices. We have built up statues in every corner of the land to Sir Robert Peel, yet what principle did that eminent statesman start with which he did not abdicate in the course of his eventful parliamentary existence? Genius has a creed of its own—forms of expression of its own, and if it condescends to party Shibboleths, it gives them a wider bearing. If this be true everywhere, especially is this true in practical politics, where, at all times,

> "Black's not so very black, nor white so very white;"

and where, in these times, the differences between the occupants of the Treasury benches and those of the Opposition are so few. There is a wide interval between a Hobbes and a Milton—between a Filmer and a Locke—between a Blackstone and a Bentham—between the stump orator of the Temple Forum or the Codgers' Hall declaiming on the rights of man, and the leader of the House of Commons dealing with a thousand discordant rights, the growth of the conflicting passions, and principles, and interests, and prejudices of a thousand years; but between the Whig and Tory aristocracy—between, for instance, Lord Derby and Lord Palmerston—the line of separation was so obscure that the wonder was that a respectable line could be held up to the public at all. Mr. Stafford jobbed at the Admiralty, but were Mr. Gladstone's nominees immaculate? Disraeli believes he and his party are as honest as their opponents. Evidently the English squirearchy are of a similar opinion. The Whig and Peelite writers are astonished, and one of the dullest of them, in a feeble octavo containing 700 pages ("Disraeli; a biography"), enters his protest, and begs to "recall our attention to the principles of English morality, which have done even more than the industrious energy and practical genius of the people in making England what she is. England has been a standing witness against political atheism." The Whig aristocracy, who have always been narrow in their principles and narrow in their application of them, who snubbed Burke, ignored Sheridan, only accepted Mackintosh when he gave up the doctrines of the *Vindiciæ Gallicæ,* and would have made Canning whipper-in—who deluded the nation with a Reform Bill which was to have prolonged their political existence *in secula seculorum,* and did not even carry Free Trade — are quite as open to the charge of political atheism as Mr. Disraeli. Position has a great deal to do with politics. The Whigs found out this when they carried the celebrated Appropriation Clause. If Lord Palmerston had been in office he would never have defeated Lord John Russell and caused the latter to resign on the question of general or local militia. Out of office no man has declaimed so energetically against the Income Tax as Mr. Gladstone. In office Mr. Horsman was a Whig. With the sweets of office dangling before them, as we get jackasses to move on by flourishing a bit of hay, what lofty patriots do middle-aged barristers become. On one side of the Speaker's chair there are men especially bound to find fault with what is professed on the other. Of course they do this unsparingly and *con amore,* because they know that if the tables were turned their own acts would be subjected to a similar unsparing criticism. The country reaps the benefit of this, for the progress thus consummated is slow—slow as public opinion. Amongst us

> "Freedom broadens slowly down
> From precedent to precedent;"

but to argue that on one side of the Speaker's chair are the sheep, and on the other the goats—on one side the knaves, and on the other the honest men—that, for instance, a barrister speaking on the Whig side is a patriot of the first water, and a barrister speaking on the Opposition benches a dishonest partisan—to believe, for instance, that a manufacturer with his hands red with the blood of factory children (see the evidence submitted to the House when Mr. Crook gained his victory) is an enlightened philanthropist, and that a country gentleman, with his horror of democracy and change, is a selfish ignoramus, betrays a verdancy rare in well-informed circles. It is not because Mr. Disraeli sits on the side of the House that is unpopular, and must be unpopular, that he is to be censured. In office he was civil and eminently disinterested, and that is more than can be said of every leader. Partisan hacks may cast no stone at him. A more august tribunal there may be even than that of the House of Commons. For a man not born to rank to be on an equality with men of rank, nay more, to be their leader, is a triumph, but there are grander triumphs still; if Mr. Disraeli has missed them, there are few that have found them, and those few rarely have a chance of catching Mr. Speaker's eye.

LORD STANLEY.

(King's Lynn—Stanley, 1256; Bourke, 1119; Sir T. F. Buxton, L., 1015.)

Gibbon tells us, "of the various forms of government which have prevailed in the world, an hereditary monarchy seems to present the fairest scope for ridicule. Is it possible to relate, without an indignant smile, that on the father's decease the property of a nation, like that of a drove of oxen, descends to his infant son, as yet unknown to mankind and himself?" The language of Gibbon is not altogether inapplicable to hereditary statesmanship. Why should the tenth transmitter of a foolish face be a ruler over men whose natures he cannot understand, and with whose wants it is impossible for him to sympathize? Surely the son of a lord is born no wiser, abler, stronger-minded than his fellows. Is he not very often born considerably less so, and, at any rate, does he not labour under one great damning disadvantage, that he has had no wholesome struggle from his youth upwards; that his impetuous will has never been disciplined by wise control; that the very conditions—I mean the struggle with hard necessity and adverse circumstances, without which most men would pass their days in epicurean ease—by means of which it is given to a man to become great, are denied him from his birth. An Englishman crawls in the dust before a lord. When can he hear the stern and unwelcome voice of truth? How can he understand the condition-of-England question? Poverty is almost romantic in the eyes of the rich. A great duke lives in Brighton because he cannot afford to live in one of his own palatial residences. The poor man is not thus encumbered,—he has no need to trouble himself with settlements and lawyers; nor is he required to subscribe to the county charities—to preside at anniversary dinners—to dance attendance at court,—nor has he his every movement recorded in the morning papers. See Strephon on a bank reclining, in a costume very Arcadian, and very much like what we see at the Adelphi on the occasion of a rustic fête. Hear him sing,

> "At ease reclined, in rustic state,
> How vain the ardour of the crowd,
> How low, how little are the proud,
> How indigent the great!"

Who would not be Strephon rather than your much-to-be-pitied lord! Indeed so over-weighted is the latter that he generally performs even his political duties by proxy. But we are entering on a question respecting which there may be different opinions. We imagine all will admit that Lord Edward Henry Stanley, eldest son of the Earl of Derby, born at Knowsley, Lancashire, 1826, is the ablest argument we have in favour of hereditary statesmanship. *Primâ facie,* a man who has an impediment in his speech, so that his utterance is unpleasant and imperfect, stands a poor chance of being elected into an assembly, one great qualification for which is more or less of oratorical power. To read a speech is yet more an outrage on our English ideas; yet Lord Stanley did this not very long since. To be a refined thinker—to go down to the core and kernel of things—unfits a man for the use of the usual party expressions, which unless you use you may vainly long for a parliamentary position. John Stuart Mill, our greatest writer on political and social science, has not a seat in the House of Commons; our profoundest Greek historian, Mr. Grote, we know declined to stand for Westminster, on account of the impossibility of coming to a good understanding with its noisy and vehement democrats. Lord Stanley's statesmanship is of a similar high order. Yet, when Lord George Bentinck died, he was elected his successor as M.P. for Walpole's favourite borough of King's Lynn. How is it that Lord Stanley has thus made a good start in public life? The answer is soon given—he is the son of his father, and that father one of England's leading landlords; that father, if not one of the most eminent politicians of the age, at any rate is one of the most eloquent speakers in any legislative assembly in the world.

In his "Memoirs of the Reign of King George the Second," old Horace Walpole, then Earl of Orford, apologizing for the unfavourable light in which he places many of his former characters, says:—"If, after all, many of the characters are bad, let it be remembered that the scenes I describe passed in the highest life, the soil the vices like." This is a little severe, and let us hope not quite so true in the days of Queen Victoria as King George. But when a young nobleman scorns delights and lives laborious days, it must be admitted on all sides he deserves well of his country. From his youth upward Lord Stanley has done this. He was a pupil of Dr. Arnold of Rugby; and we all know how, when Dr. Arnold's pupils came up to Oxford, there was found to be in them a thoughtfulness, a conscientiousness, a sense of duty, rare in men so young, and by means of which they were favourably contrasted with the alumni of other public schools. This was a confession, as we all know, fairly and honourably made by Arnold's opponents. In Lord Stanley's case this result is very manifest; and no doubt it was this that led him—while the unfledged lordlings of his own rank and standing were wearing white waistcoats, and writing very indifferent poetry, and astonishing heaven and earth by Young England affectation—to leave home, and by means of foreign travel to enlarge his views and liberalize his ideas. As soon as he was of age, Lord Stanley spent some time in Canada and America. His next step was to the West Indies, to study the results of negro emancipation, and the condition of the sugar plantations. He next paid a visit to the East, and was still in India when nominated, in March, 1852, Under Secretary of State for Foreign Affairs in the Derby Ministry. These visits have borne fruit. Lord Stanley learnt much; got rid of many exploded ideas, became wiser, as all men should who stand face to face with the truth of things and the facts of life. As a social reformer Lord Stanley is widely known. Few men have done more with regard to the encouragement of mechanics' institutes, the establishment of public libraries, and the promotion of popular education. When, in 1858, he was made President of the Indian Board, by his introduction of the competitive system into the service he gave an impulse to education among the middle classes which it is almost impossible to over-estimate. His philanthropy is thus of the highest and most practical character—of that character which acknowledges that human affairs are conducted on general principles, that suffering and human degradation are, as a rule, the result of a violation of law, and that the remedy is to be found, not so much in Acts of Parliament, or temporary expedients, as in the enlightenment, moral and intellectual, of the sufferers themselves. Many are the nostrums of our day. In vain are baths and wash-houses, in vain are flannel-waistcoats and thick boots, in vain are good meals and a good atmosphere, in vain are Saturday half-holidays and an abridgment of the hours of labour, in vain are the wonderful mechanical improvements of our time, if the people suffer from lack of knowledge, and the night of ignorance lies heavily on the land. As a politician Lord Stanley is hard to define. Dod describes him as a Conservative, but in favour of the admission of Jews to Parliament, of the Maynooth grant, and of the exemption of Dissenters from church-rates. When his father has been in office, Lord Stanley has been one of his most valuable supporters in the Lower House. Yet when, in 1855, the death of Sir W. Molesworth created a vacancy in the Colonial-office, Lord Palmerston, sensible of Lord Stanley's talents and popularity, offered him the seals of that department. More than once Lord Stanley was named as a probable holder of office under Earl Russell and Mr. Gladstone; and if, a few years since, he had come forward as a candidate for the city of London—and a numerously-signed requisition was got up to that effect—it is not clear but that he would have been selected by the City in preference to one of the present M.P.'s. The fact that such a belief existed indicates Lord Stanley's liberality. With another well-known Liberal of a still more ultra character, Lord Stanley is supposed to have held amicable relations. In the House of Commons smoking-room the interviews between Lord Stanley and John

Bright are said to have been of a very frequent and confidential nature. They both of them have this in common—that they belong to the higher order of statesmen, though their respective standpoints are wide as the poles asunder. They may yet sit side by side on the Treasury Benches. Lord Stanley must, sooner or later, cut the old country Quarter Sessions party that feasted so greatly at St. James's Hall the other day, under the presidency of Lord John Manners. As it is, his temporary alliance with them has damaged him, for people find it difficult to make allowances for a man of trained judgment, and with an understanding well cultivated, doing anything so unnatural as leading the forlorn hope of a retrograde party in church and state,—and surely the Indians, native or otherwise, have reason to complain that because some poor Whigs wanted to get back into office, Lord Stanley was driven out, and his place supplied by a third-rate official like Sir Charles Wood, a man who is always —what Lord Stanley never is—common-place. This leads me to the great characteristic of Lord Stanley. He has less of mere partisanship and more of elevated principle, perhaps, than any other man in Parliament. He has thought out his own conclusions; he has strength of mind sufficient to rely on them. He is superior to the prejudices of the hour. Never does he stoop to pander to the delusions of the mob; he is the last man in the world to talk what the Americans call "Bunkum." He has a system to fall back on, and this is a great advantage in these days of incoherent action and chaotic legislation.

Come into the House of Commons. Some grand display of force is expected—some question touching the hearts and arousing the passions of men is being discussed—some crisis is at hand. On the front bench of the Opposition, seated between Mr. Disraeli and Sir John Pakington, is a younger parliamentary performer, much more plainly dressed than the great exponent of the Asiatic mystery, and by no means so elaborately neat as the worthy member for Droitwich. His features are small, his complexion is light, his countenance pale, his figure stout, and the expression of his face slightly haughty; but this is not discernible in the Strangers' Gallery. You see, however, that he is an intensely earnest listener, that not a word of the debate escapes him, that he occasionally takes notes, and now and then speaks to his friends around him, as if in consultation. It may be that he rises to speak, and your curiosity is aroused. When you hear the Speaker announce Lord Stanley's name, you lean forward, for the House cheers, and the speaker is evidently a favourite. What! you cannot hear a word, though every one is silent as a cat? Ah! now you will hear; the voice is filling the place, and, by-and-by, will float up to you. Alas! alas! there is a sound, it is true, as of a man speaking: but it may be Greek, or Hebrew, or Chaldee that he is speaking, for aught you know to the contrary. Nature has not been so bountiful to the son as to the sire, yet you will see that the House listens with interest, that the argument tells, and when you read the speech in the *Times* next day, you will think that the speech was one of the best of the night. It is a fine illustration of the triumph of mind over matter, and shows, as we have said, that statesmanship may exist, of the highest qualities, without the possessor of them being an orator at all. Out of doors this would be a defect; it would unfit a man to succeed in making new truths popular. In the House of Commons, where declamation avails but little, it is a slight drawback, which is soon overlooked, when a man works so hard and so successfully, as patriot and statesman, as Lord Stanley does.

Poor Brough, who died prematurely the other day, tells us:—

> "My Lord Tomnoddy's the son of an Earl,
> His hair is straight but his whiskers curl;
> His lordship's forehead is far from wide,
> But there's plenty of room for the brains inside.
> He writes his name with indifferent ease,
> He's rather uncertain about the d's,
> But what does it matter, if three or one,
> To the Earl of Fitzdotterel's eldest son?"

Lord Stanley does not belong to this class. He accepts his rank and station, and at the same time its responsibilities. He is as much aware of the duties as the rights of property, and he is willing to lend the prestige of his name to institutions not exactly orthodox in conservative eyes. As regards sire and son, the order of nature seems to have been completely reversed. The son has an old head on young shoulders—he has been ever wise, and prudent, and thoughtful beyond his years. The father, when a commoner in the Lower House, always managed to keep Ireland in hot water —to goad on the colonies almost to the verge of revolt; and in the Upper House has been great in winning barren victories, and in leading his party into office merely to lead them ingloriously out again—after the commission of a few jobs such as those at Dover or Galway.

The present Lord Stanley is the reverse of all this—of course something is due to training. The Earl of Derby tells us he was born in the pre-scientific era. Lord Stanley has had an advantage in this respect—the politics of the present time are also calmer and less fraught with personal collision; but I imagine nature has cast the son in a more philosophical mould than the eloquent and impulsive sire. We can have no fear on the score of our foreign relations so long as Lord Stanley holds his place as Foreign Secretary of State.

SIR JOHN PAKINGTON.

(DROITWICH—PAKINGTON, 781; CORBET, L., 602.)

A TALE is told of an Eastern potentate, who, amongst the other lions of London, visited the House of Commons. The distinguished foreigner was delighted with everything he saw; the occupants of the Treasury benches, the Speaker, the Mace, the Serjeant-at Arms, the clerks at the table, the reporters in the gallery, small and incommodious, and the ladies very properly in another gallery, smaller and more incommodious still; all were so fortunate as to obtain his warm approval. His attention was directed to gentlemen sitting opposite the Treasury benches. He asked who they were; the reply was, that they were Her Majesty's Opposition. The answer puzzled him greatly, and when he did understand it, when it was explained that those gentlemen sat there to oppose everything Her Majesty's government said and did—to find fault with it, whether it stood still or moved on, he scarce knew whether most to admire the audacity that could suggest, or the lenity that could pardon, such a course. "Her Majesty's Opposition, indeed!" exclaimed the astonished spectator. "By Allah! in my country we should have off their heads in a week." Even in civilized Europe an opposition exists only by perilling its liberty. It is only in England it is safe. In times of excitement the opposition is a safety valve—in times of weakness, a source of confusion—in times like the present, principally a means of doubling the parliamentary session and reports. A clear, definite policy may receive a decided opposition, as it will insure a decided support. Free Trade, for instance, was a thing to which men might say Yes or No, as they could to Catholic Emancipation, the Reform Bill, or the repeal of the Test and Corporation Acts, or as they will say to measures which will be discussed when the people of this country awake from their sleep of political indifference and unbelief. But it is difficult to oppose a government without convictions; especially if the opposition comes from men in a similar category. In the main, both parties are agreed. Both have accepted Free Trade. Either would regale a hustings' mob with the cant phrases of "a glorious war," or "a safe and honourable peace." The fiery old thick-headed squires are gone, and the jolly old thick-headed opposition is gone with them. Sibthorpe was the *ultimus Romanorum*. One could not see why Sir John Pakington sat on one side of the House and Sir Charles Wood on the other. One could understand Sir Harry Inglis, or Sir Charles Wetherell, or a late Duke of Newcastle. They would not move the ancient landmarks. They honestly believed that it was essential to the welfare of this country that Old Sarum and Gatton should be represented in Parliament, and that Manchester and Birmingham should not; they thought, that the way to get the Irish Roman Catholics to love them, was by insulting and persecuting the professors of that ancient faith—that, to keep men honest, they were to swear to what they did not believe, and that the country would go to the bad if the starving labourer was permitted to eat his untaxed bread. At the time of the Reform Bill agitation Sir Harry Inglis said that if that bill were carried, then in ten years' time there would be no

State Church, no House of Lords—nay, more—that even Royalty would be swept away. Now, all this seems very absurd to us, but it was honestly believed then by some of the Opposition, who went so far as to take their money out of the English funds and invest it in American stock. The Opposition, then, if not very enlightened, was at any rate clear. Now that it has become wiser it is less of an Opposition. As an instance, let us glance at Sir John Pakington's political career. Sir John Somerset Pakington, born in 1799, at Powick Court, Worcestershire, very much astonished the world by accepting, in 1852, the office of Secretary of State for the Colonies. Men had only conceived of him as a respectable member of the country party and chairman of quarter sessions. Nominally a Conservative, necessity was laid upon him, and he was compelled to advance with the times. The party with which he acted has always opposed Free Trade, the Maynooth Grant, and the admission of Jews to Parliament; but in office—first as Colonial Secretary, and then as First Lord of the Admiralty—Sir John has accepted Free Trade, walked out of the House without voting on a Maynooth debate, and was an active party in admitting Baron Rothschild and Alderman Salomons to a seat in the House of Commons. We thus learn that Sir John, if a Conservative, is not an obstinate one; not of that type of Conservatism which the ever-to-be-lamented Arnold deprecated as the most revolutionary element in existence. From his attention to the subject of education—from his presence at the Social Science meetings—from his readiness to aid the philanthropic movements of the day—it is clear Sir John is a Liberal, whatever be the name of the party of whom he is one of the chiefs. Still more as a practical administrator are we under national obligations to Sir John Pakington. At the beginning of 1859, or at the latter end of 1858, the country became alarmed at the state of the national defences. Sir John, who was then in office, turned his attention to the subject. Our navy was admitted to be woefully deficient; we were badly off both as regards ships and men. Sir John made an attempt to build the one and procure the other. If Sir John Pakington fell into the usual error of exerting his influence as First Lord of the Admiralty in political matters; if he quarrelled with Captain Carnegie, because the latter would not fight for the Conservatives at Dover, he did but as other First Lords of the Admiralty have done before. No doubt there is monstrous abuse in the Admiralty. By means of its influence and expenditure the dockyards are little better than government boroughs. No doubt that in these places millions and millions of the people's money are wasted; Lord Clarence Paget has established this fact. A great statesman—a man of the first order—would have swept out this Augean stable. Sir John Pakington has failed to do so, and hence takes his place amongst statesmen of the second rank.

We hear much of the country party; Tennyson has painted the class. He describes a country squire as—

> "A great broad-shouldered genial Englishman;
> A lord of fat prize oxen and of sheep;
> A raiser of huge melons and of pine;
> A patron of some thirty charities;
> A pamphleteer on guano and on grain;
> A quarter sessions' chairman—abler none;
> Fair-haired, and redder than a windy morn."

"Jolly companions are they every one," but they are not orators; and while they will vote, and spend money, and fight at elections for their party, they have no idea of being penned up all night in the House of Commons, breathing bad air, and listening to bad speeches. Writing in 1828, of a government formed on the basis of resistance to Roman Catholic claims, the late Sir Robert Peel wrote—"What must have been the inevitable fate of a government composed of Goulburn, Sir John Beckett, Wetherell, and myself? Supported by very warm friends no doubt; but those warm friends being prosperous country gentlemen, fox-hunters, &c.—most excellent men—who will attend one night, but who will not leave their favourite pursuits to sit up till two or three o'clock, fighting questions of detail—on which, however, a government must have a majority—we could not have stood creditably a fortnight." The description is still true, and hence it is that Sir John Pakington is made so much of. A real country gentleman so patriotic is a rarity; a country gentleman able to speak English as fluently and correctly as any lawyer in the House is a still greater rarity.

In the middle of the Treasury bench you will see a gentleman seated, of the middle size, with a pale face, and rather a hooked nose. In his dress and general bearing, you gather indications of correctness and finish, rather than of greatness or genius. On one side of him is Mr. Disraeli; on the other, it may be, is Sir Stafford Northcote. What a contrast to each does Sir John Pakington present! Still, compared with the men with whom he is often matched, he rises vastly in your estimation. Nor is he so dreadfully dreary as—well, we'll give no more names. Sir John is a respectable speaker, and all respectable speakers are alike. He does not use the thunderbolts of Jove. He does not "shake the arsenal and fulmine over Greece." He does not even attempt—like Burke—to clothe Conservatism in a philosophic form—much less has he the wit and classic grace of Canning; but then he has ever a good word for the clergy—wears always unexceptionable linen, always sports a good hat, has his thin gray hair well brushed, and delights in faultless boots. I should think he always pays his tradespeople, attends punctually at the parish church, and, I should imagine, is a decorous husband, a pattern father of a family, and is regular in having the servants in to family prayers.

There will be no collection of his speeches after his decease. The student will not resort to them as models, either on account of their powerful logic or brilliant declamation. They will go the way of most speeches, and sleep in Hansard for ever; but Sir John is a useful man nevertheless. There are many lawyers who would make better speeches; but then they are not country gentlemen; and even if, as they do occasionally—like Mr. Napier—shed tears, the common sense of the House rejects the idea of sincerity where lawyers are concerned; but Sir John Pakington is a country gentleman with a large estate, and ready at a moment's notice to serve at the Admiralty or the War Office, or anywhere, and his party thankfully use his services. He does not convince them; they do not want to be convinced—they are convinced already. He does not convince the Liberals; their minds are made up to vote against Sir John before he opens his mouth: but he gives his party a decent excuse for voting. It would scarce do to march into the lobby without a discussion; to give silent votes would be a confession of intellectual weakness for which the country party are not yet prepared; but Sir John can speak on any question for any length of time, and when, towards the end of a debate, he rises and repeats the objections which have entered his head, his friends feel that they have appeared to have discussed the measure long enough, and that it is time the division takes place; and the strangers in the gallery feel that there are two sides to every question, and that they are not the worse for hearing them.

THE RIGHT HON. SPENCER HORATIO WALPOLE.

(Cambridge University—unopposed.)

It is said that when the great statesman, Sir Robert Walpole, was made a peer, and met his old political opponent, who had also been rewarded with a peerage in the Upper House, he exclaimed, "Here we are, my lord, the two most insignificant people in Europe." His lordship meant to imply that they, no longer leaders of parties in the Commons—reduced from the position which they had won by oratorical talent and indomitable perseverance—removed to an arena where there were but few laurels to be won, might be said, like veterans covered with renown, to have laid down their arms and retired from the field. In another sense, also, his lordship's language was true. From that time, but with one illustrious exception, the part the Walpoles have played on the political stage may be truly characterized as "insignificant."

The illustrious exception is the gentleman whose name we have placed at the head of this sketch, and of whose career we now give the outline. Mr. Walpole was born in 1809—was educated at Eton, and Trinity College, Cambridge, where he took his B.A. degree in 1828, and obtained two prizes, namely, the first English declamation prize, and also one for the best essay on the character of William III. In 1831 he was called to the bar by the Society of Lincoln's

Inn, of which he is now a bencher, and speedily obtained a large practice as a Chancery barrister. A successful lawyer is rarely long before he gets into Parliament. Mr. Walpole became a Queen's Counsel in 1846, and at the same time had the honour of becoming M.P. for Midhurst.

The year 1846 was a memorable time in our Parliamentary annals. Sir Robert Peel and the Anti-Corn Law League, together, were to destroy, in that year, the system of Protection which the country gentlemen believed to be essential to England's welfare. The former had just been appointed, for the third time, minister of England, and apparently was stronger than ever. All idea of opposition of a serious character was ridiculed. A witty diplomatist communicated to an illustrious personage the opinion of a member of the Government, that it would be only "a fat cattle opposition, and that the Protectionists would be unable to keep up the debates for two nights." In reality it was otherwise. Lord George Bentinck became the leader of the Protectionists, Mr. Disraeli became their orator, and Mr. Walpole lent to the new party, in a short while, his pleasant presence and his ready tongue. Lord George Bentinck's leadership was of short duration. In 1848 he died suddenly, but his followers remained faithful to his principles, and in 1849 Mr. Walpole gained quite a Parliamentary reputation by his speech against the repeal of the Navigation Laws. His position thus won, Mr. Walpole took his place as one of the chiefs of parties. In 1851, when all Protestant England was aroused by the audacious aggression of the Church of Rome, he was one of the principal orators on the Ecclesiastical Titles Bill, and when Lord Derby came into office, the Home Department was given to Mr. Walpole, who, to discharge the duties of that dignified position, relinquished—though by no means wealthy—a very lucrative practice at the bar. As Secretary of State for the Home Department, he carried through Parliament a measure for embodying the militia. When the Derby administration went out, Mr. Walpole followed his colleagues into the cold shade of Opposition, and took a warm part in the discussions on University Reform, on more than one occasion carrying amendments against the Government. Mr. Walpole, after leaving office, became Chairman for a time of the Great Western Railway.

In 1856 he was elected to succeed Mr. Goulburn, as representative for the University of Cambridge. In 1858, there was another change in the position of parties. Lord Palmerston had been beaten on the Foreign Conspiracy Bill, and had given up office. Lord Derby had been sent for to take his place. Again Mr. Walpole was Home Secretary, which office he relinquished when the Conservative Reform Bill was introduced, as he did not, and could not, approve of all the details of the measure. This was the second sacrifice Mr. Walpole had made in order to serve his country. In the House great credit was given to him for his honesty in this last matter, as it was well known that, had he clung to office a little while longer, he would have been entitled to the pension of £2000 a year provided for such members of the Cabinet as are entitled to it by three years' services, and whose circumstances require it. Once more there was a turn in the wheel, and Mr. Walpole and his friends returned in 1866 to power. He resumed his position at the Home Office—which office he resigned when harassed by the Hyde Park affair, in which he appears to have acted with the full advice and co-operation of his colleagues.

As an Ecclesiastical Commissioner, Mr. Walpole was and is a representative of the Church party—the party with which he is connected in many ways. As a layman, on public occasions, he is ever ready to appear as its champion. In the Church Extension Scheme, for instance, of the Bishop of London, he took the warmest interest. If possible, Mr. Walpole would make the Establishment the Church of the nation. He would do this by reforming its abuses—by stimulating its energies—by giving to it increased efficacy and power. At Ealing, where he chiefly resides, he is a constant attendant at the parish church, the rector of which is considered to be by all a useful and earnest man, a true Churchman—but no ritualist, or hankerer after the pagan pomps of Rome.

In 1835 Mr. Walpole married the daughter of Spencer Perceval, whose assassination by Bellingham in the lobby of the House of Commons caused such a shock all over the country in 1812, and over whose dead body, Wilberforce affectingly tells us how his bereaved wife grew very moderate and resigned, and, with her children, prayed for them, and the murderer's forgiveness. By his marriage Mr. Walpole is the father of a large family, chiefly daughters. In private he is simple, unostentatious, and leads the life of a well-bred, a scholarly Christian English gentleman.

Of his personal appearance and manner of speaking, it is needless to say much. As a young man, he must have been very good-looking, with his light, fresh complexion, well-chiselled features, and clear blue eyes. Now he inclines a little to stoutness, and his hair is thin and partly grey. In dress he chiefly affects black, and might be taken for a country vicar of good family. His manner in Parliament was eminently conciliatory; and we should imagine no man has made, in the course of a political career extending over stormy times, fewer enemies. His language is very musical and harmonious. When necessary, Mr. Walpole can make a good speech. As a scholar, a gentleman, and a lawyer, he has few, if any, equals on his own side of the House. In political consistency, and in the patient discharge of duty, he is surpassed by none. For the rough work of the

Home Office, it may be that he was too refined and feeling. For such a place a harder nature than his may be requisite. Be that as it may, no man in the House is held at this time in higher honour than Mr. Walpole.

CHAPTER III.

OFFICIAL LIBERALS.

THE RT. HON. W. E. GLADSTONE.

(Greenwich—Gladstone, 6351; Salomons, 6645; Mahon, C., 4342; Parker, C., 4661.)

MANY, many years ago, England's foremost statesman — distrusted by the multitude — feared by his colleagues for his superiority — wearied of the strife and turmoil of party—on the eve of his departure as Governor-General of India, spent a short while at Seaforth House, bidding farewell to his Liverpool constituents. His custom was, we are told, to sit in his room, for hours, gazing on the wide expanse of ocean before him; while below, a little lad played at his feet on the sand. The old Puritan tells us "Man proposes, God disposes." Canning did not go to India—stopped at home to let all Europe understand that England had done with the holy alliance; stopped at home, in a few short years to be buried in Westminster Abbey, while a nation wept—and the little lad grew, till his name became familiar in our mouths as a household word. Does it not seem as if the young Gladstone, while playing on the sand with England's great statesman, looking far on the wide sea before him, had caught something of the genius — of the individuality—of the eloquence—of the statesmanship, which has given to the name of Canning an immortality which shall be fresh and fragrant when the grave in Westminster Abbey and the statue in Palace-yard shall have crumbled into dust? Let me not be understood to place Gladstone on an equal pedestal with Canning. The genius of Canning was of the highest order; like that of all great men, it was universal in its range—it embraced the opposite poles of human thought and action. With the keen arrow of his wit he could deal as deadly blow as could others with the most vehement invective or laboured harangue. Gladstone is here wofully deficient. He neither jests, nor laughs, nor smiles, and evidently avoids, as unfair, little tricks and artifices which less scrupulous or more skilful orators would be but too happy to employ. It must also be remembered that oratorical display is less sought in the House of Commons than formerly. Year by year it is becoming more a business assembly —more and more a monster vestry meeting, and less and less a gathering of "*patres conscripti.*" The oratorical era of the House of Commons reached its climax with Canning; the House now meets for the "despatch of business," and the men who succeed now-a-days are men whose faculty of business is something wonderful, and Mr. Gladstone is no exception to this rule.

In the first reformed Parliament, as if to show the fallacy of the melancholy forebodings of the anti-reformers, to the effect that for the future all talent would avoid St. Stephen's, Mr. Gladstone, then a very young man, of ample promise, from whom much was expected by his friends and collegiate contemporaries, became member for the Duke of Newcastle's close borough of Newark. His initiation into office, under Sir Robert Peel, took place soon after. When Sir Robert was prematurely borne off the political arena by a lamentable accident, Mr. Gladstone became known to the world as a faithful Peelite, intent upon the vindication of his master's fame, and consistent in the application of his principles. It also became clear that he was somewhat more than the blind follower of a great leader. He had given proofs of unusual tenderness of conscience, of marvellous subtilty of intellect, of rare independence of spirit—for he had resigned office, though on what ground was never exactly clear, and had written upon High Church claims on principles exclusively his own. No mention is made of Mr. Gladstone in the "Orators of the Age," a book published in 1847. In 1838 Mr. James Grant could write, and reviewers could praise, the book in which such want of political sagacity occurs as follows:—"I have no idea that he will ever acquire the reputation of a great statesman." It is not very long since the above was written; and now, on all sides, it is admitted Mr. Gladstone is the ablest man in the House of Commons. It was he alone who overthrew Disraeli as the latter had just acquired the Chancellorship of the Exchequer and the leadership of the House of Commons, and he has been the mainstay of the Coalition Cabinet, and of every subsequent Liberal administration. If he does not acquire the reputation of a great statesman, it is clear no man in our age will. I fancy Mr. Disraeli has no love for the orator who triumphed over him with ease, and with a proud consciousness of rectitude more potent even than eloquence itself. But his admirers have ever been men whose praise was worth winning and retaining. Thirty years ago Bunsen wrote—"Gladstone is the first man in England as to intellectual power, and he has heard higher tones than any one else in this island."

Sydney Smith's description of Horner I have always considered peculiarly appropriate to Gladstone. "There was something very remarkable in his countenance. The commandments were written in his face, and I have often told him there was not a crime he might not commit with impunity, as no judge nor jury who saw him would give the smallest degree of credit to any evidence against him. There was in his look a calm, settled love of all that was honourable and good—an air of wisdom and sweetness. You saw at once that he was a great man, whom Nature had intended for a leader of human beings. You ranged yourself willingly under his banner, and submitted to his sway." I copy the passage, as very applicable to the subject of this article. Judge for yourself. Come with me into the Strangers' Gallery of the House of Commons. It is early yet; the hour appointed for the transaction of private business is not over; but already down at the Treasury Bench there is the great Liberal leader, with papers all around, to the study of which he devotes apparently considerable attention. All of a sudden you see him drop his papers and look earnestly at some speaker who has risen to ask him some unimportant question. Mr. Gladstone rises, takes off his hat, and advances to the table. With his plain dress and his fluent delivery you might almost take him for a clergyman. He repeats the question, answers it in language of remarkable elegance, and sits down without making the slightest effort at display. Look at him now, with full dark eyes, clear intellectual head, and a body well proportioned, and of an average size. Nowhere can you see a face more indicative of goodness, and honesty, and power. Of the latter, if you wait, you will soon cease to doubt. A motion is before the House. Mr. Gladstone rises to defend the government; and however forcible may have been the attack, equally forcible is the defence. He is a master of debate, and you are not sorry when he rises to reply. His acuteness never fails him. His voice is always good, his delivery always animated, and his language never at fault. If you were to print his speech from the reporters' short-hand notes, without any revision whatever, it would be a perfect piece of composition. On one occasion, the celebrated Dick Martin complained that the reporters had not done him justice. It was urged that they had but given the hon. gentleman's exact words. "True," he said, "but did I spake them in italics?" Mr. Gladstone never need fear the reporters giving his exact words, even with the accompanying italics. Better than any man in the House he can stand the test of ridicule. Indeed, with his serious demeanour he abashes levity, and puts aside all trifling. He would act the part of one of the Roman senators to perfection. If he cannot win a victory by fair means, he will not by foul. When the House, as it is too apt to do, forgets itself—when it abounds with sarcasm and personalities, Mr. Gladstone sits silent and sorrowful. But I have not yet given you an idea of his power. The party debate over, the House goes into committee. It is late; the House is hot; members are weary and away; but one man is at his post, and that man is Mr. Gladstone. Not a criticism is uttered but he makes a note of it. With his knees crossed so as to serve him for a table, with a pencil in his hand, with his head bent forward in the direction of the Speaker, there he sits hour after hour, save when he rises to defend, or enforce, or explain the measure of which he has the charge. I believe he may make a dozen speeches in the course of a single night on different subjects, and so silvery is his voice, so ready his language, so acute, and searching, and comprehensive his criticism, that the more you hear of him the more you are impressed with admiration. In his intellect, strength and flexibility are combined, and thus it is he is so full and elastic and effective when on his legs. The more difficult the theme, the more animated the debate, the more solemn the crisis, the more does he shine. Some of his more serious efforts are worthy of the best days of parliamentary history. When some national unrighteousness has been done, when some folly of the hour has to be pointed out and deplored, you know then that Gladstone, with "dauntless words and high," will speak as did he

> "Who shook the sere leaves from the wood
> As if a storm pass'd by."

Perhaps his greatest triumphs were when Palmerston was premier. No one but Mr. Gladstone could have reconciled the House of Commons not merely to the continuance, but to the increasing the Income Tax, at the very time the public had been led to expect its abolition altogether. Mr. Gladstone's sore-throat, which necessitated delay, was a European difficulty. Happily, nature and Dr. Ferguson proved victorious, and the Palmerston cabinet was saved. The Chancellor's speech of four hours was a master-piece of tact and ingenuity; was persuasive and eloquent and overpowering; the reply to Mr. Disraeli was complete, and for once in his life Mr. Gladstone was almost savage. "I could not stand that speech of Gladstone's," said a Conservative M.P. to a friend; "I was compelled to vote for him." In the debate on Mr. Du Cane's amendment, as if conscious of his coming majority of 116, Mr. Gladstone assumed a haughty and dashing bearing, and displayed a disposition to punish his adversaries which he seldom evinces. His budget took the world by surprise; it was, as an M.P. described it, an ambitious budget. The Opposition made but a feeble fight; Mr. Disraeli was but faintly supported by his own party. For a wonder, after he had spoken about a quarter of an hour, members flocked into the lobby, and chatted away with their hands in their pockets, as if Mr. Spooner were delivering an oration against Maynooth, or as if a Marylebone M.P. were ingloriously riding some dull hobby to death. Sir John Pakington made a blunder still worse. His advice to the aggrieved hop-growers to rally with the publicans and sinners—with all the interests damaged, or expecting to be damaged, by the budget, rendered their cause hopeless. When the question lay, as the hon. baronet seemed to imply, between the public good on one side and particular interests on the other, there could be no doubt as to the result. Theoretically, the House of Commons may be an imperfect body, but more or less it represents public opinion, and no one appeals to its public spirit in vain.

Mr. Gladstone's position is by no means a pleasant one. Mr. Fox said he would rather get his bread any way than by being Chancellor of the Exchequer. Depend upon it Mr. Gladstone would say the same. As a man of peace, he has been compelled to find the money for the Chinese war—a war against which he has more than once raised an indignant protest; he has had to swallow his objections to an income tax, and increase it; he has had to put up with a "gigantic innovation," and pocket the one-and-a-half millions of money the Lords persisted in pressing on him by refusing to repeal the paper duty. He has had, besides, to come to Parliament for money for fortifications. No wonder he is indignant,—no wonder he charges the House of Commons and the people of his country with extravagance,—no wonder he exclaimed as he did in one of his speeches towards the end of the late session:—"Vacillation, uncertainty, costliness, extravagance, meanness, and all the conflicting vices that could be enumerated, are united in our present system. There is a total want of authority to direct and guide. When anything is to be done we have to go from department to department, from the Executive to the House of Commons, from the House of Commons to a Committee, from a Committee to a Commission, and from a Commission back to a Committee, so that years pass away, the public is disappointed, and the money of the country is wasted. I believe such are the evils of the system that nothing short of revolutionary reform will ever be sufficient to rectify it."

Mr. Gladstone, it must be admitted, has his faults.

In the first place he has the logical faculty in excess, and will keep on splitting hairs till you are exhausted; and secondly, when out of office, and freed from its responsibilities, he will persist in putting before the House the unpopular side of the question. Again, he is of an enthusiastic character, and will paint a picture *couleur de rose* when the facts have a decided tendency the other way. He is very often the slave of an idea; he contemplates it till he loses all perception of anything else. His speech on the Repeal of the Paper Duty, in which Mr. Gladstone showed to what numerous uses paper might be applied, was a remarkable illustration of this. Whatever may be the subject of debate, he is sure to lengthen it and encumber it. He ignores the popular view. It must be refined, and sublimated, and in perilous mazes lost, and then Mr. Gladstone is in his glory. Of late, however, he has become a very different and much safer man. It was not till he became a member for South Lancashire that he appeared to be independent. Yet in office he will do strange things. He resigned rather than vote for an inquiry into the causes of the fearful calamities and horrors of the Crimean campaign. As the representative of the body that is least permeated with popular feeling — the Oxford University — Mr. Gladstone seemed compelled to act in this way. On the Russian war—on the Divorce Bill—on the Church Rate Bill—he thus voted on the unpopular side. Yet you feel that St. Stephen's does not contain an honester man, or one more conscientious, that

> "Neither gold,
> Nor sordid fame, nor hope of heavenly bliss,"

could lead him to deviate a hair's breadth from what he conceived to be the right. Nay, more—occasionally he will boil over with enthusiasm, as when, in his Letters to Lord Aberdeen on the sufferings of the Neapolitan state prisoner, he made

> "All Europe ring from side to side."

His mission to the Ionian Islands—unfortunate as it turned out to be in every respect—was undertaken in a similar fit of enthusiasm. Indeed, he has so much of this precious quality that it cannot all find a vent in public life. Hence a work on Homer, too bulky even for men of ample leisure and scholarship to find time to read.

Remember that Mr. Gladstone entered the House of Commons as the nominee of the late Duke of Newcastle—the Duke who asked if he might not do as he liked with his own?—admit that he is no party man—that he is very conscientious—that he is very anxious to learn, and the conclusion is that he admits now much that he opposed in earlier life. When he entered public life he was deeply attached to the great retrogressive party in Church and State, but he found much that had been clear in an Oxford atmosphere was quite the reverse in St. Stephen's. How strenuous, for instance, was his opposition to the Emancipation Act. Let it also be said that he was originally a protectionist—that he is now a free-trader —that he has given up as impracticable the doctrines he enunciated in his "State in its Relation to the Church." Strange is it now that England—low-church and dissenting—should have for her chief man a believer in Apostolical Succession. Yet Mr. Gladstone defends this doctrine, and, on account of it, is a firm believer in the Church of England. Chillingworth said, "I am fully persuaded there hath been no such succession." Bishop Stillingfleet declares, "This succession is as muddy as the Tiber itself." Bishop Hoadly asserts, "It hath not pleased God, in his providence, to keep up any proof of the least probability or moral possibility of a regal and uninterrupted succession, but there is a great appearance, and, humanly speaking, a certainty to the contrary, that the succession had often been interrupted." Archbishop Whately says, "There is not a minister in all Christendom who is able to trace up, with approach to certainty, his spiritual pedigree." Mr. Gladstone's faith in this respect, it may be, redeemed his many errors in Oxford eyes. Oxford might well be proud of the child of her training. Mr. Gladstone, in 1831, closed a brilliant career at Christ Church by taking a double first.

It was a bright idea of Lord Palmerston, getting Mr. Gladstone to be Chancellor of the Exchequer. Out of office his mind would have burst all bonds of habit and wandered far away. He would have opposed the budget, and the ministry would have been defeated.

Mr. Gladstone is one of the few men in the House who rise to eloquence of the stateliest order. He is seldom, if ever, historical and lost in precedent. He seems simply to rely upon his knowledge of the subject, and his ability to place it before the House in a commanding and attractive manner. How great is his merit we can best learn by contrast. When Gladstone brought forward his first budget, the House expected a treat; the pressure was enormous; strangers had taken their places, waiting for the opening of the gallery, as early as noon, and though the Chancellor of the Exchequer spoke nearly five hours, though his speech had to do exclusively with those generally dry things, facts and figures, the House was crowded to the last, and not a stranger left the gallery. When Sir Cornewall Lewis, a good man but a poor speaker—a speaker, however, who amazingly improved before his death—opened his budget, the very reverse was the case. I believe there were ten strangers in the Speaker's Gallery; certainly there were not more than a hundred members in the House. Yet the occasion was an eventful one. Peace had just been proclaimed, but the extra expenditure of the war had not ceased, and had Mr. Gladstone been the Chancellor, the attention of the country and the House would have been excited. As it was, a humdrum speaker performed his duties in a humdrum manner, and not even money matters aroused a dumb House into eloquence and life. On the introduction of his last and memorable budget, the desire to hear Mr. Gladstone was amazing. Strangers with members' orders took their places as early as nine A.M., and, for the first time since he had left it, Lord Brougham occupied a seat in the House of Commons.

Since the above was written, Mr. Gladstone has been emancipated from his Oxford bondage, and as the leader of the House of Commons introduced in 1866 a Reform Bill which found more favour out of the House than in it. Defeated in his attempt to carry it, he has gained a popularity of which he could never have dreamt. The people rally round him as the coming man.

THE RIGHT HON. ROBERT LOWE.

(London University—unopposed.)

Perhaps no one in this country at this time enjoys more notoriety than the Right Hon. Robert Lowe. His speech in the closing week of the Reform debate created a sensation almost unrivalled; and undoubtedly the position he maintained, and his bold and unflinching manner, did much to win over the waverers who otherwise would never have dared to vote in Parliament against what they had promised to support without. A timid M.P. might be excused, he would argue with himself, if he ventured to oppose a measure, which in the opinion of a leading Liberal statesman and quondam Member of a Liberal Administration, was to sacrifice the heroic work of many centuries "at the shrine of revolutionary passion or maudlin enthusiasm;" which was to "pull down the venerable temple of our liberties;" and which carried, at once

> "The fatal horse pours forth the human tide,
> Insulting Sinon flings his firebrands wide;
> The gates are burst,—the ancient rampart falls,
> And swarming millions climb its crumbling walls."

Those of us who have lived a few years and have good memories have heard all this before. Quite as much evil was predicted when the Corn-Laws were repealed, when the first Reform Bill was carried—when Roman Catholics were allowed to take their seats in Parliament. It does not alarm us. We exclaim, like the man in Lord Lytton's comedy of "Money," "In my day I have seen already eighteen crises, six annihilations of agriculture and commerce, four overthrows of the Church, and three last, final, and irremediable destructions of the entire Constitution." Yet, in spite of this argument, always answered by the logic of events, poor and worn threadbare as it is, Mr. Lowe's speech was the speech of the debate. For a day it was the entire talk of London; in the City or at the West-end, in gay clubs or dull counting-houses, on the tops of 'buses, or on the Underground Railway, wherever man met man, people said, "What a speech was that of Mr. Lowe last night!" It made Reformers vastly angry. Of the 175 electors of Calne,

61 took the trouble publicly to protest against it. Equally indignant was the Reform League. A glance at Mr. Lowe as he sits, white-haired and ruddy-faced,—hair white, not from age, but constitutionally,—will show that he is not the man to be frightened in a storm. Hark! he is named by the Speaker; and the House fills, and he is the point of attraction of every eye. What do you see? A plain man, in theprime of life, dressed in black, speaking in a plain way, in a voice clearly audible all over the House, yet in a style almost conversational, and as far removed from the school-boy's idea of oratory as it is possible; no timidity, no nervousness, no stumbling sentences at first, to be followed by a lofty burst of declamation afterwards. That is not Mr. Lowe's style. Apparently aiming at no effect, arguing, as it were, almost to himself, he holds on his way, with a slight tinge of pride as if exempt from the ordinary foibles of flesh and blood,—sarcastic, ironical, severe, making his points almost unconsciously, and as if not knowing them to be such till he is greeted with applause or laughter, and then he appears to enjoy them as much as any one else. From the appearance of the speaker, you would say naturally he liked to be unpopular, and to take the unpopular side. Guizot wrote of Lord Jeffery that he had been so long a critic that in his old age he had left to him nothing to admire. Mr. Lowe seems to have been so long an Oxford tutor, and to have towered so long above those around him,

that in the House of Commons he can recognise no intellect superior, no aim nobler, no heart beating more generously than his own. Once in his life, it is true, he had a constituency, and then he had the narrowest escape possible from having his head broken by them. When he was in office he was always in hot water with the Opposition; and when he became an independent Liberal—a Liberal who confesses that he owes no allegiance to Earl Russell—he dealt the late Liberal Administration the heaviest blow it received. Uncontrolled by the fear of constituents, not flattered by having had his name omitted from the Administration formed on the death of Lord Palmerston, conscious of his power as an administrator as well as a debater, a master of logic, and trained in all the subtleties of the schools,—Mr. Lowe's position is unique—more gratifying to his own sense of personal importance than useful to himself or profitable to the State. His triumphs are great, but it is not every one who would envy him them. And, after all, it must be remembered that the part he has undertaken to play is not a difficult one. It is easy work in an aristocratic assembly to denounce democracy—in a gathering of the rich to heap scorn upon the poor. It requires little courage to cast dirt on men who are not present to speak up and demand justice for themselves. Lord Elcho went to the meeting at St. Martin's Hall, and boldly met the working classes whom he had denounced as unfit for the franchise, face to face. Mr. Lowe, on the contrary, confines his intellectual displays to a more appreciative audience. Hence his renown, hence the ease with which he, a quondam member of an Administration pledged to Reform, could oppose it when it had a chance of being carried. In the House of Commons they are all honourable men. Selfishness cannot exist in that serene atmosphere. There the clear light of intellect separates the dross from what is sterling and noble in human actions; and there deeds are done and words uttered and applauded as the inspiration of the purest patriotism, which, outside the House, and to the *profanum vulgus*, may have the appearance of being the result of disappointed ambition or party spleen. People are so uncharitable, they do say such unkind things when a man leaves his friends and joins the ranks of his foes! It is a pity that it should be so. What, asks the satirist,—

> "What makes all doctrines plain and clear?
> About two hundred pounds a year."

As if place, or the want of it, except as a means of usefulness, was ever considered by a politician. But evidently this is a disgression, and by no means personal to the Right Hon. Robert Lowe—the merciless logician who takes good care that he shall never be led away by "revolutionary passion or maudlin enthusiasm," and yet who, as a practical man, has failed quite as much as if he had;—perhaps more so. The statesman who ignores passion and enthusiasm must fail.

All human nature is against him. Years ago Mr. Lowe found this out. He was defeated and driven from office for this alone. In his capacity of Vice-President of Committee of Council on Education, he proposed—what? Why, the most equitable thing in the world. He proposed to submit the pupils of the subsidised schools to periodical examinations, and to make the continuance of the subsidy dependent on the result of those examinations. As guardian of the public money entrusted to him for educational purposes, he proposed not to part with it till he had something for it. And what was the result? Such a storm was raised by clergymen and schoolmasters that Mr. Lowe had to give way. Mr. Lowe, in our time, repeated the blunder of Hobbes, of Malmesbury, in his. In many things they resemble each other; especially in this—that in their political systems they forget how in real life man is "flesh and blood," not a machine to chop logic; they forget how

"the fiery passions tear—
The vultures of the mind."

Intellect by itself has never ruled the world, and never will. It is seldom it has the chance. Locke, it is true, tried his hand at constitution-making, but his experiment did not succeed. Mr. Lowe himself knows that he is alone in the House; that the men whose applause he has won to-day by his uttering what they felt and had not the power to express, yesterday were his enemies, and to-morrow will be the same. They fear his intellect, his knowledge, and his scorn. Mr. Lowe has nothing in common with the Newdegates, the Bentincks, and country squires. Altogether, life with Mr. Lowe has been a success. He does not in cloistered cell or academic hall contemplate the battle from afar, but he rushes into it, and gloriously wears its sweat, and dust, and scars. Of respectable parentage, he has made himself what he is. His father was a clergyman in Nottinghamshire; his mother was the daughter of a clergyman. He was born in 1811, educated at Winchester and University College, Oxford, where in 1833 he took his B.A. degree. In 1836 he married and began the battle of life. In 1842 he was called to the bar at Lincoln's-inn. In 1843 he made a short trial of colonial life. Speedily he made his way in Australia. From 1843 to 1850 he was a Member of Council at Sydney, and for the latter portion of the time M.P. for Sydney. He came back to this country, where he at once took a high position. In 1852 he entered the House of Commons as M.P. for Kidderminster, and he represented it in Parliament till 1859. He has now the gratification of being the first member returned by the London University. Of official life he has had ample experience. Originally he was Joint Secretary of the Board of Control. Then he became Paymaster of the Forces and Vice-President of the Board of Trade, and from 1859 to 1864 he was Vice-President of Committee of Council on Education, till driven from office by the very men who now hail him as the saviour of the State, yet who would not return him to Parliament if they had the power.

And this brings us to this suggestive fact—that Mr. Lowe's Parliamentary existence was one of the best arguments for Reform. He could not be said to have had a constituency. Calne had but 175 electors, and was the property of the Marquis of Lansdowne. As it happened, the Marquis sent to the House of Commons a gentleman and a scholar; but what are we to say of the system which allowed the Marquis, if he were so disposed, to return his butler or his groom?

THE RT. HON. JAMES STANSFELD.

(Halifax—Stansfeld, 5281; Akroyd, 5201; Greening, L., 2847.)

It is now nearly thirty years since there were studying in University College, London, some young men of ample promise, which in after-life they have fully redeemed. Their presence in Gower-street was to a certain extent a pledge of their Liberal opinions and of the conscientiousness with which those opinions were entertained. I am not aware that, as regards pecuniary considerations, a residence at University College was cheaper for students from the country than one at Oxford or Cambridge;—other reasons, then, must have led to the selection of the London University. It was the result of Liberal opinions; that might be one reason for supporting it. Again, the course of instruction was more careful, and embraced a wider range of subjects than that comprehended in the curriculum of the older Universities; and then, again, no subscription of a religious character was required from students. Young men were not as a matter of form asked to give their assent and consent to articles of belief which they did not hold, and thus to violate that virgin purity of conscience which is essential to all true excellence of character. This, I imagine, was the true reason why many selected the London College. *Prestige* was of course all the other way. Ambition pointed to Oxford or Cambridge as the portals through which fame and wealth were to be won. The price to be paid by the student was not great in one sense, but tremendous in another. The many paid it willingly, caring little, like Hook, whether the Articles were thirty-nine or forty that they were called upon to sign; others, the thoughtful few, hesitated, and shrank from recklessness or thoughtlessness in such matters. For them there was the college in Gower Street, at which the wealthy snob sneered, and to which the Tory press gave the unpleasant appellation of *Stinkomalee.* It was here that the late Under-Secretary of State for India laid the foundation of his future fame.

Mr. Stansfeld is of a Yorkshire family. His uncle, Hamer Stansfeld of Leeds, was a man at one time well known in political life. His father had—I believe yet has—a legal official position at Halifax of a very respectable character. His son was also intended for the bar, and was called at the Inner Temple in 1846, though he did not practise. In 1844 he took his LL.B. degree. In the days of Stansfeld's youth, the impulse given to the political world by the great wave of Reform, which had swept all before it for a time, was still felt. Men believed in national regeneration by means of Parliamentary Reforms, and it is clear that at that time there was much for statesmen to do, or, rather, undo. Privilege was strong and outrageous in its defiance of right. The commercial policy which has since fertilised our land with wealth, and found food for all who would work, did not exist. Kind, tender-hearted Christian men and women, who wept over the sufferings of the black slave, had little sympathy to spare for the white. The knowledge which could alone elevate the working classes was denied them. Their restlessness and discontent, their readiness to obey such leaders as Feargus O'Connor, were viewed with suspicion and fear. The capitalist, and the Member of Parliament, and the parson, seemed to the operative his natural enemies. "The condition of England question," as it was then called, was indeed sad and pitiful. The masses were burning with the sense of intolerable wrong. They had helped the middle classes to win Reform, and then had been left in the lurch. Prisons were full and union-houses were full, and in the manufacturing districts the soldier superseded the police; and yet the people exclaimed against the injustice of which they had been the victims, and lean, and pale, and ignorant, and uncared-for, rallied round the Charter, and madly talked of physical force. Old men trembled, and men like Lords Sidmouth and Eldon went down into their graves believing that the greatness and glory of England had departed for ever. The young, and the generous, and brave, took a more cheerful view. For this evil there was, in their opinion, a remedy, for this disease a cure. Of this number James Stansfeld was one. It was true that

> "Many an old philosophy
> On Argive heights divinely sang;"

but new times needed new philosophies, and surely in some or other of them would the age gain what it required. The new seed fell upon good ground. By the press, by public meetings, by active organization, a kindlier spirit was created and the way prepared for victory. The dangerous chasm between the rich and the poor was bridged over. There was no longer a yawning gulf with Lazarus on one side and Dives on the other.

Thus as a student Mr. Stansfeld was something more than a mere plodding pedant. It was not success at the bar at which alone he aimed. He cared far more for literature and politics. With the people he sympathised, and for them he laboured. His father-in-law was a man of similar ideas, and at his house Mr. Stansfeld would meet many to encourage him in his political career.

In the battle of freedom as fought in other lands Mr. Stansfeld took his part. In the associations formed on behalf of Polish, or Hungarian, or Italian nationalities he was a cordial worker. When the revolutionary years of 1848-9 had ended disastrously, and London was crowded with refugees, he and his lady were the first to receive them. At his residence they were greeted with the solace which preserves the patriot from despair and rekindles the heroic flame. Kossuth, Mazzini, and others scarcely less illustrious, and equally deserving, found guidance and friendship. Mrs. Stansfeld translated Mazzini's writings into English, and by thus popularising his ideas in this country, an impulse was given to the cause of Italian regeneration which in time paved the way for the statesman who reaps the fruit of the thinker's thoughts.

Thus it came to pass that without seeking fame Mr. Stansfeld became famous, and the result was that, when a general election took place, the people of Halifax, having first consulted the father, asked the son if he would be their representative in Parliament. The latter returned an affirmative reply. Accordingly he was elected in the handsomest manner. It is said a prophet has no honour in his own country; Mr. Stansfeld is an exception to this general rule.

In the House of Commons he took his seat below

the gangway on the Ministerial side, near Cobden and Bright, and the few but powerful men who cared neither for Whig nor Tory, but emblazoned on their banners popular rights and progress. The member for Halifax speedily gained the ear of the House. His style of speaking was eminently Parliamentary. His manner was singularly pleasing and attractive. There were traces in him, too, of a higher culture than that of the party to which he belonged. He had attained to a richer and a fuller vein of thought, a broader platform, a wider range of sympathy. Let it not be understood that we have one word of reproach to utter against those noble leaders who had reluctantly, and at great personal sacrifice, entered the senate in the midst of an angry contest to plead before a hostile audience an unpopular cause. But circumstances had been favourable to Mr. Stansfeld. Literature, and philosophy, and science, and art, had enlarged and enriched his mind. He belonged to a younger and a better school. Of that school he was the first and ablest exponent. Prejudice was disarmed when the House saw that the new speaker was no blatant demagogue, but a polished, amiable, unassuming gentleman, sincere, self-possessed, equal to the occasion; and when by his motions on national expenditure, he skilfully made himself master of the situation, it was felt that in offering him official responsibility Lord Palmerston had acted wisely and well. Mr. Stansfeld became a junior Lord of the Admiralty in 1863, and was no sooner in office than his capacity for it became clear. He had mastered all the difficult questions connected with the Admiralty; he had given great satisfaction to the House by the way in which he performed his duties; the Duke of Somerset, his chief, was delighted,—so it was understood; but Mr. Stansfeld had committed a fault—he had not thrown overboard the friend of his youth. In spite of the foul slanders which had been associated with the name of the illustrious Mazzini, he still retained his friendship for the Italian exile. The Tory party, aided by Mr. W. Cox, raised a storm, and Mr. Stansfeld went his way into an honourable retirement, but he did not fall unavenged. At the general election for 1865 Mr. Cox, "your old and long-tried friend," as he termed himself pathetically, was unseated for Finsbury, and in the House of Commons his diminutive figure is seen no more. When, on the decease of Lord Palmerston, Earl Russell was entrusted with the seals of office, it was evident to all that Mr. Stansfeld's services would be required in the new Administration. Accordingly, he was appointed Under-Secretary of State for India. It seems to the outside public an undesirable arrangement to take a man from an office the duties of which he has perfectly mastered, and to place him in one where he has to begin anew; but we may presume Earl Russell had reasons satisfactory to himself; and India is a noble field for statesmanship of the highest and most ambitious order.

Mr. Stansfeld is now in the prime of life. He was born in 1820, and is remarkably youthful for his years. Though guilty of the Dundreary affectation of wearing his hair parted in the middle, he has nothing of the fop about him. In his student days he was rather negligent in his attire, but he is now always neatly dressed. He is of medium height, and by no means robust. His hair is brown, and I fancy his eyes are of a greyish cast. The perpetual smile upon his face indicates the gentleness and good-nature of a character, I believe, as pure and lofty as that of any Member in the House. On several occasions he has appeared upon the platform in connection with the meeting of the Religious Liberation Society. Of whatever Liberal Administration may be formed it is clear he must be one. Of another thing also we may be sure—that he will side with no Ministry that does not attempt to translate into legislative acts all that is best and truest in the spirit of the age.

MR. H. AUSTEN LAYARD.

(SOUTHWARK—LOCKE, 6489; LAYARD, 6371; COTTON, C., 2587.)

No one who studies public men and public affairs can doubt the doctrine of the resurrection. When, a few years since, Lord Palmerston was defeated on the Chinese war, and appealed to the country, what a crushing defeat was sustained by his opponents! To borrow the language of the turf, they were "nowhere." Manchester rejected Bright and Gibson; Mr. Cobden dared not attempt the West Riding, and actually was rejected by Huddersfield; Mr. Layard lost his seat for Aylesbury, and, for a time, had to submit to parliamentary extinction. I can scarce imagine a heavier calamity for an able or ambitious man. He who is accustomed to parliamentary life must feel existence a blank without it. To play a worthy part in the senatorial drama finds employment for the greatest energies of our greatest men. In the morning there are committees to attend, blue books to study, speeches to prepare; in the evening there are eight hours of talk to be endured, deputations to be conversed with in the lobby, and endless business, miscellaneous and otherwise. For all common life a member of Parliament is unfitted. What greatness lies in his name! how he is reported in newspapers! how much is made of him at Exeter Hall! what a boon he is on the direction of a public company! and in dining-rooms and drawing-rooms what delight attaches to his every word! How unhappy must be an American President after his four years at the White House are over! What a settled melancholy must lie in the heart of hearts of an ex-Lord Mayor! How flat, stale, and unprofitable must have been existence to Alexander when he found there were no more worlds to win! How suicidal must have been the feelings of such an one as Tom Sayers when his hour was gone—when we never mentioned him—when his name was never heard—when our lips were forbidden to speak that once familiar word! But with an M.P. dissolved into common clay it is worse, far worse. However, let him not despair; his turn may come—if he be a man of mark and merit it must come. Mr. Layard at length found his way back into St. Stephen's, and Southwark has done well in sending to Parliament an M.P. worthy to occupy the seat of Sir Charles Napier, of Sir W Molesworth, of Daniel Whittle Harvey.

Mr. Henry Austen Layard, in a book published in 1853, I find, is described as "traveller and author." A few years make a great change in the position of clever men. Time brings opportunities, and opportunity is a goodlier gift of the gods than an ancient heritage or an honoured name. The Russian war broke out, and opportunities came to all. Aged generals grasped them in vain; timid admirals saw them, and their hearts quailed; quarter-master-generals, and heads of departments, and old fogies, whom England had ignorantly worshipped for half a century, for once found themselves face to face with them, and ignominiously, and amidst universal contempt, let them go by for ever. In the midst of this wreck and ruin Layard's figure, rapidly emerging from the palpable obscure, became firmly fixed before the public eye. As I have already said, he was known to the public as an author and traveller. He had been attached to the embassy at the Porte, and afterwards, on the retirement from the Foreign-office of Lord Palmerston, and the accession of

Earl Granville, he filled the office of Under Secretary of State for Foreign Affairs. In 1852 he was returned to Parliament for Aylesbury, and in the following year he was presented with the freedom of the City of London, in consideration of his enterprising discoveries among the ruins of Nineveh. Truly, Layard's lot has fallen amongst pleasant places. I am not aware that the public made much of Captain Cook, or that the freedom of the City of London was presented to Belzoni, or that Mungo Parke had a place in the Foreign-office; but those were not days of Hudson testimonials, and now Virtue is sulky if she is her own reward.

In the session of 1855 Layard played for a higher stake. Hitherto he had been fortunate in the extreme. He made a desperate effort to be the man of the time. With the intelligent public out of doors, upon whom loose declamation is sure to tell, he had already become that; but he aimed in the House of Commons to attain a similar place—a game infinitely more difficult, and to be played with a caution and coolness which Mr. Layard unfortunately did not possess. His antecedents were in his favour, and the House lent him a willing ear. When he rose to speak it grew full; it gave him credit for a knowledge of the affairs of the East possessed but by few of its members. Unfortunately, he stated facts and instances at random. He attacked men who had relations in the House ready and willing to defend them. He excited much aristocratic indignation, and his vehement assertions were met by contradictions equally vehement, and more correct. Still, he was a favourite with the House. He then put his name down to specific motions and questions innumerable. On such a day he would call the attention of the House to the condition of the army, to the state of affairs in Asia, to the mismanagement of the Horse Guards, as the case might be. The administrative reformers believed that their hour of triumph at length had come. In its weak simplicity the radical press avowed that the nation, at length, was about to be saved, and the teeming rabid radicalism of the metropolis smiled with unwonted glee. The night came, the Strangers' Gallery was crowded; and, in their mistaken confidence, the long rows of St. Stephen's Hall were crowded with individuals waiting to take their turn. Alas, alas! the night came, but the dashing Layard held back. Not once but frequently was this the case. In the language of the field it was said of Mr. Layard that he "craned." When a horse will not take a fence he is said to "crane." No man can do this repeatedly with impunity, and Mr. Layard cannot be much surprised if, in consequence, he sank somewhat in the opinion of his admirers of the better sort.

It is charged by indignant Protestants that the Church of Rome admits and maintains the doctrine of reserve—but who does not? Is it pleasant for the lady of the house to hear her pert child inform Mr. Smithers that yesterday Ma said he was a bore, and wished he were at Hanover? Is not a candid friend the most irritating creature on the face of the globe? Do you think Anna Maria would forgive you if, in her album, instead of comparing her to blue-eyed Minerva, you simply expressed the honest wish that she would no twear her hair in curlpapers—that she would mend the holes in her stockings? Would you tell the wife of your bosom that you had made a mistake in marrying her, and that you were pining for one who now never could be yours? It is just so in the House of Commons. Often silence is golden there. Mr. Carter forgot this when he was member for Tavistock, and he never would have been listened to again; so did Robert Lowe in his debate on the Corporation Tolls, and the result was a storm of indignation that nearly shelved Mr. Lowe himself, and completely shelved his bill; so did poor Duffy on a memorable occasion, and the House was in hot water for six weeks after. But Layard made another blunder. His truth, substantially right, was often circumstantially wrong—right in its essence, wrong in its accidents. He thus committed a double offence, and gave the Philistines reason to rejoice. Yet the House lent him a willing ear; to no man was it more generous or forgiving. Mr. Layard did not do himself justice; he ought to have been more guarded in his language; less off-hand and desultory; his matter should have been more carefully prepared. His hot temper also appears to have been in his way. He has travelled in Italy, and the East, and in India, and there are vital questions touching all these places. He thus returned to Parliament under peculiarly advantageous circumstances. Mr. Layard should remember, after all, it is a fine thing to be able to lift up one's voice in the Parliament of Great Britain and Ireland, to stand up there, in the midst of principalities and powers, to speak history, and what may be quoted a hundred years to come. A foremost place there is no mean thing; not without difficulty to be attained unto, nor lightly to be whistled away.

His difficulties have been many and discouraging. There have been in his career times when he has been alone in the House—when he has had alone to bear the brunt of indignant colonels and irate officers of militia. Some men would have cowed before the storm. The House, in its harsh and angry moods, is not a pleasant place to speak in—not a bear-garden, nor yet exactly a rapturously applauding Exeter Hall; but the worst of it is, the independent members fight on their own account. They take good care that their enemies do not act on the old maxim, "Divide and rule," for they divide of their own accord, and therefore are overruled. Hardly half-a-dozen of them pull together, but every one of them does that which is right in his own eyes. If this be a blunder in military warfare, it is criminal in the House of Commons, where a band of united men, one in heart and aim, can do so much, and where the existence of such a band, in the name of right to protest against the doing of wrong, is so imperatively required. But each man is disposed of by himself. He makes his charge. It is flung back in his face—heavily by one, historically by another, pedantically by a third, flippantly by a fourth. From the Opposition benches comes a loud and fierce denial, not unmixed with scorn—all around is an atmosphere charged with thunder. There is the low, deep murmur of dissent; the inattention, which is more confusing than open interruption; heavy impotence, unassailable and conscious of its strength. From back benches on both sides, what a cluster of aggrieved rise to speak! uttering what common-place, and received with what cheers! To face that Macedonian phalanx requires some nerve. Layard has done this; and you may measure his claims to public favour by the extent, and depth, and bitterness of their hate. His triumph at Southwark, however, was an ample reward. It ought to make even an M.P. a patriot. It again placed Mr. Layard in office.

But you have not seen Mr. Layard? On the front ministerial row any night you may see him, with his bright, dark blue eye, and thick beard tinged with grey, and somewhat boyish face. He is an active-looking man, with a very good voice, and considerable fluency and readiness, generally very plainly dressed, and not in the oriental costume in which you may have seen him represented. It may be that Mr. Layard's opportunity has gone by; but it is clear, for some time to come, his acquaintance with the East will recommend him to the House.

THE RIGHT HON. EDWARD CARDWELL.

(OXFORD CITY.)

IN the last Ministry of Lord Palmerston the office of Secretary of State for the Colonies was held by Mr. Edward Cardwell, M.P. for Oxford City, one of the Peelites who have developed into as ardent reformers as is consistent with the growth of public opinion. The right honourable gentleman was first returned to Parliament in 1842, as Member for Clitheroe. He next had the honour of representing Liverpool, losing which, and having unsuccessfully contested Ayrshire, he became M.P. for the City of Oxford, on the appointment of Sir W. Page Wood to the Vice-Chancellorship in 1853. He has served the country in various offices. His first appointment dates from 1845, when he was Secretary of the Treasury; in 1853 he was President of the Board of Trade; in 1859 he became Chief Secretary for Ireland; in 1861 he was appointed Chancellor of the Duchy of Lancaster, and in 1864 Secretary of State for the Colonies. When he accepted the latter office he had to deal with the fatal Ashantee Expedition, and the War in New Zealand. Both questions were happily settled before he and his colleagues resigned in 1867. It is to his credit that he inserted in the Crown Colonies the thin edge of the wedge, and by insisting on payments from Colonial exchequers for British soldiers, did something to rouse the colonists to self-defence, and at the same time relieve the mother-country. In British North America the state of affairs was anything but satisfactory when Mr. Cardwell accepted office; the American Civil War had alarmed the Canadians, and made them feel the need of greater security. This alarm was also increased by the movements of Fenians on the border, and by the boast of certain orators and newspapers in New York. The idea of a Confederation was suggested to many, and speedily became popular in Canada, but it afterwards appeared that in New Brunswick and Prince Edward's Island the people were averse from it. Mr. Cardwell, however, never ceased to support it vigorously, and the main obstacle to it has, in our time, been at last removed by a decisive verdict in its favour at the late elections in New Brunswick. Nor were these the only difficulties with which Mr. Cardwell has had to contend. The excitement caused in Australia by the continuance of transportation, the outbreak in Jamaica, in suppressing which Governor Eyre appears to have been guilty of enormous blunders, and the Constitutional crisis in Victoria, were all very alarming occurrences, but which Mr. Cardwell appears to have met in the most judicious manner. We were all relieved by hearing that Governor Darling had been recalled, that a commission had been appointed to proceed to Jamaica, and that wise and sensible concessions had been made to the Australian colonists. A colonial minister wields an enormous power, and if he be ignorant, or reckless, or incapable, he may do the country an irreparable wrong. Mr. Cardwell is a man of great talent, but so was Charles Townshend, who lost us America. England without her colonial empire would be poor indeed. Happily in our days it is public opinion that rules in high places, but public opinion generally is very little exercised with colonial affairs.

The time has gone by when it is said as a sign of grace in a statesman, that he is a free trader. Protection is dead in politics, and is chiefly confined to enlightened Americans, or to the members of Trades' Unions. At a recent Mansion House dinner, no less an orator than Mr. Disraeli appealed to the commercial legislation of the last twenty years as a proof of the way in which Parliament responded to the wants and wishes of the community. But when Mr. Cardwell commenced his free trade career under Sir Robert Peel the contest was bitter. Sir Robert and his followers were exposed to the most galling attacks in all quarters. On one side there was the Anti-Corn-Law League, and on the other the county party, of which he was so proud to be at the head. It was hard for him—taught by necessity to leave them, and carry a system of free trade, under which they declared

England would sink never more to rise. Nor did the Repeal of the Corn Laws strengthen his position. A few months subsequently the Peel Cabinet succumbed under the hostile attacks of Lord George Bentinck and the Protectionists burning for revenge, and of Lord John Russell and the Whigs eager for place; and when deprived of their leader by an accidental fall from his horse, it seemed as if the Peelites—such as Cardwell and Gladstone—had lost their last chance of official life. Fortunately for the country such was not the case.

It is scarcely necessary to observe, that Mr. Cardwell speaks fluently and clearly. He came into the House with a high university reputation, and at once was listened to. Although not a professed orator, his speeches are always worth hearing. He is now at an age when his powers and capacities for work are at their highest; his services are indispensable to any Liberal administration, as he is affable and courteous to all, and especially conciliatory where his particular duties are concerned. Gentlemen with red hair are supposed to be peculiarly liable to gusts of passion. Mr. Cardwell's hair is undeniably red, but in speaking he is one of the coolest and calmest men in the House.

THE RIGHT HON. G. J. GOSCHEN.

(London—Goschen, 6520; Crawford, 6258; Lawrence, 6215; Bell, C., 6130; Twells, C., 6199; Gibbons, C., 6013; Rothschild, 5995.)

Many, many years ago there was a German Jew bookseller in Leipsic. Leipsic is the Paradise of booksellers, and till we got the duty off paper the Germans were the most outrageous bookmakers in the world. The Jews, I think, are like the Quakers, and don't take poor people into the denomination,—at any rate, most of them appear to prosper wonderfully. The old bookseller prospered, his son prospered, and became the founder of a mercantile and foreign banking-house in London. The firm of Goschen and Fruhling became a very wealthy and important one, and the grandson of the German bookseller received an education side by side with the nobles and magnates of the land. He did more—by the mere force of brain he towered above them all. From Rugby he went to Oriel College, Oxford, where he took a double first, and won the blue ribbon of the academic world.

From Oxford Mr. Goschen appears to have returned peacefully and quietly to the pursuits of trade, and to the office in ancient Austin-friars. If he had ambition it does not seem to have taken a political turn, and to have been developed rather with reference to his own peculiar vocation. His work on "The Theory of Exchanges" is said to be a very valuable one, and has reached a third or fourth edition. The young banker in time might rise to the top of the tree: in the great city in which wealth is honoured as the one thing needful, where gold pays for all, and covers all, and compensates for all, where it can command the smile of woman and the intellect of man, he might have grown to be one of the wealthiest. Money makes money. Fortune always aids the rich. The new banking-house might rival and surpass all others; on every exchange in Europe the name of Goschen might be as significant and far-famed as that of Rothschild. It is something to be a great capitalist—to be courted by princes and kings, to gather up into one's coffers the revenues of nations, to hold in one's hands the sinews of peace or war: Mr. Goschen was in a fair way of becoming this, when he was arrested in his mercantile career and returned to Parliament as the representative of the wealthiest constituency in the empire. Let us now explain how this came to pass. Mr. Goschen was not known to the political world at the time of his appearing as a candidate before the citizens of London. They were in a state of the most profound ignorance as to his ability, or his character, or his political opinions. He had no antecedents; in unreformed times this did not matter, as the proprietor of any particular borough felt that, as the Duke of Newcastle said, he might do what he liked with his own, and return whom he pleased; but the Reform Bill introduced popular election, and surely, it may be argued, to win a popular election a party must put forward a popular man. To a certain extent this is true; Mr. Goschen would not have had a chance for Westminster, or Marylebone, or the Tower Hamlets, or Southwark, or Lambeth. In the City it is otherwise. How is this? The answer is, the City is a constituency *sui generis.* In the City are the head-quarters of trade and commerce; the City rules the mercantile world, in the City wealth is popularity, in the City the Bank fashions opinions just as the Court at the West-end, and in the City the bank-parlour is an *imperium in imperio.* Whom it honours the City honours; whom it rejects and despises the City rejects and despises. Mr. Goschen was brought forward by the bank-parlour; he was a bank-director; his friend Mr. W. Crawford, M.P., was a bank director, and Mr. Kirkman Hodgson, who proposed him, was a bank director. Originally the seat was offered to Mr. Hodgson, who declined it, feeling himself safer and more comfortable in the snug little borough of Bridport. It was not anticipated that Parliament would last long; a general election, with all its trouble, and annoyance, and expense, was looming in the future; so Mr. Goschen was returned. It was said he was a foreigner, and far too young and untried a man to represent such a constituency as that of London. But the bank-parlour answered for his fitness, and that was enough; and thus Mr. Goschen entered Parliament. As M.P. for the City of London, as the head of an important firm, as a bank director, he had enough to do,—as much, one would think, as his energies could accomplish or his ambition desire. The general public knew little of him, and would not have been disappointed had he sat obscurely on the back benches behind Ministers, contented with cheering his leaders and with voting for his party right or wrong. A young man flushed with collegiate success, and M.P. for London, could not, however, sink so low. Mr. Goschen soon made his mark in the House, and increased in St. Stephen's his Oxford fame. He returned to his constituents with a claim on them, and that claim they willingly endorsed. In some quarters a different result was anticipated. A great deal had been said about Conservative reaction. We were told this would be made very clear at the General Election in 1865. At any rate, in the City we were assured that the Conservatives were in a position to carry two seats. Accordingly, two most respectable Conservatives were put forward—Messrs. Fowler and Lyall. The result soon demolished the pleasing dream of Conservative reaction as far as the City was concerned. The numbers were—Goschen, 7102; Crawford, 7086; Lawrence, 6637; Rothschild, 6525. The Conservatives, in spite of all their boasts, and liberal expenditure, and extensive organization, were far below the lowest of the Liberals. Their numbers were as follows:—Fowler, 4197; Lyall, 4086.

Lord Palmerston's sudden but not unexpected decease placed Earl Russell at the head of affairs. His lordship is supposed to believe that the territories known as Great Britain and Ireland are the special appanage of the Whigs, to be ruled by them and for them. The Whigs have always been an exclusively aristocratic party. They behaved very badly to Mr. Burke; and in the days of Mr. Brougham's prime, when his talents were omnipotent, when his popularity lifted them into popularity, when they could have made no head at all in the House of Commons against the Ministry with Peel on the one side, and the Radicals, such as Hume, and Burdett, and Hobhouse on the other,—even then they ignored his claims to leadership and took for that high post an honest but prosy son of a nobleman, known to history as Lord Althorpe. Even before then Mr. Tierney had actually been formally installed by the Whigs as their leader, when the most formidable person to the Tories was undoubtedly Mr. Brougham. Ability, no matter how commanding, has never been, in the opinion of the Whigs, deemed of itself sufficient to win for any man the formal leadership of their party. They have often availed themselves of the services of some new man of talent, but have always done so reluctantly. He has always been taught to consider himself a subordinate, not an equal; and if the irresistible energy of Mr. Brougham led him often to assume a bolder character, it is clear this activity and superiority displeased the Whig aristocracy, and they, as Mr. Roebuck has shown in after years, seized the opportunity which events offered of punishing Mr. Brougham, and separating themselves entirely from him. It is not clear that Earl Russell has grown much wiser; but he had shuffled his cards so often that they were serviceable no longer. The pack was used up; and thus, the grandson of the Jew German bookseller actually rose to be one of the Cabinet of which the aristocratic Earl Russell was the head. This is a fact which speaks well for the country. In spite of his youth (Mr. Goschen was born in 1831) he was a Cabinet Minister. His duties, of course, as Chancellor of the Duchy of Lancaster were not onerous; but as a member of the Cabinet in the House of Commons he will have no sinecure. He is committed to a political career for which his great talent and his readiness in debate fit him. In many quarters an opinion was entertained that Mr. Goschen will be the future Chancellor of the Exchequer when Mr. Gladstone will be called upon by the voice of the nation to occupy a more distinguished post.

Mr. Goschen is tall and slim, with dark eyes and hair, pale face, and a slightly foreign cast of countenance. He is a married man. A little of the old German Jew grandfather is still visible; but he gives you an idea of intelligence and power. He looks as if he was equal to his place. As the trainer would say, he is in good condition; and he stands a living specimen of the catholic, genial character of the free land in which he lives. Anybody may be an Englishman. We welcome them all, Jew or Gentile; the more the merrier; the more mixed the blood the better the breed; and if he have brain, and energy, and opportunity, any Englishman may rise to wealth, or fame, or power.

THE RT. HON. SIR ROBERT PEEL.

(TAMWORTH—PEEL, 1132; BULWER, 827; J. PEEL, 798.)

ACCORDING to Lord Macaulay, nothing is so valuable or so essential to success in the British Senate as oratory. "It has stood," he tells us, "in the place of all other acquirements. It has covered ignorance, weakness, rashness—the most fatal maladministration. A great negotiator is nothing when compared with a great debater, and a minister who can make a successful speech need trouble himself little about an unsuccessful expedition. This is the talent which has made judges without law, and diplomatists without French—which has sent to the Admiralty men who did not know the stern of a ship from her bowsprit, and to the East India Board men who did not know the difference between a rupee and a pagoda—which made a Foreign Secretary of Mr. Pitt, who, as George II. said, never opened Vattel, and which was very near making a Chancellor of the Exchequer of Mr. Sheridan, who could not work a sum in long division." Oratory has done this; but there is another power quite as potent in the State, and that is property; that has made dull men peers, and turned very flippant young gentlemen into statesmen. In the letters recently published by the Duke of Buckingham it is very amusing to see how Mr. Fremantle writes to know how he and the Marquis's men are to vote, and how great a card a Marquis was for all parties. The Reform Bill, it is true, did away with much of this evil—rotten burghs and close burghs are scarce now-a-days; they had aroused such national indignation that they were swept away. But still there is a great charm in birth and connexion. A man who has them may always be a statesman. He belongs to the governing classes, and inherits statesmanship as he does his estate. And not only does he get a place in Parliament, and very frequently office, but besides, he has an easy constituency—a constituency that will be thankful for small services, and that will be sure to give him very little trouble. At Lambeth, on one occasion, Mr. Roupell met his constituents. They assembled to hear him deliver his account of his stewardship. Mr. Roupell was very fluent and communicative—very naturally, with such a power of talking out of the House of Commons, his comparative silence in was remarkable. How long was he going to be a dummy? was the question put him by a logical and impertinent elector. Now, such interruptions do not happen to proprietors of hereditary seats in Parliament.

Sir Robert Peel is a proof of this. He is the son

of his father—a very great fact, and naturally so, when we remember the late Sir Robert was England's foremost man. Sir Robert Peel is also the eldest son—a better thing still, for the eldest son of the Peel family inherits the representation of Tamworth. He is born a statesman, and, if he live long enough, may be a real one—if his talents and training fit him for such a career. From his father he must have learnt much. From his diplomatic career—at what he calls an impressionable period of life—he must have acquired a little knowledge of the men who rule Europe at this time; and his House of Commons experiences have already given him a solidity and a power which was, at one time, not anticipated. When, all at once, from being almost the buffoon of the House, he rose to be worthy of his parentage, it was a little thing that did it. At the close of the Italian war, France annexed Savoy. Of course Switzerland was uncomfortable. If France trembled at an Italian kingdom twelve millions strong, much more reason had Switzerland to tremble at the nearness of the French Emperor and his millions of fighting men. The English House of Commons seemed cowed and spiritless. Mr. Bright, true to his peaceful instincts, treated the flagrant violation of right as a matter of the utmost insignificance. All at once rose, from the benches behind ministers, a voice—potent and unmistakeable—on behalf of the wronged, and against the wrong-doer. It was that of Sir Robert Peel. He had lived in Switzerland, he loved the country and its people; he saw their danger, and sympathized with their fears. Immediately the words were caught up, and re-echoed all over England. We were glad to hear them from the son of Sir Robert Peel. We felt that at last he had risen to the part which nature fitted him to play—that he had put away childish things, and become a man. 1860 is the date of Sir Robert Peel's conversion. He then experienced what, in theology, would be called "new birth." Still more may be said of Sir Robert. He became—at the same time begging the House to be aware that he is not a religious man—the champion of the persecuted Christians in Spain. Of course our sympathy is with such excellent people, but the question was—how were we to interfere? We have no Cromwells now-a-days, and have long ceased to "avenge slaughtered saints, whose bones lie cold." But according to the popular view, we ought to do this; and Sir Robert represented the popular view. In this capacity Sir Robert addressed a meeting at Liverpool, with the view to obtain from the Government assistance in mitigating the persecutions against Protestants in Spain. Of course there was an "immense audience, and resolutions were passed in conformity with the object for which the meeting was called." In such an agitation there is no responsibility—that alone rests with the Government, and he who heads it has much to gain, for we are a Protestant people, and sympathize warmly with Protestants all the world over.

Popular demonstration is, however, not without its effect, even if it leads to no decided action in higher quarters.

Sir Robert is a fine, gay-looking man. He has plenty of colour in his face, his hair and moustache are beautifully black, his figure is tall, and well proportioned; but he has more the look of a theatrical gentleman than of a rich English baronet. As we may suppose, he is rather dressy, and cultivates the graces—or seems to do so—to a considerable extent. A more striking contrast than that between Sir Robert and his brother Frederick it is impossible to conceive. The latter is the very picture of a model red tapist. His light hair is brushed straight down over his pale face, his arms and legs are thin, his carriage is that of a bookworm. You may be sure that he has had very few wild oats to sow, and that, like most very good boys, he is somewhat inclined to be dull and tame. There is something feminine in the appearance of Mr. Frederick Peel. There is nothing of the kind in that of his brother, who seems to say, "I am all right; I am the eldest son of the late Sir Robert Peel; I am a brick, and a jolly good fellow—why should I torture my brains? Why should I impair my constitution? Why should I rise early, and sit up late, to attain a position amongst a set of old fogies in the House of Commons, when my name is an open sesame to place and power, whenever I choose to trouble myself with such things?" Thus Sir Robert seems to argue with himself as he walks into the lobby of the house, with a great black stick in his hand, a camelia in his button-hole, and his new hat placed jauntily on his head.

Sir Robert Peel was born in London, 1822, educated at Harrow, was attaché to the British Embassy at Madrid from June, 1844, to May, 1846, when he was appointed Secretary to the British Legation in Switzerland. He was first returned for Tamworth July, 1850; he took his seat as a Conservative, though he voted for the ballot in 1853, and was and is in favour of free trade. As we have intimated, he generally votes on the Liberal side of the House, his attendance is very irregular, and his speeches few and far between. On one occasion when he addressed the House he nearly broke down. He has, however, mastered all that, and is now a speaker above the average.

> "When parsons drawl in one continuous hum,
> Who does not wish all baronets were dumb?"

Certainly, when Sir Robert is on his legs, such is not your wish. At first he forgot the great statesman's advice—"Young man, when you have nothing to say—say nothing;" but he soon got over that weakness. Even now, led away by his love of fun, he makes occasional blunders. This was apparent not very long ago, when he drew a very ridiculous picture of a fat volunteer crawling on his belly, and shooting a cat, and thus endeavoured to stifle at its birth what has proved to be the most effective and formidable movement of the time. Sir Robert has amply atoned for this by presenting £100 to the Stafford volunteers—as his subscription for four years to the maintenance of that worthy and effective corps. When he first spoke he had often a random way, intimating very clearly that he hardly knew himself what he was talking about. I have often heard him miss the right word, using instead one resembling it in sound but totally different in sense, and all the while the House laughing quite as much at, as with, the hon. baronet, who pitched alike into his friends and foes; and, as a wealthy baronet, with an hereditary title to statesmanship, took a very independent position. Will he become an authority? will he progress in his political career? will he rise to what he, with his name, fortune, and talents, might be? These are questions to be asked by the people, not of Tamworth alone, but of the United Kingdom. There is no danger of his sinking into a Tchinovick, as the Russians call their red tapists; but his short career as the Irish Secretary does not raise any sanguine expectation as to his future.

CHARLES GILPIN, ESQ.

(Northampton—Gilpin, 2632; Henley, 2105; Merewether, C. 1620; Lendrick, C., 1378; Bradlaugh, 1066; Dr. Lees, 485.)

One of the oldest Nonconformist towns in England is Northampton. There Brown, the founder of the

Brownists, was born, and in its gaol, after being imprisoned upwards of thirty times, and after having been frightened out of Nonconformity, he died, infirm, fiery, old. The Puritan element was strong in Northampton, and in the seventeenth century Baptists and Independents were in great force in the town. Dr. Doddridge settled there in 1729, and there, besides preaching himself, he trained up others to preach as well. Dr. Ryland was the pastor of the old Baptist chapel, College-street. In the old unreformed Parliament, and in the reign of the old Corporation, Spencer Perceval was M.P. for Northampton until he was assassinated. But better times came, Liberal principles grew and prospered, Dissenters became political, and then it was that Northampton ceased to return Tories, and sent to Westminster men who in Cromwell's time would have been denominated "thorough." Of this class is Charles Gilpin, its present M.P.

Mr. Gilpin is of a Quaker origin. He was born in 1815 in Bristol. His uncle was the well-known and well-remembered Joseph Sturge of Birmingham, a worthy patriot, who was himself very near on more than one occasion becoming an M.P. The nephew began life as a traveller for a Manchester warehouse. I don't know whether he knew Cobden at that time;—at any rate he breathed the Manchester air, which at the period referred to seems to have been remarkably keen and salubrious,—air under the influence of which Mr. Gilpin soon acquired hardihood and robustness.

Joseph Sturge, as we all know, was a great temperance reformer. His nephew became the same. The temperance movement did an immense amount of good. It not only taught the middle and lower classes of society to be temperate, it not only taught the working man how much better he could spend his money in buying books or furniture, or in the maintenance of his family, than in the consumption of vitriol gin and drugged and pernicious beer,—but it led to a quickening of intellect, especially in the direction of popular oratory, which was really astonishing and unexpected. The new movement required new men to advocate and enforce its claims. In its infancy it had no great names to trust to. The clergy, whether of the Establishment or Dissent, looked coldly on; the lawyer class, the only other class of trained speakers in the land, are never given to the unpaid advocacy of the platform; so in default the temperance cause had to form its own teachers and expounders. Men who had been saved by it from ruin in this world and the next, who had become decent and sober in consequence of it, learned in a forcible manner to declare the miseries they had escaped and the blessings they had obtained; others who joined for the sake of example and to do good, had also to become speech-makers;—oratory was the rule, and silence the exception. If a cause is to be deemed important according to the oratory it causes and excuses, then the temperance reformation is to be estimated very highly indeed. It was as a temperance orator that the late John Cassell first came before the public; it was in the same capacity that John Bright made his *début,* and the same may be said of Mr. Gilpin. In temperance societies he learned the use of the tongue.

But the time had come for Mr. Gilpin to settle in the world. He married in 1840 a daughter of an inhabitant of Falmouth, and opened a bookseller's shop in Bishopsgate-street. As a rule, political and philanthropic booksellers do much better than literary ones. I don't fancy Godwin made a fortune, and Charles Knight is never tired of telling us his losses. The world went well with Gilpin, bookseller. The Friends are a specialty in the quarter in which he pitched his tent: close by is the Friends' Meeting-house; in the neighbouring suburbs of Tottenham and Stoke Newington, in well-built and well-furnished houses, do they reside. Broad-street, where were the head-quarters of anti-slavery and other philanthropic societies affected by Quakers, was but a few steps from his shop-door; they all looked in at Bishopsgate-street to have a chat with Charles, and to buy their books and stationery there. He became useful to them all. He was the nephew of his uncle, and he shared in all his uncle's opinions. The way was thus prepared for him to take a part in public life. He was elected a Common Councilman. In Finsbury Chapel, where once a year the friends of peace meet to proclaim its Divine mission to a stubborn and unbelieving race, who go on quarrelling and arming as if peace principles had never been preached or peace congresses held, Gilpin's face on the platform was always expected, and in Exeter Hall his voice had also been raised. Perhaps in our time this sort of thing has been a little overdone,—people have tired of stump oratory, and of reverend gentlemen inculcating the humanities; but in the case of Mr. Gilpin no feeling of that kind was created It was clear that his advocacy was that of a sincere and enlightened citizen, who had no personal ends or private ambition to gratify.

At this time a movement was set on foot which tended further to bring Mr. Gilpin before the public. In Birmingham a James Taylor, jun., a plain, unlettered man, had made the wonderful discovery, that the working man might become a freeholder, and have a stake in the country if he, instead of depositing his money with the publican, invested it in a freehold land society. The idea took wonderfully; the plan was for a number of men to join together, and with their united subscriptions purchase an estate, which was afterwards cut up into forty-shilling freeholds, and always sold at a profit. In a little while these societies extended all over the country, and not only placed many of the working classes on the register, but put a good deal of money into their pockets as well. The Conservatives were alarmed: they declared the new system was unconstitutional; and then did as people often do who oppose vehemently a novelty or an innovation—adopted it themselves. Of the societies formed on this plan, by far the largest was the National Freehold Land Society in Moorgate-street, of which Mr. Cobden was, I believe, a trustee, and with which Mr. Gilpin was connected from the commencement. It flourished speedily; it was conducted on sound business principles, and with its success Mr. Gilpin is intimately connected, for from the first he worked heartily in its favour; and, when it had become a giant, and was found to require time and talent, as a paid director Mr. Gilpin retired from his own business, and devoted himself to the development of what has come to be the greatest land society of our age. Here he found ample scope for his business talents and tact; here, also, he became known and in request as a director. It is not true that all his efforts in this way have been successful. One honest director is of no avail where there are others, forming the majority, dishonest, or careless, or remiss. It is in vain that you war against the conditions of success. In these days of limited liability companies many have come to grief in spite of a good name or two, and among the names attached to such I have known many as honourable as any in the City of London. But I am not in a position here to chronicle

Mr. Gilpin's labours in connection with companies; I must not omit, however, his connection with the National Provident Institution, one of the most successful of its class.

By this time Mr. Gilpin was known as a well-tried man, as one whose time and best energies were freely given to the cause of the people. Shoemakers are always a keen, intelligent class of men. Northampton is full of such (it finds Australia in boots and shoes); and in 1857 the shoemakers and Dissenters of Northampton returned Mr. Gilpin to Parliament, where he took his seat, and fought side by side with his friends Cobden and Bright. In 1859 he became Secretary of the Poor-law Board. About that time Lord Palmerston was becoming sensible of the blunder made by the Whigs in always dividing office amongst themselves. On one occasion, we are told, when Mr. Brand was announcing to the House the formation of a new Ministry, and was going through the routine observed on such occasions, the late Sir James Graham was heard to exclaim, "What! another peer!" Sir James evidently being of the opinion that you might have too much of a good thing. Lord Palmerston was properly desirous to get a little of the popular element in his Ministry, and therefore he made the offer, which Mr. Gilpin accepted; but the position was not a pleasant one. Mr. Gilpin was not a free man. It is understood that he was not to be allowed any advocacy of his own peculiar opinions, except those relating to the abolition of capital punishment, and his situation was unpleasant to his constituents, who had no idea of returning a dumb dog, or a silent defender of the Ministry of the day. Mr. Gilpin acted wisely. He retired from office in 1865, and now, freed from its trammels, Northampton will expect her Member to do his duty. As Secretary of the Poor-law Board, he had no chance of doing so. It is something to be of the Cabinet and to mould the policy of the nation, but it is a poor thing (even if you get £1000 a-year for doing it) to be confined, as far as regards Parliamentary utterance and action, to making a House and cheering the Premier.

The personal appearance of Mr. Gilpin is by no means remarkable. He is invariably dressed in sober black, and is a plain, unpretending man, about six feet high, muscular-looking, and not over-fat. As a speaker, he is clear and sensible, aiming at perspicuity rather than effect. By his friends he is much esteemed for his kindness and readiness to assist or advise, and in public opinion he holds a place such as might well satisfy a more ambitious man, and of which, when a Manchester bagman, he could have little dreamt.

THE RIGHT HON. HENRY BRAND.

(Cambridgeshire—Lord G. Manners, C., 3998; Lord Royston, C., 3874; Rt. Hon. Henry Brand, 3310; Mr. Richard Young, 3290.)

Once, and once only, Mr. Gladstone was known to speak against time. The occasion was in the debate on the third reading of the bill for the Repeal of the Paper Duty. All at once it became apparent to the Government that they were in danger; by outward signs and symptoms it was made manifest to the most obtuse of them that their foes were more numerous than their friends, and that a division under such circumstances would be fatal. Lord Palmerston, who had a happy faculty of sleeping all the evening like Lord North, was wide awake; Lord John Russell displayed anxiety; Mr. Gibson, it was very evident, was ill at ease, as were the rest of the gentlemen who generally sit in very ungraceful postures on the Treasury Bench. To be beaten was the destruction of the Palmerston Administration; destruction of that administration was to every individual member of it, for a longer or shorter interval of time—perhaps for ever—loss of place; and loss of place means loss of influence—loss of rank—loss of salary—loss of everything the politician strives to gain. In such circumstances there is nothing like a Fabian policy, and there is nothing more desirable than a long speech. The man who speaks longest speaks best. Happily, Mr. Gladstone was on his legs, and there is no man who has such a wonderful faculty of speaking as himself, and on the occasion to which I refer the hon. gentleman very wisely exerted that faculty to the utmost. He (says an eye-witness) started vigorously enough, dashed with impetuous brevity through a great part of the subject, on which he might have advantageously insisted; but all of a sudden he began to wind round and round, over and over again came the same arguments in almost the same words, and for once the Chancellor of the Exchequer was—not almost, but I should say quite—prosy. To an *habitué* of the House, however, the cause was obvious. The Treasury Whipper-in was seen flitting about in and out, backwards and forwards, to the Treasury Bench, with an anxious and perturbed aspect of countenance. Sir Wm. Hayter, too, was moving about very much as he used to do when he was in office—in fact, he was evidently imitating the retired tallow-chandler, who used to go down to the shop on melting days; while ever and anon white-waistcoated gentlemen, evidently dragged from the opera or evening parties, were silently filling the ministerial benches. The whip was severe and unrelenting. However, at last the Treasury Whipper-in entered the House, and sat down upon the Treasury Bench with an air of complacent satisfaction—the thing was done—narrowly, but effectually; and then the Chancellor of the Exchequer sat down also. In spite of Mr. Disraeli's reply, all ground of anxiety had been removed, and the ministry had a majority—not a large one, but a majority, when they were on the verge of defeat. How was it that this defeat was averted, that the ministry were saved, that the bill for the Repeal of the Paper Duty was carried? The answer is—by the exertions of the Treasury Whipper-in.

It was once my good fortune to behold Lord John Russell smile and carry on a friendly conversation on the Government benches of the British House of Commons. Generally his lordship is cold and dignified in his demeanour, as becomes a man who is part and parcel of that wonderful machine—the British Constitution. The individual with whom he was conversing was rather under the average size, of slim build, very plainly dressed, and with one of those fresh, ruddy, whiskerless faces which make even an old man look young. It was clear that he was a good Whig, and of an old family, otherwise Lord John would have been a little less friendly. It was also clear that he was in office, or he would not have been sitting by the side of premiers and Chancellors of the Exchequer; and yet his was not a face familiar to me as a man who had won his position by any talent, oratorical or administrative, of his own. The name of the gentleman was Brand. A reference to "Dod" informed me that he was the second son of the twentieth Baron Dacre; that he was private secretary to Sir George Grey; that he was "averse to large organic changes;" that he was returned for Lewes for the first time in 1852; and that on the formation of the Palmerston Cabinet he was promoted to the office held so long and ably by Sir William Goodenough Hayter. After all, the general reader is still in the dark with regard to Mr. Brand. He says to me, "Here is a man, born in 1814, in the prime of life, not memorable for any great work or act, yet you give him a niche in your gallery of modern statesmen. How is this? What you quote from 'Dod' in no way enlightens me." Wait awhile, my anxious inquirer. I frankly confess that, after all, you are very little the wiser when I give you Mr. Dod's facts. There is a society called the Tract Society—of the merits or demerits of which it is not for me to speak here—the travelling agent of that society was an immensely stout man. On one occasion that agent called at a clergyman's house in a provincial town. The clergyman's daughter ran laughing into her father's study, "Papa, here's the Tract Society come." In the same way Mr. Brand was that awful personage—THE BRITISH PARLIAMENTARY SYSTEM. He smiled, and you were returned for Rottenborough, and the newspapers trumpeted the glorious triumph of liberal principles. He frowned, and you were unseated for bribery and corruption. On good terms with Mr. Brand, and you were elected into the Reform Club; you got that little place in the Circumlocution-office for your son; your wife had a ticket for one of Lady Palmerston's brilliant assemblies. When the Duke of Wellington said in the excitement occasioned by the passing of the Reform Bill, he did not see how the king's government could be carried on, he forgot the Treasury Whipper-in. By his aid nothing is easier. Sir W. Hayter, Mr. Brand's predecessor, was a model in this respect, and still, I think, does a good deal of amateur whipping-in. If

I could catch him a moment I would point him out. Here he is. "What, by the door?" No, he is in the lobby; no, he is gone into the House; no, he is out. Ah! here he comes; but you can't see him, for he is in the midst of a group. But see! he has stepped on one side to read a note. That is he—that sharp-featured, active-looking man! a cross, as it were, between a rollicking Irishman and an English merchant, all the shrewdness of the one and the fun of the other; in person square-built and not very tall, but ever agile, and seemingly a model of the art of perpetual motion. In the same way Mr. Brand was always on duty. You would see him in the lobby before the Speaker was at prayers; after the Speaker had done his prayers; long after the gas had been turned on, far into the night, ofttimes far into the early morn. Mr. Brand dwelt in the lobby. It was not known that he slept anywhere, with the exception of forty winks on the Treasury benches, nor that he partook of meals except during the parliamentary recess. He said to one, "Come," and he came—to another, "Go," and he went. He was friendly with every one, and managed to talk to a dozen people at once. He held one by the button, he administered to another a dig in the ribs, at another he winked, another he accosted in a free and easy manner. He slapped peers on the back, and shook hands even with Irish M.P.'s. His duty was, as Canning—no fourth-rate man, as a contemporary ludicrously calls him—said, "to make a House, and keep a House, and cheer the minister." On one occasion Canning wrote :—

> "Cheer him as his audience flag,
> Brother Hiley, Brother Bragge,
> Cheer him as he hobbles vilely,
> Brother Bragge, and Brother Hiley."

Brothers Bragge and Hiley were the Treasury Whippers-in of their day. The Whipper-in is, perhaps, the most powerful man in the House of Commons. Let him over-sleep himself—let him have a fit of indigestion—let him be laid up with the gout—and immediately the Liberal cabinet is *in extremis,* and the nation is plunged into all the horrors of a crisis. How comes this about? you very naturally ask. You tell me you do not hear of Mr. Brand's eloquence; you do not see his name in Hansard; it does not seem to you that he shines in debate. Well, the answer to this question will let you into one of the secrets of the British constitution—a secret that you will not discover, however attentively you may study Blackstone or De Lolme. Gentle reader, you cannot be so green as to suppose that, in any country under the sun, men are guided to their conclusions simply by means of the debates of public assemblies; you cannot be so green even as to believe that these discussions have anything to do with the subsequent decision. Pre-eminently in the British House of Commons this is not the case, and the consequence is that the debate does not influence the decision, but is merely the apology for it. The premier makes his speech, and he leaves his Whipper-in to make up the majority that is to keep the Ministry in office. Mr. Brand was the Ministerial Whipper-in; hence it is that he was always in the lobby finding pairs—laying hold of this member—preventing that one from escaping; and that his means of communication reached to the Clubs, to the Opera, as well as to the smoking-room and library of the House of Commons. The whip extends over Europe. On one occasion, I believe, Sir Robert Peel's Administration was saved by one vote, and that the vote of a member who had travelled from the interior of the Continent obedient to the summons of the whip. The fact is, we are governed by the whip; nor could it well be otherwise if we are to have government by means of party; and Parliamentary government means party government. In the theory of the Constitution Cave Adullams have no place. Mr. Disraeli, in his Life of Lord George Bentinck, speaks of the creation of a third political party as "a result at all times and under any circumstances difficult to achieve, and which had failed even under the auspices of accomplished and experienced statesmen." Sir Robert Peel understood this—that is, in other words, the hon. baronet felt that in vain he held office if his party would not respond to the whip. The French Republicans failed because they could not understand this, and for a similar reason the Metropolitan Board of Works, and the respectable parish vestries of St. Pancras or Marylebone, seem in a disorganized and chaotic state, and succeed in doing so little business. During the recent Reform Debates more than one effort was made to count out the House of Commons, and yet let there be anything supremely unimportant of a personal nature, such as that squabble between Messrs. Horsman and Walters, and the House is crammed in every part. When a discussion respecting our one hundred and fifty millions of Indian subjects is raised, I have often seen less than forty members present. One advantage of this is that even the dullest dog in the House gets his say, for if the House be thin—and why should any sane man be compelled to listen to a lawyer talking for promotion, or to a borough representative airing the dictionary for the exclusive benefit of his own constituents?—the Whipper-in knows where all his men are, and will bring them up when the division bell rings and the serious business of the evening has commenced. Without the so-called whip, Parliamentary government is almost an impossibility—the assembly, with its eternal talk, would fall into contempt, and all power would pass into the hands of the Crown. Make the experiment on a small scale—get a hundred honest, intelligent men together—each man with a theory of his own and a grievance, and what would be the result? Why, that nothing whatever could be done. There are votes taken every night in which the majority of members have no earthly interest; yet these votes are essential to the carrying on of the

Queen's Government. Now, in the House of Commons, by means of the party and the whip, actually some progress is made. Here, in England, so much business is taken off by the municipalities, that our Parliament is far less laden with details than was the French Assembly; yet, if all our legislators were honest, independent, crotchety, disdainful of party and disobedient to this influence, we should split up into helplessness and fatuity. It is the application of the whip that makes the House of Commons a working assembly, and preserves us from the horrors of despotism.

Dreamers and theorists—political babes and sucklings—may tell me that a Whipper-in is the result of parliamentary corruption—that we should be better without him—that such as he are a fearful sign of the times; but if jobs must be done—if little arrangements must be made—if, in other words, people require to be looked after, the Whipper-in is the man to do it. Parliament is a self-seeking assembly, and to buy every man at his own valuation would be evidently a bad bargain for the people. Indeed, the Whipper-in is most useful to his party. He will supply Liberal candidates to any amount; he will judiciously distribute the Government advertisements and patronage; he will make the needful arrangements with the Opposition as to the public business; he will reconcile uneasy consciences to the unpleasant task of renouncing in Parliament the pledges they made when out. I confess—unflinching patriot though I be—my mouth waters as I think of the good things the Whipper-in has at his disposal; and I rush away from the lobby exclaiming, "Lead me not into temptation; but deliver me from evil."

THE RT. HON. JOHN BRIGHT.

(BIRMINGHAM—BRIGHT, 14,569; DIXON, 15,163; MUNTZ, 14,864; LOYD, C., 8513; EVANS, C., 6926.)

SOME few years back, while the Anti-Corn-Law agitation was yet in its infancy, and being fought with a fierceness almost incredible in these more moderate days, when in agricultural circles no language was considered too contemptuous for its supporters, in a small village in one of the midland counties an unknown individual was delivering an address on the all-absorbing theme. He was dressed in black, and his coat was of that peculiar cut considered by the worthy disciples of George Fox—alas! how falsely—as a standing protest against the fashions of the world. The lecturer was young, square built, and muscular, with a broad face and forehead, with a fresh complexion, with "mild blue eyes" like those of the late Russian Nicholas, but nevertheless, with a general expression quite sufficiently decided and severe. As an orator the man did not shine. His voice was good, though somewhat harsh; his manner was awkward, as is the custom of the country, and the sentences came out of his mouth loose, naked, and ill-formed. He was not master of the situation, yet he wanted not confidence, nor matter, nor words. Practice it was clear was all that he required. The orator felt this himself. He told his audience that he was learning to speak upon the question, and that he would succeed in time. That he did learn, that he did succeed, is obvious when I mention the fact that the speaker was no other than John Bright, M.P. for Birmingham.

It is one of the effects of a popular agitation that it elevates for a time into equal importance the true man and the false. Both alike are strong in the exposure of practical anomalies or injustice—strong in the power of uttering for the dumb multitude what it travails in agony to declare—strong in the sweet voices of the sovran mob. The hour makes the man. In its tumult. and excitement, and uproar, like the spectres on the Brocken, he seems twice his ordinary size. Poor, pitiful, small, weak-minded creature though he be, for a time he wields a giant's power, and speaks with a giant's voice. For a time, of each tribune of the people it is emphatically declared—

> "In him Demosthenes is heard again,
> Liberty taught him her Athenian strain."

The Sacheverells, the Lord George Gordons, the Wilkses, the Orator Hunts, the Feargus O'Connors and Daniel O'Connells, have each seemed to the people, delirious with the intoxication of the time, what Stephano seemed to Caliban, a very god. The hour past the tumult calmed, the angry voices stilled, men's eyes opened, the dilated demagogue dwindles into his ordinary insignificance. Alas! poor Yorick, where be his jibes and gibberings? It is a painful process, this state of collapse. To have been floated into public life on a public agitation, and to continue to float when that agitation has ceased, when the political world is dull as the weeds that rot on Lethe's shore; to play Othello when Othello's occupation is gone, requires an unusually strong brain and brave heart. Mr. Bright has gone through all this and succeeded; nay, more, has triumphed, and by this triumph has placed himself foremost among the statesmen of the age.

I scarce believe, with Robert Owen and the moderns, that all men are equal, and that the only difference between a great man and a little man is that one is born on a pedestal and that the other is not. Still it is a great advantage to be born on a pedestal. With an infatuation unparalleled amongst savages and incredible in a people who profess to believe the Bible, we have so crippled the democracy, that when it enters into the arena with aristocracy it does so at tremendous odds. To attain his position John Bright has injured his health and shortened his days. Men like Lord John Russell and Viscount Palmerston attain a superior position by just sufficient healthy labour to lengthen theirs. They are born on the pedestal, and not placed there by merits of their own. Few of our noble statesmen would have been there unless born there. Either the energy, or the time, or the patience, or the talent to secure a position would have been wanting. To emerge from the mob, to rise from the respectable dead level of the Smiths, Browns, Joneses, and Robinsons, to get the advantage over them by the head and shoulders, is a Herculean task. In the first place, the men who are on the pedestal look on contemptuously if you try to put yourself on an equality with them. In the second place, the Smiths, Browns, Joneses, and Robinsons will do all that they can to prevent your achieving a higher position than themselves. The very class for whom you labour will deem you impertinent, and damn you with faint praise. Only a remarkable man could thus shake off all obstacles and climb the steep

"Where Fame's proud temple shines afar."

Whatever may be the feeling out of doors, it will not be denied that John Bright has succeeded in doing this in the House of Commons and amongst his peers. No one ever heard him in Parliament without feeling that he is a power in that House; yet such a position was one no one would have prophesied for him a few years since. Everything was against him when he was first returned as member for Durham. All his antecedents were precisely those most calculated to excite opposition and contempt. He was not merely not a landlord, but he was a cotton lord. He was not merely not of the Church of England, but of the church whose harmless peculiarities have been more laughed at than its virtues admired. He was not merely one of the Anti-Corn-

Law League, but one of its greatest men. He was not merely at the head of an agitation thoroughly revolutionary, as it seemed to its opponents, but he was one of those who let it be clearly understood that that agitation, so far from being final, was but the means to an end. He not only had no respect for Parliamentary shams and conventionalities, but he expressed that contempt in a manner the most unpalatable and undisguised. Nevertheless it was not long ere he compelled the House to do homage to his honesty and strength. At first it rebelled—it groaned when he got up—it emptied itself when he spoke; but the House, if it looks kindly on aristocratic imbecility, will not long refuse to sanction democratic capacity and pluck. The House is generous, and has a thorough appreciation of a MAN; and the result is, that now, as far as it is concerned, Mr. Bright has nothing to fear. He may damage himself out of doors; he may offend a people warlike in its instinct in spite of cotton-growing Manchester; he may alienate the cultivated mind of the country by his grovelling theory of a nation's life; he may arouse, and justly, the hostility of the press, by the degrading mission which he would chalk out for it; he may make people very angry by his praise of the Emperor Napoleon and his readiness to sacrifice Savoy; but he has taken honours in the senate, and there his position is secure.

How is this? In London generally Mr. Bright is not a popular man. In what is considered good society it is hinted that he is a demagogue, and that his dangerous mission is to set the lower classes against the upper ones. People tell you that on the platform Mr. Bright is a very different and much bolder man than on the floor of St. Stephen's—a criticism which, however, may be passed on every public man, inasmuch as platform speaking aims at creating popular enthusiasm, while oratory in the House of Commons is of a more business-like and practical character. It is undeniable, however, that at certain intervals of time the opinions of Mr. Bright are those of a minority. His peace views are decidedly at a discount. His devotion to the material interests of the nation is carried to an extreme, and is somewhat repulsive to those who believe that man does not live by bread alone. His pugnacity, reminding one of the celebrated remark of the late Lord George Bentinck, that if he were not a Quaker he would be a prize-fighter, has been an offence to the many who are prone to sing :—

> "Let us alone; what pleasure can we have
> To war with evil? Is there any peace
> In ever climbing up the climbing wave?"

To all such,—to all who believe in the traditions of the past,—to all who would rather endure a wrong than fight with it,—to all who would take the world as they find it, and only smile when told that their idols are wind-bags which collapse only with the prick of a pin,—Mr. Bright is a constant source of uneasiness and irritation. Now, in London especially these classes are numerous. London people are well-to-do: they soon make money; they soon rise to the dignity of a brougham and a country-house; they soon learn to give good dinners and to eat them. And men in this position, when they have done their day's business in the City, only desire ease and rest out of business hours. In the provinces it is different; there Paterfamilias, as soon as he puts up his shutters, or locks up his warehouse, is sure to have some philanthropic, or religious, or political employment; a London political lecturer is coming, and he must take the chair; or a Ragged School is to be formed, and he is to be the Treasurer; or a Mechanics' Institution is in difficulties, and he has to show how the requisite funds are to be obtained. These are the men who rally round John Bright; but they are scarce in London, and yet John Bright, their representative, is honoured in the House of Commons. Why? The answer is soon given. Come with me into the Strangers' Gallery, and look hard on your left. About the middle of the third bench of the gangway you see a vigorous-looking man in black. What a contrast he presents to the mass around! Lord Bacon deemed himself ancient when he was thirty-one. Mr. Bright is, then, more than ancient, but he is in the prime of life nevertheless. The debate has been drawing its slow length along, and weariness is on every face. Small men have been on their legs. The Bœotians—the lordlings whose misfortune it is to misrepresent counties, and others—have been uttering sentiments childish and commonplace; or an official underling, with languid oratory, and much allusion to blue-books, has essayed to show that everything governmental is as it ought to be, that the right man is in the right place, and that everything is for the best; or with the usual nonchalant air, has contended that no great harm has been done, and that if there had it did not matter much. Up rises Mr. Bright, with a voice something of a scream, and rushes into the very heart of the subject—scornfully tossing on one side, as irrelevant, the platitudes of preceding speakers. The question, whatever it may be, is taken up manfully and boldly. There is no display of fine learning—no Latin quotation—no subtle disquisition—no elaborated climax—no polished peroration. There is no attempt to evade the difficulties of the question; on the contrary, the speaker seems to delight in them, as an Irishman will fight for fun. He states them in all their naked literalness, and wrestles with them as an intellectual athlete. No one can pretend Mr. Bright is always in the right; sometimes he must be wrong. To most of us it seems that the Manchester policy as regards peace and war is a policy which, as Mr. Disraeli truly remarked, would degrade our ancient monarchy into a third-rate republic—a policy repugnant to the national pride and sense of honour—a policy oblivious of glorious traditions and ancient fame. But Mr. Bright is in earnest—he means what he says; you see that the speaker has heart as well as brain, and on he goes, right to the mark, uttering honestly and plainly his thoughts, calling a spade a spade, however contrary that may be to parliamentary etiquette and usage. There are times when he attempts a loftier strain, when he becomes eloquent, and appeals to the consciences of men of all parties, and carries with him the hearts of all. At such times Mr. Bright's earnestness is overpowering. You cannot resist its impetuous course, and the House, that feels rightly, if it votes wrongly, is completely subdued. On more than one occasion, when Mr. Bright has risen to speak, has there been

> "Silence, deep as death,
> And the boldest held his breath
> For a time."

This was especially apparent a few years since, during the Indian debates. I never heard more effective speeches delivered by any man, and I think the general opinion coincided with my own. Mr. Bright was well up in his subject. India can produce cotton. Manchester needs cotton. Hence it was Mr. Bright spoke with such vehemence, and passion, and power. How great the contrast between a modern House of Commons and an ancient one—between Bright and Burke! It was an ancient dynasty overthrown; an ancient people oppressed; a multitude numerous as the sands upon the sea-shore, wasting away beneath British injustice; another Verres harassing a wasted Sicily, that excited the imagination and fired the heart of Mr. Burke. It was because a splendid opportunity of growing cotton for Manchester was lost, that Mr. Bright bore down upon the government with resistless force. The stand-point of the one was chivalrous and classic, of the other modern and commercial. Sneer at it as selfish if you will, but is it not the truer one of the two? All men act from selfish motives,—the Christian who flies from the wrath to come, as much as the spendthrift who squanders, or the miser who saves. I read lately the report of a sermon preached at the consecration of Tiptree Heath Church by a distinguished divine. The Doctor's aim was to show that if a nation feared the Lord it would prosper, and hence the propriety of the nation supporting a religious establishment. Give your money to the Almighty because He will pay it you back with interest. Such is the modern gospel. If it be true that we can only attain to an enlightened selfishness at the best; and if it be true, as Mr. Bright believes, that the Manchester policy as regards India would bring with it an immense amount of good; it, at any rate, must not be despised for its selfishness, and surely, at any rate, may challenge a comparison with the Derby policy, or the Palmerston policy, or that of the Whigs. As regards India, it is clear that had the Bright policy prevailed we should have had no Indian mutiny.

"Mr. Bright," says Mr. G. R. Francis, in his careful estimate of the orators of the age, "may be said to have been dragged upwards by Mr. Cobden in his rapid and remarkable ascent to fame and notoriety. Had he been left to pursue his path alone it is more than probable that he would never have emerged from the dead level of society, or that if he had attained any eminence at all, it would have been to achieve a distinction not more illustrious than that of the most noisy and arrogant orator of a parish vestry, in whom strength of lungs and an indomitable determination not to be outbullied are the most prominent qualifications." How foolish all this seems, read by the light of the present; but when Mr. Francis wrote, such was the general feeling. And now, like another Warwick, Mr. Bright stands,—a setter up or puller down of kings. When Lord Derby is in office the Whigs are indignant, and declare that he has formed an unnatural alliance with Mr. Bright. When he supports Lord John Russell, the Conservatives hint at another Lichfield compact. Independent Radicals, men whose self-love suggests leadership, intimate that they differ strongly from the member for Birmingham. Yet I am much mistaken if that honourable gentleman do not act a conspicuous part in the House for many years to come. As old statesmen pass away—as old prejudices are forgotten—as Mr. Bright himself mellows with years—as his views form with growing experience, leadership and office must fall to his lot. His speeches during the late Reform debates were models, whether as regards force of argument or oratorical beauty and power. Even by this time is his great heresy, during the Crimean War, forgotten if not forgiven. Wise men now fail to perceive that for the anxiety then endured—for the treasure then wasted—for the blood then spilt as water—for the heroism then displayed—for the national enthusiasm then created, we have received an adequate result.

The *Times* is occasionally very angry with Mr. Bright, yet he has never said harder things of the aristocracy and the British Constitution than the *Times*. Hear our officers on the army and navy. According to them our rulers are blind, and the country is going headlong to the devil. It was only the other day that a military man assured us that the most conservative of officers were fast becoming radicals in consequence of their disgust at the waste and mismanagement in high quarters. If Mr. Bright's object be a good one, let him have the same licence allowed to others. Public agitation requires enthusiasm, and exaggeration is the necessary result. All members of parliament on the platform speak in a different manner to what they do in the House, and this is still more the case with the Radical Reformer, since on the platform he publishes his extreme views, but in the House of Commons, where there is a majority against him, he is compelled to take what he can get. It is clear, for some time to come there must be political agitation out of doors. If it be true that in the counties the tenant farmers are under the influence of their landlords; or as Lord Derby, when Lord

Stanley, said, you can always tell the politics of the representative of a county if you know the politics of the leading landlords,—if our borough constituencies be many of them venal and corrupt, he who would endeavour to wipe away from us this reproach and shame, and advocates reform, is acting a patriot's part; and the men who stand by what they call the British Constitution, who shut their eyes to its defects, who cry "Esto perpetua," are the real fomentors of class disunion and revolution. Can any one doubt that the majority of men, whether in the House of Commons or elsewhere, act from interested motives? If so, why should Mr. Bright be sent to Coventry for saying so? Mr. Bright, sorrowing from the grave of a beloved wife, was urged by his friend Mr. Cobden into the political arena—not to forget his grief, but to gain a solace for it by his splendid exertions for the happiness and welfare of the poor. He represents a class who have been denied their rightful position in politics, to whom it is of actual consequence that taxation be lightened and commerce freed—a class to whom Great Britain must look more and more to find employment and sustenance for her swarming sons. The charge of self-interest sometimes brought against him comes with an ill grace from lawyers who move heaven and earth to prevent law-reform, or from landlords who sing with might and main,

> "Let learning, laws, and commerce die,
> But give us back our old nobility."

The perpetual abuse of Mr. Bright in some quarters is ungenerous. Men who are dumb in his presence are ready enough to bark behind his back. However, from a hostile press and hostile orators, Mr. Bright, if he be wise, will learn somewhat. "Caius Gracchus," writes old Plutarch, "was rough and impetuous, and it often happened that in his harangues he was carried away by passion, contrary to his judgment, and his voice became shrill, and he fell to abuse, and grew confused in his discourse. To remedy this fault he employed Licinius, a well-educated slave, who used to stand behind him when he was speaking, with a musical instrument, such as is used as an accompaniment to singing, and whenever he observed that the voice of Caius was becoming harsh and broken through passion, he would produce a soft note, upon which Caius would immediately moderate his voice and become calm." Our Caius may learn a lesson from him of Rome.

CHAPTER IV.

INDEPENDENT LIBERALS.

JACOB BRIGHT, ESQ.

(Manchester—Bazley, 14,192; Bright, 13,514; Jones, 10,662; Henry, 5236; Birly, C., 15,486; Hoare, C., 12,684.)

A SHORT while since a thrill of joy ran through the land when it was found that Manchester, after a temporary flirtation with another party, had been consistent with the policy associated all the world over with her name, and had, by an enormous majority (8260 to 6409 polled by Mr. Bennett and 612 by Mr. Mitchell Henry), returned to Parliament Mr. Jacob Bright, the brother of England's greatest orator, in preference to a mild Liberal and a Conservative nobody. When the new Member took his seat, as we happened to be in the House at the time, we will describe the ceremony for the benefit of our readers. About five minutes to four the Speaker entered the House, and, standing at the table, not in his chair of state, listened while the Chaplain read the prayers. This ceremony being over, the Speaker still standing at the table, with his three-cornered cocked hat in his hand, with which he points at each M.P., counts till he has assured himself of the gratifying fact that there are forty legislators present. If that number be not present there is no House, and M.P.'s and reporters steal a holiday. On the day in question, taking his seat in his proper place, the House was made, and business commenced by the Speaker declaring that there was a new Member to be sworn, and asking him to come to the table for that purpose. At this announcement there was no little cheering on the Liberal benches, not very well filled, however, and silence amongst the Conservative ranks, represented at that time by no less than four individuals on the back benches. Not the ghost of a minister was present. The cheering was renewed when Mr. Jacob Bright was led up to the table, his brother on one side, and Mr. Bazley, his colleague, on the other. The clerk, in long black gown and with official wig, advanced to the new Member, standing on the side of the table next the Treasury Bench, and read to him the usual declaration, which being done, Mr. Bright signed his name, advanced to the Speaker, who gave him a congratulatory shake of the hand, and then retired to the second bench below the gangway, where, seated next but one to his brother, he received a cordial welcome from many to whom common fame or personal acquaintance had indicated the worth of their new ally. Of course in the lobby, when the new Member made his appearance, there was not a little whispering and much anxious scrutiny on the part of spectators, and no wonder. Time and hard work are beginning to tell upon John Bright. Is he once more to have by his side a fitting supporter? Is the aching void, left by Cobden's death, to be filled up, and by a brother? These are questions, at any rate, to be asked, questions that must have come into some men's minds on that particular night.

In personal appearance there is very little resemblance between the brothers. Mr. Jacob Bright is more delicate-looking than his brother, is of slighter build, does not wear a coat of quaker-cut, and has a thick beard and moustache. He is also balder than you would expect in a man of his age (he is but forty-six), and when he speaks to you you observe a little hacking cough, which indicates a delicacy of chest very undesirable in a champion of the people now-a-days. His features are sharper and his eye is keener than that of his brother. Evidently he has been a hard-working man all his life, and till his health broke down, about seven years ago, was indefatigable in promoting the industrial and moral welfare of the town of Rochdale, in which he lived, and where he is still engaged in business. Mr. Jacob Bright was the first Mayor of Rochdale. He was for years one of the most active promoters of the temperance cause in that town, and was noted in religious opinions for a liberality which at the recent election was made a matter of reproach to him by those who ought to have known better. A few years ago he left Rochdale and went to reside in the neighbourhood of Manchester. At the general election of 1866 he contested the city, but after polling 5562 votes was beaten by the late Mr. E. James, Q.C. Since then he has been more prominent as a public man, and has taken part in most of the Manchester meetings on the Liberal side; otherwise, with the exception of his share in the labours of the Anti-Corn Law League, he had till his appearances at Manchester confined himself to business, and to the advocacy in every way of the interests of the industrial population, amongst whom his lot had been cast. Such is a brief outline of Mr. Jacob Bright's personal career. Let me add, he has achieved a good reputation as a platform orator in the provinces, and that there is every reason to believe that in the House of Commons he has justified the anticipations of his friends. Certainly, on the few occasions on which he has spoken his remarks were well-timed and were respectfully received.

Of Mr. Jacob Bright's political opinions but a very brief notice is necessary. The men sent by Manchester to Parliament give no uncertain sound, the name he bears is also a guarantee that he belongs to the advanced school, and that he will steadily and earnestly labour with his voice and vote on its behalf. He is of those who look to the future rather than the past; who have little sympathy with the territorial system which England has long outgrown; who believe that from a people educated and possessed of political power we have nothing to fear, and that onward gloriously we shall

"Sweep into a younger day."

Mr. Bright is in favour of the ballot; he says we must have "such a redistribution of seats as will take away the monopoly of political power from rotten boroughs, and from small communities;" the Universities must cease to be sectarian; and we must have "such an educational system as that any man in Great Britain and Ireland will become an educated man." He would approach the Irish problem by dealing with her Church, equalizing her educational institutions, and by giving "security to every man who endeavours to earn an honest living by tilling the soil of his native country."

PETER TAYLOR, ESQ.

(LEICESTER—TAYLOR, 7152; HARRIS, 6825; GREEN, 2474.)

LEICESTER is a place memorable in Dissenting circles. There, if anywhere, we may expect to find its essence in its purest and most unadulterated form. Traditions of Robert Hall yet linger in that ancient town. There Edward Miall preached and matured his plan for the establishment of the *Nonconformist;* there yet preaches his faithful ally, the genial Mursell. Mr.

Baines, who has had the honour of being its Mayor, was a Church-rate martyr. Leicester is almost, in its way, as notorious as Manchester, on account of its school,—a school of which the old Noncons who believed in Josiah Conder were at one time terribly afraid. Leicester, then, is a noteworthy place, and since 1862 has been represented in Parliament by a noteworthy man.

Mr. Peter Taylor—for it is of him we write—must have been born into the world purposely to represent Leicester. His father was the Chairman of the League Conference, and one of the most active members of the London Anti-Corn-law Association. His maternal uncle was Mr. Courtauld, the gentleman who so widely distinguished himself by carrying the famous Braintree Church-rate case until the final decision was given in the House of Lords, which for ever settled the right of a majority of rate-payers to levy or refuse a Church-rate; upsetting the previous decisions of the lower courts, which declared the churchwardens and a minority of the ratepayers to possess the power to make a Church-rate.

In another way Mr. Taylor is also well qualified to represent Leicester. It may not be true that he who drives fat oxen should himself be fat; but it is true a business town requires for its representative a business man. Mr. Taylor was a partner in the well-known firm of Courtauld and Co., the extensive silk and crape manufacturers at Bocking, Halsted, and Braintree, in

Essex. In his character of master-manufacturer he was known as a sincere philanthropist and practical friend of the working man, before it was the fashion or a good advertisement of one's business to appear in such a capacity. The firm in question have long been conspicuous for the fair and enlightened conduct they have pursued towards those in their employ. As far back as 1858, the latter invited their employers to a festival, as a spontaneous demonstration of their good will and respect. Proceedings so creditable to the manufacturer and the operatives are much more common now than then. The firm in question have the honour of setting an example which others have followed, and by means of which a great scandal has been removed from our land.

Leicester, then, found in Mr. Taylor what she required. Leicester, however, was not her Member's first love. He had already wooed but not won Newcastle-upon-Tyne.

> "Thebes did his early years engage;
> He chooses Athens in his riper age."

But it is time that we now speak of Mr. Taylor himself. 1819 is the date of his birth, and at a very early period he began to take an interest in public affairs. His father was, as we have already intimated, one of the advanced Liberals of the city; and at his father's house he would meet with many of the leading Liberals of the day. Chief among these was Mr. Johnson Fox, the well-known Unitarian minister, afterwards M.P. for Oldham, with whom, to the close of his life, Mr. Taylor was on the most intimate terms. No sooner had Mr. Taylor left school than he began to cultivate his oratorical powers with great success, and became an active member on the Radical side of various debating societies, especially at one in connexion with the University College, London, where the writer remembers to have been struck with the ease and force with which he expressed his views, and with the readiness with which he combated opponents. Most of our eminent debaters began to be such in early youth. Pitt and Canning were accomplished speakers long before they commenced their Parliamentary career. We all know how early Sir Robert Peel became an orator. And such was Mr. Taylor's youthful fame that he delivered several lectures for the Anti-Corn-law League, and, at the suggestion of Mr. Cobden, became one of the founders of the Metropolitan Young Men's Anti-Monopoly Association, prior to the removal of the offices of the Anti-Corn-law League from Manchester to London. But Mr. Taylor's sympathies were by no means confined to the cause of free trade. Noble as that was, he was an advocate for freedom as well,—for the rights of man wherever he existed. In 1846 he was one of the most active founders of the People's International League; and when, in 1847, the Society of the Friends of Italy was formed, Mr. Taylor was the chairman of the executive committee. Subsequently he became chairman of the executive committee of the Garibaldi Italian Unity Committee, which met at 17, Southampton-street, Strand, the old offices of the Friends of Italy. For years Mr. Taylor has taken a deep interest in foreign affairs, especially in connexion with those of Italy. In 1845 he became an intimate friend of Mazzini, in consequence of the treatment the latter received at the hands of the late Sir James Graham. In 1858 Mr. Taylor contested Newcastle-upon-Tyne. In 1860 he made an unsuccessful appearance at Leicester; but he obtained on that occasion the reputation of "a Radical, outspoken, thorough-going, and honest;" and on the strength of that character got in due time to be returned.

As a speaker Mr. Taylor at once made his way in the House. His maiden speech was delivered on the occasion of his taking his seat, and at any rate displayed no sense of the speaker's being nervous or ill at ease. Perhaps, if anything, his coolness and self-assurance were somewhat too evident for the members of an assembly which believes itself to be the noblest senate in the world, and expects the *débutant* to be not a little afraid of its august character and power. Since then he has spoken many times, and with effect. One occasion the writer especially remembers. The debate had reference to American affairs; and no less a personage than Mr. Mason, the author of the Fugitive Slave Law, and the representative in Europe of the Southern Confederacy—then flushed with success, not, as now, an exploded sham—was present. Mr. Taylor, I take it, was aware of this. At any rate, he took the opportunity of speaking, and uttered a sentiment to the effect—I forget the exact terms—that he would rather be the most degraded creature in existence, than be the author of so infamous a measure as the Fugitive Slave Law. The speech told with wonderful effect. Mr. Mason, it was evident, listened with the utmost attention, and the hit at himself—of course quite unexpected—seemed utterly to paralyse him. All at once his face blanched, and his emotion was painful to witness. He turned to a Member sitting next him, and essayed a sickly smile; but the attempt was a failure, which but feebly covered his feeling of mortification and his sense of shame. That speech was an oratorical success of which any one might be proud. Of course, the reader need not be told in what part of the House Mr. Taylor sits. His place is in the neighbourhood of Mr. Bright, to whom he renders a hearty allegiance, and in whose opinions shares.

Apparently Mr. Taylor is destined for many years of active service. His health seems good, and he is generally to be found at his post. He has a spare figure, keen blue eyes, long dark hair, and bushy beard,—a thoughtful, earnest-looking man, evidently intent on other matters than personal appearance or display. His voice is sharp and powerful; he always speaks as if he said what he meant, and as if he meant what he said. There are, it is to be feared, many Reformers—pledged Reformers, I mean—in the House who do not care one iota about Reform. To that class Mr. Taylor cannot be said to belong.

JAMES WHITE, ESQ.

(BRIGHTON—WHITE, 3351; FAWCETT, 3086; ASHBURY, C., 2092; CONINGHAM, 408; MOORE, 1243.)

To spend other people's money in a handsome way, and thereby to get credit for generosity and liberality, is to not very conscientious people one of the pleasantest things in the world. The economical reformer is always in a minority. The subject to which he devotes himself is not an attractive one; the figures with which he has to deal are not those of rhetoric, and it is rarely that he gets the support of any considerable party on either side of the House. The reason of this is not far to seek. The ministry for the time being have no great horror of having a large revenue in their hands. It gives them influence; it enables them to employ a large number of officials, and thus strengthen their parliamentary influence and connexion. The Opposition have always the hope of being in office themselves, and they have not only the pleasing chance of having the income of the nation at their disposal, but they have also to remember that if, out of office, they bind themselves to economical reforms, they may be called upon, in a very inconvenient manner, to fulfil the pledges they rashly gave. One of the most artful things ever done by that sagacious statesman, the Duke of Wellington, was to accept defeat when it was inevitable on a question of economical rather than political Reform. In 1830 he saw that his administration did not command support in the new parliament, and when, to the amazement of Sir H. Parnell, his amendment on the Civil List was carried, the Opposition found themselves hampered with pledges which they had given, never dreaming of such a sudden turn of affairs. In his fall the Duke contrived not a little to damage his adversaries. Hence it is that regular party men have ever been very chary in demanding reduction of national expenditure, and, unlike the flower-girls of Paris, immortalized by Biddy Fudge, have been averse to

"Disturb a romance with pecuniary views."

It is all very well to say that the country is rich and prosperous; that the middle and upper classes don't feel the weight of taxation; that our operatives are well employed, and at remunerative wages, and are willing to contribute to maintaining the honour and glory of Old England. We know better. Look at the weaver in Bethnal-green, the widow stitching shirts at 4d. per day for a Jew slop-seller, the agriculturist with his large family brought up on wages seldom exceeding 12s. a week; think of a little child of four years old earning her own living! It is for these and such as these, and there are far too many of them, that taxation is a heavy burden. But they are not a powerful class, and their friends are few. Joseph Hume was one of them, and Mr. James White, member for Brighton, is another.

My own impression is that a financial reformer should be a very big man, and Mr. White has this essential qualification, as he is certainly one of the biggest men in the House. He should also be a very good-natured man, and Mr. White is this; and be prepared in an assembly inclined to extravagant expenditure to be considered a bit of a bore. "Who have you been listening to?" said a gentleman to me one night, after I had heard Mr. White's speech on his motion to the effect that the expenditure of the Government has of late years been excessive, and that it should be, in justice to the working-classes, reduced—"who have you been listening to?" "To Mr. White," was my reply. "Ah!" said he, "I'll be bound to say that there was some good stuff in his speech." And so undoubtedly there was; yet few M.P.'s, comparatively speaking, cared to hear it; and the debate was got over as quickly as possible. Joseph Hume, as we can all remember, was served in the same way; yet we have in the diaries and memoirs of the leading statesmen of that day, subsequently published, ample evidence that they were all terribly afraid of Hume's criticisms in the House of Commons—criticisms often delivered to an almost empty House, and to an audience by no means admiring or sympathetic; and more than once it is very evident that

George IV., or those who managed the affairs of the nation for him, wished Mr. Hume at Hanover. Let this be an encouragement to Mr. White, who is following in Mr. Hume's steps, and has the field almost entirely to himself. The part may not be an ambitious one, but it is a useful one. It may not lead to office, but it will surely gain for him who acts it successfully the reward of a nation's thanks. London-super-Mare has reason to be proud of her member. He is a man of business, and he sticks to it. He speaks on business subjects, and in a business way, with no ambitious flourishes, and no laboured rhetoric, but with all the force and effectiveness of earnestness and common sense.

Mr. White has the good sense to understand this. It must be remembered that he entered Parliament when he had arrived at mature years—after a life spent in the acquisition of wealth and independence in a distant quarter of the globe.

In the small band of advanced Reformers Mr. White occupies no mean place. The readers and purchasers of penny newspapers are under great obligations to him. It will be remembered that the Lords objected to the repeal of the paper duty, and that there was danger lest that important measure should be defeated. A Constitutional Defence Association was formed, round which rallied the friends of cheap knowledge in all parts of the country. Of this association Mr. James White was the indefatigable and untiring chairman; the committee met, I think, daily. Mr. White was never absent from his post, the country was thoroughly roused, Mr. Gladstone was cheered on his way, and the abolition of the paper duties was the result. The good thus effected I think it is impossible to overestimate. We have just passed through a great struggle for Reform; yet how peaceful was the situation! how different to what it was in 1830, when the Birmingham political union was a standing menace which frightened the privileged classes and compelled them reluctantly to yield Reform! What has made the difference? The answer is, The cheap press, which has taught the working man to reflect, and shrivelled up the pride of the blatant demagogue. The boon was not won one minute too early. Just as the cheap press got into existence there came the American war, and the cotton-spinners of Lancashire were struck down with bitter poverty and biting want. Did ever a people under similar circumstances behave with such noble, such Christian resignation? How was it that they did not do as they were wont to do—rise up in masses and frighten all above them? How was it no special constables were sworn in? that no dragoons were quartered in Manchester and Blackburn? that no shops were pillaged and no gentlemen's mansions burnt? The answer is, that they knew better, that they were educated by the Sunday-school, by the preacher, and, last and not least, by the everywhere-circulating penny press. It has often struck me with surprise how in the hurry and bustle of life so little recognition has been taken of the men who created a cheap press, who rolled away the stone from the door to let in light and knowledge in the darkest corners of the land. Especial thanks, at any rate, are due to Milner Gibson, and latterly to Mr. White.

In the House Mr. White's seat is generally below the gangway, whoever may be in office. If you are not in a position to see him, you can tell where he is in a storm of "Hear, hears," or "Divide, divides," as his full deep voice wells up out of his capacious chest (when he was M.P. for Plymouth his loud cheer was known as the Plymouth Sound). He is a man to catch your eye anywhere, as few have a jollier or more portly presence. It is true his black whiskers are tinged with grey; that his curly short hair has become thin at the top of the head; but nevertheless his beaming, rosy countenance indicates a vitality far from exhausted, and a power of work which promises endurance for many years.

GEORGE MELLY, ESQ.

(Stoke-upon-Trent—Melly and Roden, Liberals—unopposed.)

Last session a new Member made a maiden speech. Apparently he was, comparatively speaking, a young man, of ordinary stature, with fresh face, dark eyes, and dark hair. A maiden speech is always a trying occasion. A member can rarely do justice to himself at such times. His voice is generally thin, owing perhaps to his having not at once got the range of the House, and possibly to a nervous dread of the august assembly before whom he rises to speak. The gentleman to whom I refer, Mr. Melly, the new M.P. for Stoke, was, however, equal to the occasion; at any rate he did not break down amidst universal laughter, as men sometimes do. The subject of debate happened to be Mr. John Abel Smith's measure for the curtailing the sale of liquors on Sunday, a subject on which considerable interest has been excited in all ranks of the community, the publicans considering any legislation on the matter an interference with the rights of the working man to get beastly drunk, whip his wife, and starve his children; and the religious, and especially the temperance section of the British community, failing to see any need of a public house being open on a day when all other shops are closed. The new M.P. did not make a long speech, but what he did say was to the point. In supporting the Bill he said its object was to close the avenues as far as possible which were now open to the working man to spend his wages in drink as soon as he received them. Mr. Melly then adduced Liverpool, the place with which he was more immediately connected, as an illustration of what might be done by stringent regulations.

Stoke, whose new M.P. has thus broken ground, is the capital of one of England's grandest and most successful industries. Its Parliamentary limits comprise Burslem, Tunstall, Hanley, Shelton, Stoke, Longton, and Lane-end. The town is in the centre of the Potteries, and its chief manufacture is china, earthenware, ornamental and encaustic tiles. Taste, capital, industry have spread the fame of the Potteries all the world over. Its history is deeply interesting. Not two hundred years ago a small business was established at Burslem for making earthenware of a coarse description, coated with a common lead glaze. About the year 1690 the manufacture was improved by two Dutchmen, the brothers Elers, who introduced the mode of glazing ware by the vapour of salt, which they threw by handfuls among the ignited goods into the kiln. But these were rude, unscientific, and desultory efforts. It is to the celebrated Josiah Wedgwood that this country and the world at large are mainly indebted for the great modern advancement of the ceramic art. It was he who first erected magnificent factories, where every resource of mechanical and chemical science was made to co-operate with the arts of painting, sculpture, and statuary, in perfecting this valuable branch of trade. So sound were his principles, so judicious his procedure, and so ably have they been prosecuted by his successors in Staffordshire, that a district formerly bleak and barren and unprofitable, but ten miles long and two or three broad, now returns two members to Parliament, contributes immensely to our national dignity and wealth, and is inhabited by a population of considerably more than a hundred thousand. Nor do the people at the Potteries rest satisfied with the *éclat* they have already gained. At the last Paris Exhibition, where British manufacturers were unfairly treated, as Mr. Eugene Rimmel himself confesses in his interesting little work on the subject, after all, gold medals were awarded to Minton and Co. and Copeland and Sons. We are all proud of the Potteries. You would not go there for rural beauty, for retirement, for sunny skies, green fields, and silvery streams. It is not a place for fashion and high life to resort to. It is not there the languid belle or the used-up swell would hasten to drink the waters or participate in the pleasures and sports of country life. It is a monster beehive, swarming with civilization and intelligence and life, where the fair humanities bloom and bear fruit in spite of chimneys vomiting forth smoke all day long, of waste plots heaped up with cinders, scoriæ, and fragments of broken pots which have not stood the fire, and coal all around. A place of such persevering industry should return a persevering man. Mr. Melly is pre-eminently such. He has already fought three Parliamentary contests. In 1862 Mr. Melly was defeated at Preston by Sir Thomas Hesketh. In 1865 he was in a minority at Stoke, the numbers being—Beresford Hope, 1463; Grenfell, 1373; and Melly, 1277. Last session, in consequence of Mr. Beresford Hope coming forward for Cambridge, there was a vacancy at Stoke. Again Mr. Melly appeared as a candidate. The occasion was an eventful one. A Reform Bill had been carried, and it was left to Stoke to decide whether the men who passed that measure were the earnest friends of the people they professed to be. The clear-headed men of the Potteries gave a decided answer in the negative. The numbers were: Mr. Melly (Liberal), 1489; Mr. Campbell (Conservative), senior partner of Minton and Co., 1428. Great excitement of course prevailed, but there was no disorder. In thanking the electors, Mr. Melly observed that he accepted the victory in the names of Mr. Gladstone, Earl Russell, Mr. Bright, and the great Liberal party. The Potteries now return two Liberal M.P.'s; such is their confidence in the "truly Liberal policy" of Mr. Disraeli and his friends, in spite of the fact that it was objected to Mr. Melly that he was a Unitarian, and that, besides, his opponent was a local candidate, representing one of the leading industries of the district.

One word about the election. It was a model one, and deserves to be held up to public admiration. The candidates pledged themselves to abstain from all forms of treating and undue pressure, and especially from that greatest of all sources of demoralization at contested elections, the holding of committee meetings at public-houses. "The result," says the *Staffordshire Advertiser*, a neutral journal, "has been one upon which the district may reflect with honest pride and just satisfaction. Probably no election in the Potteries was ever more sturdily contested; and certainly on no former occasion was there such a marked absence of insobriety, violence, and intimidation." The *Staffordshire Sentinel* declares that the speech of Mr. Melly at the declaration of the poll was "so becoming as to satisfy his political opponents that in him the borough has elected one who is worthy and well able to represent it in Parliament."

The Melly family are, I believe, of Swiss extraction. The father was the founder of the mercantile house which has existed at Liverpool for half a century, and which early attained a great success. To Charles, the elder brother of Mr. George Melly, the British public —especially the temperance section of it—are under great obligations, as to him we are indebted for the origin of the Drinking Fountain Movement.

Of Mr. Melly himself we add a few further particulars. He was born August 20, 1830, and is the second son of Andrew Melly of Liverpool, merchant, and Ellen Greg, daughter of the first Member for Manchester under the Reform Bill of 1832. Mr. Melly was educated at Rugby, under the present Archbishop of Canterbury. His commercial education was commenced under a firm in the City—Messrs. Morris, Prevost, and Co.—of the highest standing. In 1853, on the death of his father during a tour in Southern Nubia, Mr. Melly became a partner in the house of Melly, Romilly, and Co., Mr. Henry Romilly, his guardian, and the then senior partner, being a son of Sir Samuel Romilly. It will thus be seen that his political education was under sound auspices.

Mr. Melly is author of "Khartoum and the Blue and White Niles," 1852, two editions; "School Experience of a Fag," 1856, one vol.; of about twelve pamphlets on Education Compulsory, 1859; Reformatory Schools; Future of the Working Classes, &c. &c. &c. He was Hon. Secretary of the Social Science Congress, Liverpool, 1859; Major commanding the Fourth Lancashire Artillery Volunteers, 1859—1866; Member of the Mersey Docks and Harbour Board. Besides, he is member of the Committee of Akbar Reformatory Ship; of Discharged Prisoners' Aid Society; of Ragged School Society; of that on Compulsory Education, Liverpool; he is also a member of the Council of Social Science; and a director of the Union Marine Insurance Company.

THOMAS HUGHES, ESQ.

(Frome—Hughes, 571; Sleigh, C., 476.)

In the lobby of the House of Commons you may often see, while Parliament is sitting, a tall, light-faced, light-haired ("auricomous" I believe is the proper term, if I may borrow from Mrs. Borrodaile or Madam Rachel), gentlemanly-looking man in the prime of life, of pleasant manner and active temperament. He is always neatly dressed, and seems to have many acquaintances of an humbler position in society than that to which he himself evidently belongs. All the out-of-door agitators who get up the steam, or at any rate who think they do, in the metropolis, are familiar with him; and you see him shaking hands with deputations clearly of an industrial origin, and representing co-operative societies or trades unions. The gentleman to whom I allude is Mr. Hughes, better known as Tom Hughes, author of "Tom Brown's School-days," "The Scouring of the White Horse," and other books that were very popular in their day and generation. It does not follow that a gentleman who writes a hearty and healthy book for schoolboys should make a good Member of Parliament. The tale-writer and the statesman have very little in common. Mr. Hughes, however, had been something more than a writer. He had had much to do with working men; he had been one of the few earnest workers associated with Mr. Maurice in bringing together the middle and upper classes of society and the working men; he had devoted to the latter much of his energy and time. Nor were they ungrateful. Under the old system there were few boroughs in which the working man had so much influence as Lambeth. At the 1865 general election they placed Mr. Hughes at the head of the poll. The numbers were: Hughes, 6373; Doulton, 6280; Lawrence, 4743; Haig, Conservative, 514. As regards Mr. Hughes, the expense was, comparatively speaking, very small, the principal part of the work was done by friends and unpaid canvassers. Even that expense, however, Mr. Hughes considered was more than a candidate ought legitimately to be asked to incur. An M.P. who has been in Parliament ought at any rate to be able to appeal to his past services, and to rely upon them as a fair claim to re-election. In conformity with this principle, recently Mr. Hughes left to his rivals to hire public-houses, to placard the borough, to organize an expensive system of canvas—in short, to move heaven and earth to gratify an honourable ambition, and to get themselves returned for Lambeth. While we were anxiously and hopefully awaiting the result of this novel and manly action on the part of Mr. Hughes, all at once it was announced that there had been a change at head-quarters. Sir Henry Rawlinson accepted a seat in the Indian Council. This appointment vacated his seat for Frome, and Mr. Hughes at once and with marvellous agility transferred his affections to the latter locality. Nor is he to be blamed for so doing. The step, I believe, was taken to advance the interests of the Liberal party. Mr. Hughes's success at Frome was certain, but it was not so certain that if Mr. Hughes had kept to Lambeth a Liberal would have been returned for Frome; as it is, Lambeth is certain to return two Liberals, and Frome thus has the honour of being represented in person by no less a distinguished personage than Mr. Thomas Hughes.

As a politician Mr. Hughes has not made much way in the House. He is there considered more of an authority on social matters. Certainly it is on these latter questions he feels himself most at home; nevertheless, as a politician he has been a steady, an earnest, a consistent Liberal. He has been in Parliament during three eventful years, and as his working class admirers say in their address to the working men of Lambeth, "On every occasion when the great question of improving the representation of the people was before the House, he was at his post urging their claim to full enfranchisement." He is sound on the vital matters, the redistribution of seats, and the mischievous rate-paying clauses. As regards the ballot, Mr. Hughes wishes to see the electors placed in a position of political independence, and therefore capable of voting freely and openly. He has pledged himself to support any measure which would enable any constituency to decide for itself whether it would have its electors vote by ballot, and perhaps that is as much as can be expected. The ballot is not a measure to which any one would lightly or very willingly resort. In a free country we expect a man boldly to proclaim his political opinions, and as boldly to support them with his vote. We must all abhor the necessity which requires the ballot. On the Irish Church Mr. Hughes is sound. In Parliament Mr. Hughes has ever given a hearty support to the policy of the great leader of the Liberal party, and he is not likely to desert the latter now that his triumph seems sure. But we need not dwell on Mr. Hughes's merits as a politician. "In conclusion," say the working men of Lambeth, "the conduct of Mr. Hughes during the whole of his political life has been of the most exemplary character."

As we have said, the questions in which Mr. Hughes is peculiarly interested, and on which he is most forcible in the House, are questions of an educational or social nature. He has supported Mr. Coleridge's praiseworthy efforts to make our sectarian Universities truly national. He was also very efficient in carrying Mr. Torrens' Bill authorizing the Government to advance money to provide improved dwellings for the working classes. As a friend of justice to all classes of the community alike, Mr. Hughes has devoted a considerable portion of his time and ability to protect honest tradesmen from the dishonest competition of dealers who cheat the public by using unjust weights and measures. It was said that by this course Mr. Hughes had endangered his seat in Lambeth. We can scarcely believe this. The supposition that in that borough there are more dishonest tradesmen than honest ones, to say nothing of the working-class voters who suffer from these practices, and might be supposed to rally round any one who would expose such dishonesty, is simply ridiculous. On such questions as these in the House of Commons he is second to no one. In another respect he stands also alone. By moral means alone the working classes placed him at the head of the poll on his first election. It is to be questioned whether in the late Parliament there was another M.P. similarly returned. We hear much of the need of sending working men Members to Parliament, Mr. Hughes is a model of what a working man M.P. should be; firm in principle, conciliatory in utterance, ready to express his convictions and to carry them whether they are popular or the reverse. On the Sunday question, for instance, Mr. Hughes's opinions are not those of a majority of his Lambeth friends,—but they do not think of him anything the worse for that.

Mr. Hughes is young comparatively speaking. He was born in 1823, and is the second son of the late J. Hughes, Esq., of Donnington Priory, Berks. In 1847 he married the eldest daughter of the Rev. James Ford, Prebendary of Exeter. He was—as we need scarce remark—educated at Rugby in its palmy days. In 1845 he took his B.A. degree at Oxford, where he had been a student in Oriel, and in 1848 he was called to the Bar at Lincoln's Inn. In that year, as we know, society was moved to its lowest deep. No wonder that since then a new spirit has been abroad in the land, or that a man like Mr. Hughes should seek especially to represent it in the British Senate.

ACTON SMEE AYRTON, ESQ.

(TOWER HAMLETS—AYRTON, 9839; SAMUDA, 7849; BEALES, 7160; COOPE, C., 7446; NEWTON, 2890.)

IN the old unreformed Parliament the Tower Hamlets —or rather the Parliamentary borough of that name —had a population of 647,845 and an electoral body of 29,799, a constituency, in short, the largest in the kingdom. Under the new dispensation the population has been divided, and the new borough of the Tower Hamlets will consist only of the river-side parishes from the Tower to Bow Creek, together with the eastern parishes of Bow and Bromley. It is clear the new borough will be large enough. It will have a population of 337,000, and an electoral body not much smaller than before the division. In Poplar, Limehouse, Stepney, St. George's-in-the-East, and Whitechapel, places where men live by hard work, and have little interest in great Government expenditure or in aristocratic institutions, people are mostly Liberal. For the borough at the recent election there were four candidates in the field, all very Liberal. One was Mr. Beales, another was Mr. Samuda, another was Mr. Newton, and a fourth was Acton Smee Ayrton, Esq. It is of this latter gentleman we propose to speak. Other things being equal, no sensible constituency would make a change merely for the love of change. No man willingly gets rid of a good servant. Most wise men believe it to be better to bear the ills they have than fly to those they know not of. Tried men, at any rate, are infinitely to be preferred to untried ones. A man who has made his mark in the House of Commons, who is listened to when he speaks, who cannot be snubbed or put down, who, at any rate, has shown superiority to the rank and file around him, it is clear has a kind of moral right to say to the electors, "I have served you faithfully; I have been laborious in my exertions for your welfare: I have a right to expect that you will return me again." The fickleness of the multitude is proverbial. Their passion for new brooms, which do not after all sweep cleaner than the old, is matter of history. But it is to be hoped in the enlightened region of the Tower Hamlets, where democracy has it all its own way, it may be shown that the people of the present age can appreciate and reward loyalty to their interests. In this respect the claims of no new man can for an instant be compared with those of the present Member. In the old Parliament Mr. Ayrton was almost a model M.P., never absent from his post, ever ready to do the best he could with his tongue or by his vote.

Nature has not fitted Mr. Ayrton to act the part of a demagogue. Nor has he any of a mob orator's qualifications. He has very much the appearance of a hard, dry lawyer in a good state of preservation, not given to let his tongue run faster than his thoughts, or to talk more than to do. He has not much enthusiasm himself, nor is he calculated to create much enthusiasm in the minds of others. His private history is soon told. He is the third son of F. Ayrton, Esq., formerly of Gray's-inn, and late of Bombay, by Julia, only child of Lieutenant-Colonel Nugent. He was born in 1816; he was called to the bar by the Middle Temple in 1853. He was elected for the Tower Hamlets about the same time, and is a member of the Reform Club. In a long speech which he made the other day he referred to his political life since his first connexion with the borough, now sixteen years ago, and reminded his hearers of the fidelity and consistency of his conduct with regard to the rights of labour, reform, education, the Irish Church, and other questions of the day.

As regards the future, it may be safely affirmed Mr. Ayrton will follow the party of which Mr. Gladstone is the leader. It is true, he tells us, the Conservatives have given us on compulsion a Reform Bill —but as bad as it could be. It is true they have adopted the great principle of household suffrage, but at the same time they had so complicated it by ratepaying clauses and conditions of residence, as to render it to a great extent nugatory. The redistribution clauses must be considered only as temporary, and more than ever will the voter require the protection of the ballot. On the question of the reduction of our national expenditure Mr. Ayrton is equally decided. On Church questions he is unwilling to admit that the New Testament is not applicable to present circumstances, and that Christians could not support their own places of worship and ministers on the voluntary principle, just as in the Tower Hamlets the dissenters do theirs. He anticipates in the Church of the future a Presbyterian element. As regards local taxation, Mr. Ayrton declares that it is monstrous that fashionable people should build houses where none but they could live. He is for placing the poor charges upon the whole metropolis, and not upon separate districts. On the delicate question of ladies voting, Mr. Ayrton's answers are not satisfactory to the advanced females of whom Mrs. Harriet Law may be said to be the leader. With regard to the Permissive Bill he will allow the inhabitants of a district to exercise their own discretion, and would not leave the licensing to the discretion of the magistrate. He is in favour of the continuance of the Income-tax; and referring to the opening of places of public amusement on Sunday, he said it would be an unfortunate thing if the Government were to set their servants to work on that day. On these questions Mr. Ayrton's opinions were satisfactory. At the last election he coalesced with no other candidate, but threw himself on the intelligence of the great body of electors. He was quite right in doing so. We were sure, as it turned out, that the Tower Hamlets would not reject him for an untried man. A metropolitan M.P. is in one respect deeply to be pitied. He is never out of the reach of his constituents. He is expected always to be at their beck and call. He never has a moment to himself. How far happier is the man who represents the Orkneys or the Land's-end. If he offends his constituents their anger is appeased by the time he makes his appearance among them. It is only occasionally he has to assume a respectful attitude towards the constituent body. The metropolitan M.P. has always to mind his manners, not only once a week, but all the year round.

It was in this last Session of Parliament that Mr. Ayrton more particularly came to the front. Ever since he had been an M.P. he had taken an eminently respectable position, but in the temporary disorganization of the Liberal ranks Mr. Ayrton's fidelity and perseverance placed him in a new position. Some time ago, when the great meeting of the Liberal party was held at the house of the present Prime Minister, Mr. Ayrton declared that an increase of the number of voters, without a redistribution of seats, would be a national injury rather than a benefit, and true to this idea he triumphed more than once over the Conservative Ministry. Again, Mr. Ayrton signally distinguished himself as a leader in the opposition made to the Metropolitan Cattle Market Bill—a Bill which in spite of the enthusiastic support of the country gentlemen, was ultimately withdrawn,—a Bill which, had it been carried, would have materially increased the cost of meat to the poor of London, and besides was a violation of free trade. That Mr. Ayrton is not deficient in moral courage is clear from the fact that on one occasion he actually dared to beard Mr. Beales and his friends at one of their gatherings in St. James's Hall. He differed from them on some particular question, and took the liberty to tell them so. Clearly such a man as Mr. Ayrton, by faithful and independent service, by well-tried ability, has proved his right to be at any rate one of the men for the new Parliament.

EDWARD BAINES.

(LEEDS—BAINES, 15,946; CARTER, 15,105; WHEELHOUSE, C., 9437; DUNCOMBE, C., 1621.)

LORD HOLLAND was a Whig nobleman, and we dare say gave on appropriate occasions "the Liberty of the Press." Tom Moore was a gentleman of the press, and in common with more exalted literary gentlemen had the run of Holland House. We read in Moore's diary an account of a breakfast in that headquarters of Whiggery in 1831: "Talked of the state of the press, the great misfortune of the total separation that had taken place between those who conduct it and the better rank of society; even from literature it had become in a great measure separated, instead of forming, as in France, a distinguished branch of it. Now you," he said, "and all the other eminent literary persons of the day, keep as much aloof from the gentlemen of the press as we of the political world do, and they are therefore thrown, with all their force and their virulence unsoftened by the commerce of society, to form a separate and hostile class of themselves." We have here the accepted creed in good society. It is true Lord Palmerston told us he had met Mr. Delane, of the *Times*, in society, that he had had the honour of receiving him at his own house, that he found him a very agreeable and intelligent gentleman; but then Lord Palmerston had happily reached a time of life when people are not very particular as to what company they keep.

In England journalism, like virtue, is its own reward. Wordsworth tells us,

> "We poets in our youth begin in gladness,
> Whereof comes in the end despondency and madness."

But the poet may become a lion, may have a pension, may die poet-laureate. All abuse the literary man. Lord John Russell says he is prone to be discontented with the Government under which he lives—a feeling as natural to him as the attachment of the Bedford family to Woburn Abbey and the glorious Reformation. Undoubtedly the proper place for the journalist is the House of Commons. Did we proceed upon the supposition that governing was a science and not an hereditary gift; not a freak of nature, as the thick upper lip of the House of Hapsburg, but a capacity only to be found in men of strong natures, a capacity, moreover, becoming stronger and wiser, as it is wisely nurtured and exercised, the journalists in the House of Commons would be a numerous class. As it is, the loss is chiefly that of the nation, for perhaps the journalist is the only man in England who studies politics for their own sake. The scion of the aristocracy looks upon the representation of his division of the county as one of his hereditary rights and duties—a bore perhaps, but one of the penalties he must pay for being so immensely cleverer and wiser than the rest of humanity. His father is the largest proprietor in Blankshire, and the estate always returns the M.P. That honour is transmitted with the family spoons, and will be till such time as future reformed constituencies shall ask of a man—not what acres are his by the accident of birth, but what are his capabilities and brains. The lawyer would laugh at you as a simpleton if you supposed for an instant that he goes through the expense and trouble of a parliamentary election for any other purpose than that of his own promotion. The soldier or the sailor seeks a seat in Parliament for the same reason. The merchant and the contractor and the manufacturer are more prone to look after their own interests than those of the public. There are many well-meaning men blessed with long purses, who are returned on account of local influence and unlimited expenditure, merely for the sake of a little natural and not discreditable vanity, but the journalist is the only man whose days and nights are devoted to politics, who knows better than all other men the state of public feeling, the ignorance or the prejudice and the passions of the hour, who can best distinguish the genuine wants and wishes of the age, and is most given to the solution of temporary problems by the application of abstract principles and eternal truths; and yet this is the man who most rarely enters the walls of St. Stephen's. In politics, it seems as if there was a dead set against newspaper writers. It is true that we suffer for this; that if we go to war our armies perish, as in the Crimea or at Walcheren; that we hold India by an army where mutiny seems chronic; that our taxation has reached a climax which to all thoughtful men is appalling; that we have forfeited our continental friendships; that nowhere are the poor so poor, so depraved, so ignorant, as in this land of enormous wealth, where we have an aristocracy and a State Church the richest in Europe. It is true we suffer all this in good company, and that so indomitable is English pluck that we keep right in the main; but this could be achieved at a much less expenditure of precious treasure and still more precious blood and brain. Tom Moore tells us of a party at which were present a country squire and a poet; the former was wonderfully polite to the latter, and in adjourning to the next room offered him precedence. When told, however, the individual was a mere poet, "Oh!" said he, "I know my place," and rudely pushing in before, left the poor poet to follow. Our statesmen treat the journalist in the same way. If we are ruined we are rejoiced to learn that it is not by what Lord John Russell termed, when he was making such a mess of it at Vienna, "the ribald press." Of the institution thus termed, Mr. Edward Baines is one of the most distinguished members.

Let me observe, in the first place, Mr. Baines has the great merit of being the son of his father. Years and years ago, when Leeds was unrepresented, when Parliament was unreformed, when the most hideous class legislation prevailed, there went into Leeds a young lad born near Preston, in Lancashire, of whom his schoolmaster prophesied that he would be either a great man or would be hanged. This lad married, and settled in Leeds as a printer. He began by laying down the rule that he would not spend more than half his income, and he acted on it. He always drank water; he took no snuff; he never smoked. Neither tavern nor theatre saw his face. Yet he was not an earthworm; he was a man of great public spirit, but the pure joys of domestic life, the pleasures of industry, and the satisfaction of doing good, combined to make him happy. The lad did not end his days on the gallows, nor did he become great in the general acceptance of the term, but in his way, and for him, he was a great man. He became prosperous; he won many friends; they assisted him to purchase the *Leeds Mercury;* the proprietor, who had taught himself to speak when a lad by being a member of a discussion class, threw himself heart and soul into the struggle for Reform. Leeds and Yorkshire felt deeply on this matter; not a meeting on the subject scarcely was held at which he did not assist. When Leeds had the franchise first extended to it, it was owing in a great measure to him that Messrs. Marshall and Macaulay were returned; and on the appointment of the latter to a seat in the Council of the Governor-General of India, he, after a pretty close struggle with Sir John Beckett, was elected in his place. Such was Edward Baines, senior,—a model middle-class man, an illustration of what industry, and energy, and integrity can effect. What the old Hebrew book says is true—the children of Baines, senior, were trained up in their father's steps. Mr. E. Baines, the present M.P. for Leeds, inherits not only his father's claim upon his native town, but his father's virtues; and follows in his father's steps.

The present M.P. for Leeds was born in the year 1800, and married, in 1829, a daughter of Thomas Blackburn, Esq., of Liverpool; was educated at Manchester, and has been all his life connected with the journal of which I believe till lately he was the head. He is a J.P. and Deputy-Lieutenant for the West Riding of Yorkshire, and President of the Yorkshire Union of Mechanics' Institutions. He is also author of the "History of the Cotton Manufacture," a book which the late Sir Robert Peel, at a very critical period of his own history, found time to study with certainly more than average attention; and of a Life of his father, still deserving circulation, and of which

I believe some years ago there was a cheap edition published. If the youthful swells of the present day would read it, they would be all the better for its perusal, and the philosophical Radical might also study it, as it would teach him how useful a school are the local institutions he would put down by his system of centralization. The memorial raised by the filial piety of the son was worthy the parent, and was such a work as should find a place in young men's libraries at the present day. If it is out of print, a cheap abridged edition would be found to contain some useful reading.

It was late in life when Mr. Baines entered the House of Commons. He was first returned for Leeds in 1859. The election was honourable to himself and honourable to his native town. The true theory of representation is a burgess representing his own borough. Often a fitting man is passed over and a moneyed or titled stranger preferred. Out of his own borough, Mr. Baines had long been known and esteemed. Years ago there were fierce contentions in the land about education, about Maynooth, about the voluntary principle; and in the contest one of the most earnest, and one of the hardest hitters on the Dissenting side, was Mr. Baines; and his work on the voluntary principle in education, and against Government interference, was deemed unanswerable by those of his own way of thinking. As a Sunday-school teacher Mr. Baines had practical experience of the power of the voluntary principle in education. As a member of a Congregational church, it had been demonstrated to him how much purer and more powerful were the ministrations of the Gospel messenger when he set forth on his Divine mission untrammelled by the fetters of the State; and in a similar spirit and with a similar faith he would legislate for the body politic. And he is quite logical in this; for if the voluntary principle can grapple with the spiritual wants of the day, surely it is sufficient for the removal of temporary and minor ills. Out of this religious faith has grown Mr. Baines's political creed and career. The moment he became a member of the Legislature, he obtained a parliamentary committee to do away with what was called the Bible monopoly, a monopoly by which no one was allowed to print the Bible in England but the printers of the Universities of Oxford and Cambridge, and the printers to the Queen's Most Excellent Majesty. Nor does Mr. Baines rest his faith merely on a form of words. Not merely would he have the State retire from the field of labour where its presence is a doubtful benefit, but he would have an energetic voluntaryism occupy its place. Surely, whatever may be the nation's needs, there is that in the heart of the nation that can grapple with and overcome them all. He would raise temperance societies to abolish drunkenness; he would have educational societies disseminate that knowledge without which true civilization cannot exist; and with the living faith of voluntary Christianity he would clothe the land with Gospel life and light. His political creed is a hopeful one. He has faith in humanity, which is dwarfed and poor indeed when taught to rely upon the aid and resources of the State, but which is grand in its aspect and lofty in its aims if left to itself, to listen to and respond to the voice of duty and of God. Faith can do all things: it can move mountains; it can shake the world. The State can offer but place and pay. The hireling seeks them alone and is content. Instead of raising men he degrades them. If he teaches, it is but mechanically; if he accepts the priest's office, it is but for a bit of bread. It is only by love that religion can gain its trophies or win its way. As a practical politician, Mr. Baines has interested himself chiefly with endeavouring to get the franchise in boroughs extended down to six-pound holders. That his argument on the subject was considered by the ministry as unanswerable is clear from the new Franchise Bill the session before last carried through the Commons. Strengthen the foundations of your political edifice, says Mr. Baines, widen the basis, include within it those whom you now exclude, make friends of those whom you treat as enemies; and the time came when the labours of Mr. Baines and of Mr. Locke King produced their proper effect, and Liberals and Conservatives alike voted for Parliamentary Reform.

Mr. Baines appears to have led a laborious life. He

has much the appearance of a student and a thinker. As an orator he is effective because he is painstaking and persevering; and if not the leader of orthodox Dissent in Parliament, at any rate is accepted there as one of its most eminent representatives. His place is behind the Ministerial benches, and his support is always given their occupants. He has been nurtured in pure Whig principles, and cannot forget that to Lord John Russell we owe the repeal of the Test and Corporation Acts, Parliamentary Reform, and negro emancipation. Leeds, with its mighty industries and well-taught operatives, could have no better representative of its Liberalism and Dissent,—a Liberalism which means more than finality,—a Dissent which is always thirsting after practical result.

HENRY SELF PAGE WINTERBOTHAM, ESQ.

(STROUD—DICKENSON, 2826; WINTERBOTHAM, 2734; DORRINGTON, 2180.)

IN the year 1793, while all true patriots were despairing of their country, and Mr. Pitt was blossoming fast into a furious anti-Reformer, Sir Richard Perryn, one of the judges of His Majesty's Court of Exchequer, and a special jury, assembled in the ancient city of Exeter to try a poor Baptist parson for seditious words uttered while preaching a sermon in Plymouth on the previous 5th of November. Defendant was charged with having declared that the laws made at the Revolution "had been abused and brought into disuse." Actually it was sworn by some witnesses, though denied by others, that he had said, "I approve highly of the Revolution in France." He had asked, "Why are your streets and poorhouses crowded with poor and your gaols with thieves, but because of oppressive laws and taxes?" And besides, he had actually the audacity to declare that the English "had as much right to stand up for liberty as they had in France;" and to promulgate the unheard-of doctrine that His Majesty, good George III., as our fathers called him, who wished every child in his dominions might be able to read the Bible (it was a pity he neglected to teach it to his own children), "was placed upon the throne upon condition of keeping certain laws and rules, and if he does not observe them he has no more right to the throne than the Stuarts had." In those times it was a perilous thing to talk in that strain. In a speech which was endorsed by all present, for it was concluded amidst vehement applause, Sergeant Rooke, the counsel for the Crown, implied that the defendant "had been guilty of blasphemy against the Majesty of heaven;" and that such low-bred persons as himself and his hearers had no business to indulge in political discussions, for when they do, said Rooke the lawyer, "they endanger the constitution under which they have long been happy, and which has been the envy of surrounding nations." After this the jury had an easy time of it, and found the defendant guilty. Nor was this all. The next day the poor unfortunate Baptist parson was again placed in the dock for a similar offence. Sergeant Rooke was again the prosecutor, and a verdict of guilty was returned by the same jury. The defendant had next to appear in London to receive sentence. Lord Kenyon, in the height of his judicial fame and wisdom, and with a view to the preservation of our glorious constitution in Church and State, adjudged him to two years' imprisonment, and a fine of one hundred pounds, for the first offence, and to a similar punishment for the second offence, besides, at the end of that term, compelling him to find surety for his good behaviour for five years, himself in £500, and two sureties in £200 each. The name of this unfortunate victim of Georgian loyalty and prejudice was Winterbotham, and his grandson is now a prosperous equity draughtsman and conveyancer; and as M.P. for Stroud, by a speech delivered on the occasion of the debate on Mr. Coleridge's Universities Test Abolition Bill, obtained at once an enviable Parliamentary reputation. As an able writer in the *English Independent* well observed, his speech "was listened to with equal delight and surprise, the leaders on both sides paying him the compliment of marked attention. At its close it was felt—and indeed said—by Sir William Heathcote, that in Mr. Winterbotham the House had gained an addition to its debating power, and the Dissenters to their influence in that assembly. He spoke with ease, self-possession, and wondrous emphasis both of voice and of action; and in an address which occupied nearly half an hour, put several new points which told well." Nor are we surprised at this eulogium. It is certainly well deserved. It but expresses what all must feel. The talents and the principles of the grandfather have been handed down to, and inherited by the grandson. Society has got to be a little wiser than when good old George III. reigned. We honour the grandson, and put him in Parliament. Our grandfathers put his grandfather in gaol. Let us be grateful to the brave men who suffered imprisonment, transportation, death, for English freedom. Let us see to it that in these lukewarm days we guard our sacred rights as valiantly as they.

There are few more pleasant or agreeable men in the House than Mr. Winterbotham. There is nothing sectarian in his manner or appearance. With his cheerful smile you can scarcely fancy him to be a Chancery barrister at all. He has a smart and fashionable air, looks young, is in stature rather small. He has no beard, and his hair is rather inclined to the colour which may be said to be sandy or golden, as the writer is of a poetic or prosaic temperament. He comes from a commercial and manufacturing centre where Dissent and Liberalism have long flourished. Mr. Poulett Thomson, one of our leading advocates of Free Trade, ere Cobden and Bright had taken the field, was representative of Stroud. Earl

Russell was glad to find refuge there when he was ousted from Devonshire by its Tory landlords, and that Mr. Horsman has so long represented it is due rather to his early and celebrated attacks on ecclesiastical abuses than to his more recent coquettings with the discomfited politicians who in vain sought refuge in Cave Adullam, which unfortunately proved to be no place of shelter after all. Mr. Winterbotham became M.P. for Stroud in the year 1867, just as the session was about to terminate. He was opposed by a "Constitutionalist," in the person of a Mr. Dorrington. The numbers were—Dorrington, 508; Winterbotham, 570. The Constitutionalist party are now no more. Having, under the guidance of Mr. Disraeli, abandoned the constitution, they now take their stand upon the Church in danger. Is it not Mr. Tadpole who in "Coningsby" expresses his preference for a good Church in danger cry by the plea that it means nothing?

For one thing Mr. Winterbotham is to be commended. In these shoddy days, as soon as Brown has made his fortune as a soapboiler, or Smith has become a successful speculator and alters his name to Smythe, somehow or other they find they had what no one gave them credit for the possession of—grandfathers, and astonish the weak eyes of their poor relations with coats of arms. In a work recently published on the House of Commons, a list of members is given, with an account of each, a little after the manner of Dodd. In the part devoted to each member, space is left for the insertion of his coat of arms. Mr. Winterbotham leaves that a blank, and intimates that he bears none. We might expect this from the son of his grandfather; but it is not always our reasonable expectations are realized. Mr. Winterbotham's father was a banker at Stroud. He is the second son, and was born March 2, 1837. He was educated at Amersham Grammar School, Bucks, an extinct Parliamentary borough, once represented in the Senate by the illustrious Algernon Sidney and the poet Waller. It is to be hoped as a boy the future M.P. for Stroud there imbibed somewhat of the spirit of the celebrated martyr for liberty. At any rate, he has soon become a rising man on the popular side. At the London University he graduated with honours, and took his B.A. degree in 1856, and his LL.B. in 1859. At University College, to which place he went after leaving Amersham, he certainly led no idle life. In 1858 he won the Hume Scholarship in Jurisprudence, and in 1859 the Hume Scholarship in Political Economy. A little while after he was elected Fellow of University College. In 1860 he was called to the bar by the Society of Lincoln's Inn. He travels the Oxford circuit. For the information of our lady readers, let us add that he is unmarried; and like the great William Pitt, finds, at any rate for the present, in his country his wife. Whether the country is the better for such extreme devotion is a question the writer on the present occasion declines to discuss.

JOSEPH COWEN, ESQ.

(Newcastle—Cowen, 7057; Headlam, 6674; Hammond, 2727.)

Friday nights in the House of Commons are generally busy ones. I always tell the stranger to get his order or his name down on the Speaker's lists on a Friday, as generally on that occasion there is a great deal of extra skirmishing. Members are anxious to unburden their breasts and to do their duty to their country. They seem to get thus a weight off their minds, and are the better prepared to enjoy their Saturday half-holiday and their Sabbath repose. On the night of which I write, however, it was clear that the miscellaneous skirmishing would be by no means permitted. The House was intent on business—and very important business too. There was the Representation of the People Bill to be discussed in committee, and some five or six pages of proposed amendments to consider. My heart sank within me as I took up the paper. Considering that we don't live to the age of Methusaleh—considering that a Reform Bill had to be passed—considering that we were getting rapidly into June, said I to myself, how are these amendments to be fully debated? Who is sufficient for these things? Foolish man—or person—for that is Mr. Mill's phrase, and I always like to talk like a great philosopher when I can—foolish person, replied I, that I am. Is not the House of Commons the concentrated essence of the wisdom of the nation, and cannot it do everything?

except, as Lord Coke said, make a man into a woman, or reverse the process and reduce the porcelain of creation into common clay. Well, on the night in question I got a good idea as to how the House gets through its business. It had, I have said, a great deal to do, and it was very full indeed. There was Mr. Gladstone and the Liberal party, which had come down the tree "by particular desire" and "for one night only," all around and about. There were the country gentlemen whose mission it is to resist the democratic spirit of the age, seated behind the then Chancellor of the Exchequer, who has played many parts in his time, but who did never such a strange trick as that of the session before last—that is, turning squires

> "With brains made clear
> By the irresistible strength of beer"

into the supporters of household suffrage and a lodger franchise. His work was all the harder that he had to do it all himself. The only vacant seats when I entered the House were on the Treasury Bench. There was a sad lack of talent there. The harvest was bountiful, but the labourers were few. Well, as I have said, that night gave one a good idea of how the House could work. The first amendment discussed was that of Mr. Watkin, of Stockport, defining a dwelling-house for the purpose of the Act to consist of two rooms. To this a further amendment had been added by Mr. Pease, of Durham, requiring that the rooms should contain at the least sixteen hundred cubic feet of space, and then the stream of talk began to flow. One of the first to protest against Mr. Watkin's definition of a house was Mr. Cowen, of Newcastle-on-Tyne, who told how in his own borough there were 14,000 persons who would be disfranchised if the amendment were carried, and described feelingly how in Newcastle many a respectable working man and his wife occupied but one room till the growth of a family necessitated more accommodation. The honourable member had little to say—nor did he take long in saying it—but he was listened to with the utmost attention, as if words of wisdom dropped from his mouth. How was this? Mr. Cowen is no professional orator—no barrister talking for a place—and at his time of life it cannot be that he is led away by the desire of fame and seeks the applause of listening senates to command. His appearance forbids our entertaining a supposition of the kind. He rises from his seat on the third bench, where he has been sitting by the side of Peter Taylor, and at once every eye is directed to him. It is known that he will not speak long, that he will not speak unless he has something to say, that he represents a great constituency far away, and that though sprung from the ranks, such has been the integrity, the perseverance, the patriotism of his life, that in his own neighbourhood no man is received with more respect. Well, in the House of Commons there is the profoundest political equality, and in his place Mr. Cowen is listened to as attentively as if in his veins there ran the blue blood of our oldest families; there was no attempt to cough him down, no groans as when a Conservative Darby Griffith or a Protestant Whalley appears upon the stage. Nor did Mr. Cowen seem in the least degree embarrassed by his peculiar situation. His speech was strong and clear, with just enough of a Northern accent to give it individuality. He stood up firmly as a rock; evidently he is no novice at public speaking, and though getting on for seventy—he was born in 1800—and crowned with grey hairs, his tall muscular frame and his big head denote a more than average amount of physical and mental strength. Of the former indeed he has already convinced the House. There is no man so regular in his attendance. Indeed, he may be termed the constant member. He assists Mr. Speaker in his devotions—he is there while private business is discussed, or petitions presented, or notices of motion given. He listens to what is said on both sides of the House by honourable gentlemen. When others are dining he retains his seat—and when others have dined and have come back with livelier spirits in consequence, Mr. Cowen is there still, patient, unwearied, vigilant, like one of the lions in Trafalgar Square. Such are the sort of men we want in the House. His place is the proper one. Wilberforce used to say when the debate came to him, he just joined in it—that was all. That is the right way in the House of Commons, and that is why Mr. Cowen has succeeded when he has spoken. Many a member has a speech ready, but the debate does not come to him, and he has no opportunity of delivering it. I knew of more than one instance on that very night in which an M.P. had determined to take part in the discussion, but somehow or other had no chance; the front row of the Opposition was crammed with M.P.'s waiting to speak—who, alas, after all their preparation had to put their speeches into their pockets, and go home, to the great loss of the country in general, and the reporters in particular.

And here let me say Parliamentary attendance is not so easy a thing as at first sight it may appear. Some country people fancy it a fine thing to be a Parliament chap, and to sit in a big house in London with lots of great people, in the presence of a Speaker in a big wig and with a gold mace before him. Oh, my brother bumpkin, it is harder work than you imagine, especially when the weather is sultry, and it is pleasanter to be riding in Rotten Row, or lounging about the Parks. It is no joke breathing a House of Commons atmosphere terribly deficient in oxygen and ozone—from four or six till the twilight is gone, and the dim grey of morn is glimmering in the east. It is unpleasant to go to bed just as Smith's red carts with the papers are rushing along the Strand to catch the first down trains, and chubby red-faced milkmaids are commencing the distribution of their highly adulterated and questionable beverage; or as the British operative patronizes his cup of "early purl." But worst of all is it to hear Wishy succeed Washy with his everlasting small talk, and to split your skull (I mean metaphorically) in the vain endeavour to extract one particle of sense out of that waste of words, one needle out of that stack of hay. A lawyer may do this for the sake of office; a vain man because he is ambitious; a party politician because he is sure of his reward; but the case is very different with a man like Mr. Cowen, who belongs to the advanced Liberals, who is independent of party—who has nothing to wish for or hope from it; who can gain nothing but the reward of his conscience, and the pleasure which springs from the faithful and laborious discharge of duty.

MR. ALDERMAN LUSK.

(FINSBURY—TORRENS, 13,159; LUSK, 12,503; O'MALLEY, C., 6137; COX, L., 1238.)

AT the last unreformed election, Finsbury had a population of 387,278, and as many as 22,530 electors. There was a severe contest for the honour of representing it in Parliament. Five Liberals were in the field (the Conservatives dared not put in appearance; they had not, and they have not now, a chance). The successful candidates were Mr. Torrens, a well-known literary man, and Mr. Alderman Lusk. It is of the latter gentleman we propose to speak. He is one of the many examples of which the metropolis is full of what may be done by perseverance, patience, and prudence. He came to London poor, he is now rich; unknown, he is now one of the most influential and respected of its leading citizens. Few men have had a more successful commercial or political career.

Mr. Lusk was born in Ayrshire in 1813. He lost his father, who was a farmer, very early in life, and had to trust wholly to his own energies and abilities; but his mother was a very superior woman, and to her the son was much indebted for advice, encouragement, and example. As the eldest of a large family, he had soon to leave home to make his way in the world, and he began life as an active lad behind the counter in a little northern town. To a certain extent all Scotch lads are educated and ambitious, and Andrew Lusk aimed at something higher than provincial reputation. He came to London, tried reporting and writing for newspapers, and then decided to devote his energies entirely to trade. If we are to judge by the result, the decision was a wise one. Fortune smiled on the young Scotchman bravely fighting the battle of life. He became a shipowner and provision merchant. In due time he was elected to represent the ward in which he lived in the Court of Common Council. Four years afterwards he was chosen to fill the office of sheriff to the City of London. He was then elected Alderman, and, as we have already said, M.P. In the promotion of several important commercial undertakings Mr. Lusk has taken a very prominent part. Amongst these we may mention the Commercial Union Assurance Company, and the Imperial Bank. Of the latter undertaking he was the chairman and ruling spirit from the first.

Sydney Smith was once asked what were the duties of an archdeacon. To perform archidiaconal duties, was his reply. The answer left the questioner as wise as before. If asked what were the duties of a London alderman, we should reply after the manner of the worthy Canon of St. Paul's. One of the duties of an alderman, however, as we all know, is to take the chair at public meetings, and from a list lying before us we get an idea of what Alderman Lusk has done in this respect, of his truly Christian spirit, and of his desire to promote the best interests of his fellow-citizens. It appears in one year, 1864, he presided at the meeting of the Holloway Ragged-school, the Commercial Travellers' Benevolent Society Dinner, the Surrey Chapel Lectures, Seamen's Mission, Commercial-road; Sunday-school, New North-road; Lectures to Young Men (Church of England), Islington; Sunday-school, St. John's-square (Wesleyan); Aged Pilgrims' Friend Society; Sunday-school, James-street, St. Luke's; Ragged-school, Hoxton; Ragged-school Golden-lane; Sunday-school, Leather-lane; Silver Trade Pension Society, Philanthropic Society, Pensions for Aged Newsvendors' Association; Exeter

Hall Lectures, Young Men's Christian Association; Christian Young Men's Association, Islington Branch; Spa-fields Sunday-school, Bermondsey Sunday-school, Britannia-fields Sunday-school, Working Men's Club, Golden-Lane; Christian Relief Society, Barnsbury Hall; Sermon-lane Ragged-school, Kingsland Ragged-school; Fatherless Children's Asylum Election, Primitive Methodist Annual Meeting. Besides all this, the Alderman acted as steward at twelve hospital festivals, and assisted at various other Ragged and Sunday-school meetings. Surely this of itself is a fair amount of work, independently of the routine business which must take more or less of an Alderman's time.

In Parliament, Mr. Lusk, by his good sense and industry, soon obtained a respectable position. The first year he was put on a Gas Committee, and pertinaciously insisted on certain views which at the time were thought extreme, but which have since, after two years' thorough investigation of the subject, been virtually adopted. In 1867 he was an active supporter of the Bill for amending the Merchant Shipping Act. He suggested several of the most important amendments, clauses which the head of the Government confessed were for the benefit of the public in general, and that of sailors in particular. In his attendance he is most unremitting; during the last two sessions he was not absent from his place a single day, and his name appears in almost every discussion. As a Liberal he is always sound and staunch. He votes steadily with his party; is led away by no personal aims or petty crotchets of his own, and takes a deep interest in all questions connected with free trade and popular education. As a Presbyterian his views on the Irish Church may be depended on. He sees no danger to religion from the destruction of a system which more than anything else in Ireland has hindered the spread of the Gospel, and has alienated the mind of the people from England's Protestantism and England's rule.

Much more may be said of Alderman Lusk: he is a fair speaker, he is in the prime of life, he takes a pleasure in hard work. But besides, he has assigned to himself a special task, and that is, while others talk of the extravagance of Government, and on the hustings especially denounce our profligate expenditure, he practieally endeavours, by moving amendments in Committee of Supply, to reduce that expenditure and curtail that extravagance. This is no easy matter; financial reform is always, as a matter of fact and not of theory, unpopular in the House of Commons. We all like to be generous and liberal at other people's expense. All men like Hume, or Williams of Lambeth, are unpopular, simply because they contend, bit by bit and in detail, for economy with respect to national affairs. Great orators rarely appear as financial reformers when there is a discussion on the estimates. In matters of figures there is no room for oratorical display; besides, the discussion comes on at unseasonable hours, when few Members are present except the Government subordinates whose duty is not to speak, but to vote. It is much to the credit of Alderman Lusk that since he has been a Member of Parliament not a vote of supply has passed in his absence, whether taken at the hour sacred to dinner, or at the equally inconvenient small hours. Almost alone, there sits the Alderman, as if he were administering justice at the Guildhall, and as if the small band seated on the Treasury Benches voting away millions of money in the twinkling of an eye, were so many delinquents awaiting sentence. It really is a disgrace to the Liberal party that he is not better supported. It is all very fine to say that it is no use nibbling at details. Our answer is that if the Liberal Members, as guardians of the national exchequer, made up their minds unanimously to nibble at details in preference to supporting abstract resolutions, many a poor man's heart would be lighter, and many a poor man's home happier. As it is, the Queen's Taxes are often the straw which breaks the camel's back. All honour then be given to financial Reformers! The poor man's true friend is such an M.P. as Alderman Lusk.

SIR FRANCIS CROSSLEY.

(YORKSHIRE W. R., NORTH—unopposed.)

THE West Riding of Yorkshire is the parliamentary blue ribbon. A king can make a belted knight, but it is not in the province of king or queen to create any man, however gifted, knight of the shire for the West Riding. It returned Wilberforce, and struck the knell of the slave trade. It returned Henry Brougham, and inaugurated the triumph of Reform. By its return of Richard Cobden, in 1847, all England felt that free trade had been secured. To canvass the West Riding a man must have a considerable amount of spare time, and energy, and cash, and if he be an unknown man, even these will fail him in the hour of trial. At the last election of Wilberforce, in 1807, upwards of 23,000 persons voted. The poll was kept open for fifteen days, and the costs of the contest were estimated at half a million. Elections are not quite such costly affairs as they were, but they are still far too expensive and wearying; the consequence is, the public have but a limited choice. People select not the best man, but the best man with cash. In 1852 the registered electors for the West Riding were 37,319. It is not easy to reach this mass of people—a people perhaps less dominated over by landlords than any constituency in the kingdom—for little more than four per cent. of them live by agriculture. The candidate, it is evident, must be well known—he must have money, for that is a *sine quâ non* in a West Riding election—he must have brains, for in Yorkshire people mostly have big heads—and his politics must be popular, for as the aristocracy send their sons and scions into Parliament to preserve the governing power in their own hands, it is evident that the democracy when they have the chance will expect their candidate to do battle on their behalf. Now with all these conditions Sir Frank Crossley complies. By honest labour and the exercise of his brains he has got to be where he is. He is a representative man. In our villages and towns there are many such, but they have not chosen the better path. They have become intemperate or dissipated, they have missed the tide, which taken at the flood, leads on to fortune, and they have listened to the Circe voices which wreck men's careers and ruin men's souls. All along our land they lie in swinish repose, the men who might have won for themselves fame and power, and conferred benefits untold on their fellows. If they have become rich, with ineffable littleness they have turned against the class from whence they sprung, and have vainly endeavoured to ape the fashions of those by whom they are justly derided and despised; but it is chiefly under the cloud of adverse circumstances that the capabilities which lie hidden in all men, as much in the Saxon peasant as in the Norman lord (for wonderful is the generosity of nature), are obscured and blotted out. Of too many it may be said, in the language of Gray, language likely to be applicable to large masses to the end of the chapter, that

> "Chill penury repressed their noble rage,
> And froze the genial current of the soul."

Happily, in Frank Crossley's case the "chill penury" of the poet existed only in a comparative degree, as contrasted with the wealth he and his family were in time to attain, and was soon turned into a genial affluence. Happily, we say, but it is not always that affluence has a genial effect; it acts on some as an east wind, and withers up all the graces of human character. Some men it altogether ruins. God grants them their desire, but sends leanness to their souls. If they were Dissenters they become High Church, and sneer at the conventicles. If they were Liberals, they become Conservatives, and think Lord Derby the most sagacious politician under the sun. If they have poor relations they despise and cut them; they treat them as Jeames de la Pluche did poor Mary Ann. "Once for all," as that distinguished individual informed the Lady Angelina, "once for all, suckmstances is changed betwigst me and er; it's a pang to part with her, says I, my fine hi's filling with tears; but part with her I must."

As an active philanthropist Mr. Frank Crossley was well and widely known. Halifax, which he first represented in Parliament, and where his manufactory is situated, bears witness to his munificence. These Lancashire and Yorkshire people, when they make money, make it not as most of us do in petty fractions, by hard and unremitting industry, but on a grand scale. And they spend it on an equally grand scale. Go to Scarborough and see the expenditure of these men; it quite pales our London extravagance; fortune has been liberal to them, and they are liberal to all around. No ladies are so splendidly dressed, so expensively educated, so well provided with handsome equipages, and the other outward signs of wealth, as their wives and daughters. And the wealth they have freely won, they freely distribute; charity finds in them willing friends; misfortune rarely appeals to them in vain. If the town in which they reside requires a literary institution, arboretum, or a park, they are not backward in giving it. A thousand pounds or two is of little consequence to them. And thus Mr. Brown gives Liverpool a free library, or Mr. Strutt presents Derby with an arboretum, or Mr. Frank Crossley bestows on Halifax a free park. And we all admire the generosity, and feel that such use of wealth—to the credit of our great merchants and manufacturers be it written—is by no means rare. For the successors of the Medici we have to look now-a-days to the merchants and manufacturers, who, in defiance of Mr. Ruskin, have become rich.

As a politician, Sir Francis Crossley may be defined as belonging to his class. He is a manufacturer, not a landlord; and he represents a manufacturing, not an agricultural constituency. It is just such men we want in the House of Commons. Men who have no connexion with trade and commerce are sure to make a mess of it when they come to legislate respecting such matters. For such matters practical men are required. "It appears," said a late writer in the *Times*, "a statement was published a few months back to the effect that a large trade might be opened up by a short land route from our Indian possessions to the western frontier of China, and the project excited very favourable attention among the commercial classes in London and the provinces. Any one glancing at a map of Asia will be struck with the proximity we have already attained to China by means of our acquisitions in Pegu. From the port of Rangoon our territory extends towards China a distance of 250 miles. We then come to the territory of the King of Burmah, and across this, which is also about 250 miles in width, we come to the Chinese frontier town of Esmok. We are thus brought into direct communication with that people almost at our own doors, the whole of the navigation *viâ* Singapore and the Chinese Sea would be saved, and we should, moreover, reach a class of the population with whom we could never otherwise come in commercial contact, even if our political relations with the Chinese Government were of the most unrestricted and cordial character. What, then, is the difficulty? The first idea likely to occur is that the King of Burmah would throw obstacles in our way. Such, however, is not the case. The King of Burmah seems to understand commercial interests better than some English statesmen, for he is represented to be friendly to anything that will promote traffic through his dominions. Apparently there is no difficulty except the old one. Our Foreign Office are not fond of new questions, and least of all of commercial questions. The Leeds Chamber of Commerce recently memorialized the Government on the subject. They represented its important bearing on the interests not only of our home manufacturers, merchants, and shipowners, but of our traders in all parts of India. The Chambers of Commerce of Bradford, Halifax, Huddersfield, and Liverpool had previously made similar representations. The reply has been such as to damp as far as possible all effort in the matter. Nothing was required but a civil negotiation with the King of Burmah, which the Government alone can make, and that in any future diplomatic arrangements with the Chinese authorities the town of Esmok should be recognised as a legal place of trade. Lord John Russell, however, thinks that 'much inconvenience' might arise from such a 'novel' proposition. Moreover, it would be 'impossible to protect British trade at so inland a city,' or 'to exercise due control over British subjects.' Next to the possibility of anything that might cause 'inconvenience' to the Foreign Office, the idea of allowing 'British subjects' to run without leading-strings has always been most distasteful to that department. The Chambers of Commerce have likewise been furnished with a hint that they know nothing about the true interests of trade, since the very measure for which they are now praying, under the idea of extending it, would only bring it into jeopardy. 'Redress for any wrong done in such a remote quarter as Esmok,' observes his Lordship, 'could in all probability only be obtained by applying pressure at places more accessible, and so placing in jeopardy the more important interests of British trade on the seaboard of China.'" Gentlemen of rank in the Government departments do not see—as people connected with trade and commerce see and feel—the importance of little things—the advantages of even the slightest reduction in taxation; that where the farmer feeds and maintains ten families, the manufacturer, or large employer of labour, can do the same for a hundred, and that the primary care of a statesman or legislator should be that, in every way possible, the taxes on industry should be annihilated and the sources of labour set free. Gentlemen fail to understand these things as great employers do. The latter have not had their fair share in Parliament. A change is taking place in this respect. It is time it were so, for so eager is the rivalry of commerce, that it is quite impossible we can maintain our position at the head of the world's markets unless we reduce our national expenditure, sweep away all vexatious imposts and unnecessary regulations from our statute book, and give the working man and his master all the help we can. If we do not do this, America, France, Germany—where the cost of living is less—will day by day surpass us, and we shall decline, as did Tyre and Sidon in days gone by. It is for this reason that men like Sir Francis are so useful in the House of Commons, and need to have their number increased. As to dogmatic polities, of course he is decidedly an advanced Liberal. We know what are the politics of his class; the spread of education, the protection of the ballot, and the separation of Church and State. The temperance world find in him an uncompromising champion, and the dissenting religious public is familiar with his face when May arrives, and Exeter Hall is thronged. Dissenting ministers who have gone down to Halifax to preach have told us of their surprise at finding an M.P. and a rich and great manufacturer acting as a clerk, and giving out the hymns.

In the House of Commons Sir Francis Crossley is easily discernible. He is a strong, well-looking man, in the very prime of life—just such a powerful-looking man as you may often see in the streets in fustian; and his black beard and white waistcoat render him conspicuous from afar. You can see Sir Francis is not a man to be daunted—has true Anglo-Saxon capacity for work and true Anglo-Saxon decision of character—if the time comes when statesmanship will be synonymous with administrative capacity, such a man will be in request. Surely it is no bad test of a man's qualification for office, that as a manufacturer, or merchant, or shipowner, he should have organized and carried out successful operations in many lands and amongst many men. Surely such an education is at least equal to that which can be acquired by contact with grooms and stable-boys, and game-keepers, and ballet-girls, and the toadies who always prey upon elder sons. Surely some of our ablest legislators—the men most potent in the Commons—are men of Sir F. Crossley's class. The admirers of our aristocracy tell us that it is the finest race in the world. You would not get this idea from a glance at the Commons. There are few more puny-looking men than Lord John Russell. You pass Lord Stanley in the street without giving him a second look. We know more than one lord in the House who, all curled and scented, and bedizened, reminds you rather of a baboon than a man. In Sir Francis's pale and full, yet determined face, you read that his life has been one of hard endeavour; that he has had little time to waste. As an orator, you see that he is in earnest; that he has no words to spare; that he is not a professional talker—that curse of our age and country—and that when he has said what is in him, he will not detain you one moment longer. Hence it is seldom that he speaks in the House of Commons; but he is regular in his attendance, and votes always—according to the opinion of his constituents—on the right side.

CHAPTER V.

THE PROTESTANT PARTY.

MR. NEWDEGATE.

(North Warwickshire—Newdegate, 4545; Davenport, 4374; Muntz, L., 3406; Flower, L., 3317.)

THERE was a time when people believed in protection to native industry—which, stripped of all its verbiage, meant that the consumer was to be taxed for the benefit of the producer. This theory, as regards agriculture, did not come into operation till the close of our great war with France. War prices had raised the prices of provisions, and every one turned farmer, deeming agriculture the most lucrative of all callings. Orator Hunt, then a young man, tells us how the farmers of his day lived riotously—riding the finest of horses, and drinking the costliest of wines, and how hundreds of men turned farmers, who knew no more about farming than the man in the moon. Well, this golden age came to an end. When peace was made, bad times came for the landlords and the farmers; the latter had spent all their money, and the former were in fear of not getting their rents. At that time the Parliament of England was almost exclusively a landlords' Parliament. They made the laws, and, as all men will do, they took care of themselves. The proper course would have been, as rents went up artificially in time of war, with the return of peace to have lowered the rents. But this did not suit the landlords. Instead, they made a law to keep up the rents by forbidding the importation of foreign corn, except when corn had reached starvation prices. The public rather laughed at political economy then (we know, for instance, Charles Fox could never read Smith's "Wealth of Nations"), but they knew enough to feel that such a prohibition was injurious to themselves. The people were very indignant, yet the minority in Parliament opposed to it was miserably small. Sir Samuel Romilly, in his diary of the 6th of March, 1815, says, "Great outrages have been committed against the members of both Houses of Parliament, who are supposed to be friends to the Corn Bill. The populace broke into the houses of the Lord Chancellor and of Mr. Robinson, and destroyed part of their furniture. Other houses were, too, attacked—such as Lord Darnley's, Lord Ellenborough's, and others." Again, next day we read, "The same outrages and riots in different parts of the town, and a few persons killed or wounded by the soldiery." Miss Cornelia Knight remarks—"The people are discontented with the Corn Bill, and write horrid things on the walls, such as

'Bread or Blood;' 'More Bellinghams;' 'Bread, or else the Regent's head.'" Nevertheless the Bill became law, and as England, year by year, grew less agricultural and more manufacturing, the dwellers in towns began to perceive that not only were they, in consequence of the Act of Parliament, paying more for their bread than otherwise would have been the case, but that, besides, we were compelled to refuse to trade with an immense population in Europe and America, who would be capital customers, if we would take their corn in exchange for our cotton goods. This state of things lasted till the days of Chartism, the potato disease, and the Anti-Corn Law League, and then the artificial impediment to trade, and national plenty and well-being, was swept away. How great has been the gain has been very apparent in severe winters, when the poor have suffered frightfully, when under the old system we should have had bread riots, appeal to physical force, the lower classes excited and revengeful, the upper alarmed and ill at ease. As it is, we have nothing of the kind to record. There often is, it is true, much suffering, but that suffering is bravely borne by the poor, and fully and warmly sympathized with by the rich. At Birmingham, or Manchester, even in Coventry, there has been no agitation of an alarming character. This arises simply from the fact that the poorest feel that they have not to impute their sufferings to class legislation. Lately, within ten months, corn, in mere grain or flour, costing no less a sum than 22,862,916*l.* was imported into these islands from America, Russia, and Egypt. If this quantity be reduced into quartern loaves, how great the number! And then recollect that all these hundreds of millions of loaves have been eaten in excess of what would have been eaten if the old prohibitive Corn Laws had survived to these times. To this bread we must add all the meat from cattle from foreign parts, and then recollect all this has gone to the poor, for the rich are never in danger of starvation; and then we get but a faint idea of the blessings of free trade, as a means of giving to one country its superfluity in exchange for that other country's superfluity, and of building up all the nations of the earth into a common brotherhood. When we think of these things we are not surprised to find how rare is a genuine protectionist. Yet such, undoubtedly, was Mr. Newdegate, who sat side by side with his grey-haired and venerable friend and colleague, the late Mr. Spooner, on the third bench of the Opposition. Like the latter gentleman, he has been very much abused by certain parties, merely because he sticks to his principles, and will not move with the times. Mr. Newdegate does not believe in progress, thinks the former days were better than these, and would have England as she was in those days when Pitt, the pilot, weathered the storm. Mr. Newdegate forgets that what is good for the country at one time is bad at another; that the days of Pitt and Fox are gone, and that their politics have gone with them; that we have gigantic hives of industry and life to maintain; that we have a people becoming increasingly educated; and that we must adapt the legislation of modern times to the requirements of modern society rather than to exploded prejudices. Now-a-days a manufacturer thinks himself as great a man as a landlord, and the operative considers himself as good as his master. The operative and the manufacturer may be wrong, but as you cannot make them think so, it is vain to treat them as if they were conscious of an inferior position. In acting as if they were, Mr. Newdegate wars with a progress he cannot resist, and makes himself very unpopular as well. At one time there was a talk of ousting him from the representation of North Warwickshire. When the freehold land societies commenced their career, their aim was chiefly (they have since become a profitable investment) to give men votes. The working-men of Birmingham joined them in large numbers, and the Liberals of that district were delighted at the idea of unseating their Tory members. However, Messrs. Spooner and Newdegate were too strong for them, and remain secure. An important lesson is taught by this—viz., how desirable it is that politicians should live in mutual harmony, and bear and forbear. Mr. Newdegate represents North Warwickshire, yet Mr. Bright represents its chief town. Of course Mr. Bright will tell you he represents public opinion; but surely Mr. Newdegate represents public opinion as well. The one has a party to back him in the same way as the other. It is true every man thinks himself in the right; but when decent men differ so much as they do on matters of science, or religion, or politics, we must feel that it becomes no man to be high-minded, or arrogant, or dogmatic. Both Mr. Newdegate and Mr. Bright are too apt to forget this, and scold their opponents instead of arguing with them. Mr. Newdegate generally speaks in that way. I consider him a very irritating speaker; he never seems to think that other people can by any means think they are right, if their opinions do not square with his own. As a speaker he is wonderfully one-sided. He may not be narrow-minded, but he seems so to you. With his tall, thin figure, he looks it; and as he stretches out his long arms, and drops his bony hands, you feel inclined to agree with West, who tells us that there is a great deal of character in the way men carry their hands. Mr. Newdegate is by no means a pleasing speaker. He does not hesitate or stammer, nor is his voice bad, but he does not fill you with admiration, nor does he carry you away with him. Nor do you feel inclined, like Bottom's Duke, to exclaim—"Let him roar again—let him roar again." The country gentlemen may have all the learning, but they have not all the eloquence of the House. Mr. Newdegate's oratory is of the character which may be termed bucolic. You can easily fancy him babbling of green fields, of fat oxen, of draining on a large scale, or discoursing learnedly, and beautifully, and bountifully on the importance of manure to the farmer, and of its various kinds, and their various properties. You can easily fancy him in scarlet, a bold rider across country, and stopping for nothing in the shape of fence, or brook, or five-barred gate, or feasting his tenantry on rent-days, like a fine old English gentleman, all of the olden time. You would expect from him a strict regard to the decencies and conventionalities of society, a regular subscription to the National Schools, and a devout attendance at his parish church—but that is all. As to looking at all sides of a question—as to his supposing that there is more than one side to look at, or that his one side may possibly be the wrong one—no one who knows Mr. Newdegate would ever deem him guilty of such a thing. From the speeches of such a man you would expect no display of literary ability, no wide induction, no skilful marshalling of facts and figures, no chain of argument subtlely contrived and skilfully measured out, no wit that moves to laughter, nor pathos that stirs to tears. Mr. Newdegate's oratory—it must be confessed even by his warmest friends—is conspicuous by a singular absence of all these qualifications, so desirable to a public speaker. Arguing hypothetically we may go further, and say, to such a man the advocacy of Conservative and High Church principles by one not of an old English landed family, by one whose political antecedents do not favour the idea that he was trained up a Pharisee of the strictest sect of the Pharisees, by one remarkable for the ambiguous and cloudy nature of his speeches on the gravest political questions of the day, by one who impresses you with an idea rather of the graceful agility with which he can explain away, than of the earnestness with which he can battle for a party—would be particularly unpleasant; and the result would be, that rather than rally under such a leader, he, Mr. Newdegate, would fight the battle alone. All acquainted with the political world know such to be the case, and that Mr. Newdegate is one of the heads of the Tory few who deprecate Mr. Disraeli's submission to the spirit of the age, and repudiate his policy almost as much as the men of Manchester themselves.

Mr. Newdegate's career, or, rather, such part of it as concerns the general public, is soon told. He was born in 1816, and is the son of the late Charles Newdigate-Newdegate, of Harefield-place, Middlesex. In 1843 he was returned for North Warwickshire, and ever followed in the wake of his Church and Protestant colleague, Mr. Spooner. Since then Mr. Newdegate has taken a more prominent position—a position in which he has contrived in a singular manner to obtain for himself the utmost amount of parliamentary opposition and respect. At one time, he was reported to have purchased and carried on at his own expense the *Press* newspaper. He has thus made pecuniary sacrifices for his party, and let us hope will not be forgotten if their hour of triumph should arrive.

GEORGE H. WHALLEY, ESQ.

(Peterborough—Wells, 1289; Whalley, 1124; Hankey, 837; Wrenfordsley, C., 159.)

Once upon a time the writer was standing in the lobby of the House of Commons in close propinquity with a young man from the country, who evidently had never been in that august locality before. As one popular M.P. after another appeared our young friend grew vastly excited, much to the annoyance of the *genii loci*—the police, who like the deities in Olympus approve

"The depth but not the tumult of the soul."

One of them was particularly indignant and observant of our friend, whose enthusiasm seemed to know no bounds. X.Y.Z.—for we will call him such—could stand it no longer. Said he, placing his official hand upon the stranger's shoulder, "My young friend, if you can't control your feelings, you had better go outside." Now Mr. Whalley can't control his feelings, but unfortunately for the cause he upholds he is inside, and will remain so as long as Peterborough returns him as her M.P.

If the possession of moral courage constitutes greatness, Mr. Whalley has few equals, and no superiors, in Parliament or out A good fellow is occasionally described as a brick, but Mr. Whalley is a rock. Argument is lost on him; of ridicule he is unconscious; anger simply provokes his pity. No man is oftener on his legs in the House, no man is seldomer heard. Hume tells us all the sciences have a relation to one another. In a similar way, in Popery Mr. Whalley finds the *ultima ratio*—the final cause of every disaster under heaven, including of course railway accidents, the cattle plague, the Schleswig-Holstein war, the Fenian conspiracy, a war in New Zealand, and a City panic. Hence is it that there is always an occasion for him to rise, whatever may be the subject of debate. Popery is to him the tree of evil, whose roots extend to every land, and whose branches darken and poison the atmosphere of the globe. An aged nobleman, not long deceased, was in the habit, if anything went wrong in the fashionable world, of asking, "Who is she?"—believing firmly, but ungallantly, that no mischief would exist unless a woman was at the bottom of it. To the Pope, Mr. Whalley assigns that bad pre-eminence. At every turn he takes he sees that incarnate evil. Destroy Popery and the world will be at peace, and the lion will lie down with the lamb, and the poor's rates will be diminished, and, better still, the income-tax will be reduced. Our readers may have forgotten the name of Mr. T. Fitzgerald. If we may credit the Loyal Effusion in "Rejected Addresses," his style of reasoning seems to have supplied Mr. Whalley with a model, which he has faithfully imitated. He asks—

> "Who burnt (confound his soul) the houses twain
> Of Covent Garden and of Drury Lane?

Who, while the British squadron lay off Cork,
(God bless the Regent and the Duke of York!)
With a foul earthquake ravaged the Caraccas,
And raised the price of dry goods and tobaccos?
Who makes the quartern loaves and Luddites rise?
Who fills the butchers' shops with large blue flies?

Well, it is thus that Mr. Whalley reasons, and it is thus in sober prose he declaims, or appears to declaim, for the chances are if Mr. Whalley speaks half an hour you will never hear a dozen consecutive words all the time. His appearance is always the signal for a storm. It is amusing to see him biding his opportunity,—his dark head and white waistcoat are conspicuous from afar. Up he rises; yet, alas, he fails somehow or other to catch the Speaker's eye. He is not disappointed. He knows that in time his turn will come—the Speaker must see his white waistcoat. Another speech is made; up again is the white waistcoat. Alas! again, burdened and unrelieved, to sit down. The House thins off—members are at dinner. The hour is come, and behold Mr. Whalley rising from the back benches on the Liberal side. Groans loud and deep are heard everywhere. Apparently Mr. Whalley heeds them not. In vain does the storm of disapprobation rage—in front, behind, on every side; he has the testimony of an approving conscience within. Mr. Whalley is not a bad speaker; he delivers his opinions with a great deal of force and energy, and in his speech what lack of argument there may be is completely compensated for by vehemence of manner and exaggeration of language. Amidst the fiercest signs of impatience he holds on his unfaltering way. He has, it is clear to him, his duty to do, and that he will discharge, whether men smile or frown—whether they applaud or condemn. Generally, for some minutes not a word is audible; you see Mr. Whalley wildly gesticulating. Perhaps you are permitted to hear a sentence, in which Popery is described in uncomplimentary terms, and then all is lost in the Babel of chaotic sounds. Cries of "Divide, divide—vide—vide!" spread from one side of the House to the other; then there is a lull; then comes a roar of groans, in which Liberals and Conservatives, who have by this time greatly dined, all gladly join. Eager Irish M.P.'s cry "Question, question!" Then above the storm is heard the full deep voice of the Speaker calling "Order, order," and perhaps for a few minutes, or till he has again aroused the antagonism of his audience, Mr. Whalley is permitted to proceed without interruption. My own opinion is, that Mr. Whalley thinks these exhibitions highly creditable to him. I believe he is unconscious of the ridicule he creates. My reason for arriving at this conclusion is, that on the nights when Mr. Whalley has been unusually ridiculous and sincere, he has generally had a lady to escort home from the House.

Is Mr. Whalley a Jesuit in disguise? Can he be a sound Protestant who makes Protestantism ridiculous? Mr. Newdegate, who represents the old Church of

England anti-Popery party in the House—who has many a time and oft been cheered and upheld by Mr. Whalley's voice and vote, implies as much; and his ingratitude led to an appeal to the public, or rather to the editor of the *Times*, from the injured Whalley. The letter referred to was as follows: "Sir—The unprecedented attack made upon me in the debate on the Transubstantiation Bill this evening, I was prevented by the forms of the House from replying to, and I have to rely upon your courtesy to insert in the same paper in which the debate is reported the following observations:—Mr. Newdegate was not justified in imputing to me indifference to religious sentiment. Nothing that I have ever said or done can in the slightest degree justify such imputations. In such efforts as I have made to resist or expose the political action of the Romish priesthood, I have ever endeavoured to suppress everything that could give offence to religious sentiments honestly entertained, and I shall continue to act upon that principle. To impute to me on that account indifference to religious sentiments, without, as I assert, the slightest justification from any word or act of mine, and untrue as it is to the utmost degree, is in itself alike opposed to the courtesy of a gentleman and to the credit of whatever form of Christianity Mr. Newdegate may possess." No wonder Mr. Whalley was indignant. To have doubts cast on his Protestantism—and by Mr. Newdegate, with whom he had so often fought shoulder to shoulder—that was "the unkindest cut of all." It really was too bad to raise the question. Mr. Whalley not sincere in his Protestantism! Well, then, sincerity has left the world. No one can doubt Mr. Whalley's sincerity. It is only equalled by his indiscretion. He belongs to that numerous class who love not wisely but too well.

On secular questions, if such exist for Mr. Whalley, he generally votes with the Liberals, by whom he is considered a good fellow, except where the Scarlet Lady is concerned, and then Bishop Corbet's distracted Puritan, who exclaims—

> "I am not mad, most noble masters,
> But zeal and godly knowledge
> Have put me in hope
> To deal with the Pope
> As well as the best at College"—

is sobriety itself compared with the member for Peterborough, who may yet turn out a respectable M.P. if he will ignore the existence of the Roman Catholics. As I have said before, Mr. Whalley can speak very well. He is now in the prime of life—a man of very good temper—active and persevering. For a Jesuit in disguise he is not a bad-looking little man, though of a slightly Jewish cast of countenance.

The world shall know something of its greatest men. Mr. Whalley was born at Gloucester in 1813. He was educated at University College, London, in the Literary and Philosophical Society of which his Protestant zeal more than once led him into angry collision with the Irish law students, of whom there were many belonging to the Society. In 1836 he married Anne, daughter of R. Attree, Esq., and was called to the bar at Gray's Inn in 1839. He is a magistrate and deputy-lieutenant for Denbigh, and besides a magistrate for Montgomery and Carnarvon. In 1852 he was high sheriff of his county. In the same year he was returned for Peterborough, in spite of very strong opposition on the part of the Earl Fitzwilliam, who is supposed to exercise much influence in that ancient city. Peterborough has a cathedral, from the top of which you could see over the fen country, and in old time tell of coming danger. So its member on his watch-tower discovers the faintest effort of Romanism, and calls on England to beware. Happily, England, in spite of an unfaithful State Church, needs not the warning voice. A man who has emancipated himself is not likely to be a slave. Protestantism is safe as long as England guards and preserves her free press and pulpit. In his glorious dream the Bedford tinker represents Popery as toothless and in its dotage; John Bunyan was a wiser man than Mr. Whalley.

CHAPTER VI.

NEW MEMBERS.

CHARLES REED, ESQ.

(HACKNEY—REED, 14,785; HOLMS, 12,243; BUTLER, 6825; HOMER, 2021; DICKSON, 2575; WEBB, C., 2669.)

IN religious and philanthropic circles no name is better known or held in higher honour than that of Reed. At Hackney lived, and in the east of London preached with a power and unction the memory of which has not yet passed away, Dr. Andrew Reed. Of his life and labours we need not speak here. In the battle ever being fought between good and evil, right and wrong, God and the devil, he was a valiant soldier on the right side. Enriched with the legacy of his example, the sons have trodden in their father's steps. One has drawn to himself a large congregation in one of England's pleasantest watering-places, and another has long been one of the band who, to the honour of their age, find success in business and activity in public life, perfectly compatible with philanthropic effort and Christian zeal. It is of this son, Mr. Charles Reed, we write.

In the Reform Bill lately carried, one of the new boroughs called into existence is that of Hackney, comprising Bethnal-green, Cambridge-heath, Clapton, Dalston, De Beauvoir Town, Hackney, Haggerstone, Homerton, Hoxton, Kingsland, Shacklewell, Shoreditch, Stamford-hill, Upper Clapton, and portions of Spitalfields, Stoke Newington, and Victoria Park. It appears, some time before the new borough was called upon to exercise its privilege of returning two members to Parliament, the note of warning had been sounded, and strenuous preparations for the great event had been made. In compliance with a numerously signed requisition of electors, Mr. Charles Reed offered himself as a candidate. Long resident in the parish of Hackney, his opinions were pretty well known in the district. We may briefly say, however, here, that he expressed himself prepared to support "a more equitable distribution of seats than could be carried in the present House of Commons;" that he had arrived at the conclusion, "though very reluctantly," that for the free exercise of the suffrage the voter must have the protection of the ballot; that he is "opposed to all compulsory exactions, and to the appropriation of public money for religious purposes." Mr. Reed further declared himself in favour of "strict economy in the various departments of the public service;" he has "a strong conviction of the necessity for the extension of the principle of local self-government;" "the national universities," he considers, "with all their honours and emoluments, should be thrown open to all, without distinction of rank or creed," and in Ireland he would "support any measure for the impartial disendowment of all religious bodies." On the great question of education Mr. Reed says nothing; but a glance at his active life will show that no one has worked harder for the education of the people than himself. A firm, yet moderate Dissenter, associated with Churchmen as one of the committee of the Bible Society and in other ways, it is clear, from his enormous majority, he received the support of the religious public whether of the church or the chapel.

Mr. Reed is somewhere about forty-seven years of age, of ready speech, and a pleasant presence. All his life he has been a working man. He is now at the head of one of the oldest and largest type foundries in London; but in his youth, after a careful training at Hackney, and then at what is now University College, but what was then the London University, he went down to Leeds, and was five years in a woollen manufactory in that town, commencing at the very bottom and working his way upwards, thus gaining a practical acquaintance with the habits, and the wants, and the condition, and the capacity of the industrious classes, eminently desirable in any one aiming to be a member of Parliament under the new dispensation inaugurated by the last Reform Bill. It is to be presumed at Leeds Mr. Reed found time for other, and, to a young man, more congenial occupation. We infer so from the fact that he married the youngest daughter of the late Mr. Baines, M.P., father of the present well-known Member for that great town. Leeds, with its narrow streets, and tall chimneys, all day and night vomiting forth clouds of smoke, does not look much like a place to make love in, but as philosophers have profoundly remarked, human nature is much the same all the world over, and people fall in love and get married in Leeds as well as in Belgravia, as they did when Noah told them the deluge was coming, or when Lord Derby made all England take what he described "as a leap in the dark."

In 1842 Mr. Reed commenced business in the City of London. At once he appears to have become a distinguished member of its ancient corporation. It is to him is due the merit of getting the freedom of the City presented to Lord Clyde, Sir J. M'Clintock, the hardy explorer of the North-West passage, and Mr. Peabody, the friend of the poor. As one of the Corporation Mr. Reed was selected to be the deputy governor of the Irish Society, and in that capacity did much for education in Londonderry. Our readers will remember the gallant stand Mr. Reed made on behalf of Bunhill-fields, which he was at length enabled to save from the grasp of the Ecclesiastical Commissioners, who would have otherwise built over that truly consecrated ground. For his activity in this matter we hold the religious public to be under lasting obligation to Mr. Reed. As one of the conservators of the river Thames Mr. Reed has also responsible duties to perform. We may add here that he is one of the Deputy Lieutenants of the City, that he has been chairman of the Corporation Library, and is one of the leading members of that truly excellent establishment, the City of London School.

At the age of twenty-six Mr. Reed was elected a Fellow of the Society of Antiquaries. Of his literary merits, the Life of his father recently published, and which rapidly reached a second edition, is a fair specimen. It is a book well known and liked in religious circles. For many years Mr. Reed has been an incessant writer, especially on topics connected with education. In his "History of the Irish Society" he evinced a capacity for historical research of no common order. For a twelvemonth, we believe, he was the editor of a well-known religious newspaper. In 1851, under the title of "Why Not?" Mr. Reed published a pamphlet in favour of a free library for the City of London. On the question of rating he was defeated; but he still looks forward to the successful accomplishment of his scheme. Philanthropically, Mr. Reed may be said to have devoted himself to the carrying out of his father's plans. The Orphan Asylum, and the Institution at Earlswood, are the special objects of his care. On the retirement of Sir Morton Peto from the chairmanship of the deputies of the three denominations, Mr. Reed was selected to fill the vacant post. Mr. Reed has also the honour to be the chairman of the London Missionary Society. In the cause of Sunday-schools he is also an earnest labourer. From his youth upwards he has been connected with them.

Such is a brief outline of the career of the man who, with every chance of success, became the candidate for the representation of Hackney, and who aspires to be one of England's legislators in the eventful days that are to come, when an enlarged constituency will require statesmanship of a very different order to that which has hitherto prevailed; when the Constitution of the country will have to undergo a searching scrutiny; when Democracy will raise the cry of equality; and labour, admirably organized and conscious of its physical strength, shall demand, what it assumes to be, its rights. The old soldiers of the Commonwealth trusted in God, and kept their powder dry. As much as ever in the future, the men who fight England's battles in the senate will have to trust in God, and they will do so if the constituencies return to Parliament such as Mr. Charles Reed. In London there are few men more honourable in business, more able in public life, more devoted to the spread of that religion which has made England greater, and grander, and freer than any other nation on the face of the earth. Trained to public speaking, to such an orator Hackney may well trust her interests, be they large or small;

and over his return the friends of religion and education, of peace and progress, rejoice.

SAMUEL MORLEY, ESQ.

(Bristol—Berkeley, 8768; Morley, 8720; Mills, C., 6682.)

Men's lives are books, and to be read as such. It is by the study of them we learn how to live ourselves. Montaigne would have a father teach his children to inquire into "the manners, revenues, and alliances of princes." In our days we have learnt to look elsewhere for examples. Addison, when he sent for his stepson, the young Earl of Warwick, that he might see how a Christian could die, had a better perception of the true need for training children than the old philosopher of France. In our time a riper knowledge has taught us that it is better to know how men live than how they die; to know what they are doing for their age, what for the sake of truth, what for their Lord and Master, than to be cognizant even of the faith and hopes by which the Christian is cheered and sustained in the dying hour. It is action rather than contemplation, life on the platform, or in the pulpit, or in the market-place, rather than in the cloister or the closet, that the age requires. It is well to read of this; better still is it to see it in the living form. Of some such in our day we would speak, without impertinence or unseemly prying into private affairs. No one blamed John Milton when he told his friends and foes how, when there was civil war, and the time had come for his native land to contend for faith and freedom, he hastened home from the blue skies and pleasant companionship of Italy; listened no longer to the allurements of ambition, laid down the harp that in his blind old age he was to wake up to melody and power, and took his part as a common soldier in the common strife. Such knowledge was useful and beneficial. It made many a man a better worker in the cause. In like manner, if we say for others what they might but do not say of themselves—in many ways a beneficial result may be produced.

Mr. Samuel Morley belongs to a class of which there have been many in the great city of London, but of which there have been, alas! still too few, and of which it is to be feared that the number in these days of wealth and luxury does not increase. The great merchant, when he has left his counting-house, is too ready in his suburban mansion to forget what are the claims of the age upon such as he; he is tired and weary, and asks to be permitted to remain at home, entertaining, it may be, his immediate friends with costly hospitality, and subscribing liberally to charitable purposes. You can't get him to lend his personal aid to a Reform meeting, or a temperance association, or a religious society; yet there must be men to make a speech, or take the chair upon such occasions.

Christian citizenship requires that a man should do this—should lend himself to every good word or work, however unfashionable. And, whatever may be the personal sacrifice required, a Christian should at all times be ready to denounce wrong, by whomsoever it may be done, and upon whomsoever it may fall. The Romans cherished patriotism as a cardinal virtue. Citizenship with them was a high and holy thing. They were ready to live and die for it. When the city had become enervated with wealth—when citizenship meant class privileges for the few and bitter injustice for the many, Rome fell, as she deserved to do. If the decay and decline of England ever be a fact, it will be from a similar cause. It is to men of Mr. Morley's stamp that it is due that such has not been the case. A man of business may be a Christian and a politician at the same time. Indeed, England can never be what she ought to be till her merchant princes become such. Algernon Sidney, speaking of the Florentine republic of his day, wrote: "It was for a short time the most perfect republic that ever existed. In the morning they used to attend to their counting-houses in the humble garb and manner of citizens. In the evening they used to attend in their places as legislators, with their *gonfaloniere,* who was elected every three months, at their head, and at night, when necessary, eighty thousand men, at the sight of the war-fires on the hills, assembled in the Vale of Arno to march against the foe." Such was Florence in her day of lustre—such will England be when her leaders are such as Samuel Morley.

Born in 1809, a magistrate for Middlesex, the principal in a business which, under his care, has become gigantic, Mr. Morley has, perhaps, worked as hard as most men of his age and time. There are few such businesses in London as the great hosiery establishment in Wood-street, which was founded at Nottingham, and conducted by his father, Mr. John Morley, and his uncle, Mr. Richard Morley, before him. Happy and well looked after are the young men in it. They are not merely as much as possible preserved from the perils of London life, but they are stimulated to Christian life and activity in many ways; a kindly superintendence is everywhere exercised, and a cordial spirit seems to animate all. But, as a Nonconformist and a citizen, Mr. Morley found that he had something else to do than attend to business or the young men in his employ. The Liberals of London soon learned to claim him as one of their leaders. He shared in the Anti-Corn-Law League agitation; he took a part in the various movements with Cobden and Hume for the further extension of Reform; and when the Crimean war broke out, and our old system of red tape and circumlocution broke down, Mr. Morley was placed at the head of the citizens, who, at the London Tavern, or at old Drury-lane, held monster meetings in behalf of administrative Reform. At their first public gathering—held May 5,

1855—so crowded that hundreds of persons, including many Members of Parliament, were unable to obtain admission, Mr. Morley, as chairman, said the "aristocracy had as much right to share in the Government as any other class, but only as they exhibited the sterling qualities of honesty and efficiency. The assemblage of that day had no direct connexion with the question of the war, but the hideous disclosure of mismanagement which the history of the war revealed seemed to identify the movement with the contest with Russia; and even when that contest was over the all-important question would recur, How are we to be governed? Let them go to any one of the public departments they pleased, and if they chanced to meet the head of it without his intelligent underling at his elbow to cram him, they would find him displaying an amount of gross ignorance, incompetence, and superciliousness about any given subject which was actually eating into the very heart of the country, undermining its greatness, and would, if continued, be its ruin." This strong language was justified by the facts which appeared at that time; nor were they spoken in vain. Great administrative reforms were introduced, and an impulse was given to that other question of Parliamentary Reform which, in spite of the treachery of friends and the hostility of foes, may be said to be now settled. Ten years after these words were spoken Mr. Morley was returned at the head of the poll as M.P. for Nottingham. How he fell into bad hands and was unseated is known to all. But he was in Parliament long enough to achieve a Parliamentary reputation, and to leave it regretted by so distinguished a man as Mr. Gladstone, then Chancellor of the Exchequer. With his career in the Senate thus rudely cut short, Mr. Morley did not retire from the political arena in disgust. On the contrary, he renewed his activity. Immediately after he presided at a highly influential meeting, convened by the National Reform Union at the Westminster Palace Hotel; and in many quarters the hope was cherished that at the next election Mr. Morley would be returned to Parliament. Bristol has fulfilled this hope.

Good people in our young days used to say that to be political was to cease to be spiritual. Such was the formula in pious circles. At any rate Mr. Morley is certainly an illustrious exception. It appears to us that it is his religion which has driven him into political life, as it did the heroes of the Commonwealth, or the Presbyterians when they rose up against the unfortunate Mary, whose fatal charms poets yet live to sing. As a Dissenter, Mr. Morley believes in the power of the voluntary principle, if it can have but fair play. He is a zealous advocate of temperance as a means of removing the drunkenness which has been the bane of the English. He is an advocate of the political emancipation of the working man; he is a dear friend of popular education: but, above all, it is his aim that the Church should awake from her lethargy, and seek to fill the land with Gospel light and life. Though a Congregationalist, he is ready to aid with his purse or his presence the earnest worker, to whatever sect he may belong. The claims of home, especially, Mr. Morley loves to plead. To that end he subscribes thousands annually, and sacrifices much of the ease of domestic life. There is hardly a chapel built to which he is not a subscriber, and there is not a county association at which he has not been present. For the last eight years especially, has much of his time been spent in this manner; nor has he laboured in vain. A great revival of home missionary efforts has been the result. Intensely earnest and practical, he has held conference after conference with pastors and people in all our chief towns and cities. His one great ruling idea is, that it is the duty of the Church of Christ to bring the world to the rule of Christ. The State cannot do this, and the Church must. In this work all can do something. The poor man can give his time or talent, and the rich man his wealth. He is but a steward. The question with him, while a world is waiting to be evangelized, should be not how much he should give, but how little he should retain. "'There is that scattereth and still increaseth.' No man," said Mr. Morley recently, at a public meeting, "more than I, has realized the truth of this passage of Scripture." In 1841 Mr. Morley married a daughter of Mr. Samuel Hope, of Liverpool; but this is not the place to speak of him as a

Paterfamilias. "I have known many great and good men," said a gentleman to us the other day, "but for strength of mind, depth of sympathy, and sincerity of character, I have met with no one like Samuel Morley." As his well-made person and clear, business-like oratory must be familiar to most of our readers, we need not say more. In the month of May, as chairman at one or other of our religious anniversaries, Mr. Morley is sure to be in his right place.

HENRY RICHARD, ESQ.

(Merthyr Tydvil—Richard, 11,565; Fothergill, 7513; Bruce, 5691.)

Perhaps nowhere more than in Wales have we an illustration of the inefficiency of the existing system of representation and of the pressing need of the reform just effected. Under the old system swept away in 1832 there were many anomalies. It was a great anomaly that Old Sarum and Gatton should be represented in Parliament, while Manchester and Birmingham and Leeds were not. It was a great anomaly that most of the boroughs should be in the hands of a few noblemen, who sold them, and did what they liked with their own; it was a great anomaly that it was in the power of two or three lords or dukes to decide as to who should or who should not represent any particular county in Parliament; but it was a greater anomaly still that Wales, emphatically the land of Dissent, where you never see a cluster of houses without finding a Baptist, or Independent, or Calvinistic Methodist chapel in their midst, had not a single Dissenter to represent it in the British House of Commons.

At the head of the picturesque Taff valley, in a region of coal and iron, is a town called Merthyr, which assuredly no traveller for pleasure would visit, especially on a rainy day. The town seems to stand upon coal. You dig down a few yards and you find the invaluable article at once. There is coal in the air you breathe, in the water you drink. By day the streets, which are narrow, and the houses, which seem run up wherever an eligible or ineligible building site could be found, are empty. At night the scene is changed. By thousands you see around you the colliers from the pit, or the puddlers from the great ironworks famed all the world over. Some of them are on the way to the beershop to smoke tobacco and to drink a beverage by no means to be compared with that brewed in Burton or Bavaria. The larger proportion, however, are thinking of better things. With their wives and children they are flocking to the temperance hall, or the singing-class, or to some plain but capacious chapel, where, in a tongue unintelligible to the Saxon, and with a fervour of which we can give the reader no idea, the orator will unfold the blessings of temperance, or tell the wondrous tale of redeeming love. In a Parliamentary sense Merthyr is the chief town of a district comprising Dowlais, Aberdare, Mountain Ash, Hirwain, Cefn, &c. Our description of Merthyr more or less applies to them all. In all of them is cherished an enthusiastic nationality and an hereditary Dissent. The Eisteddfod preserves the one; but for the other, such was the apathy of the Church by law established, Wales would have been a land of heathens. Betrayed by their representatives, who have suffered their dearest institutions to be insulted, Welshmen have long chafed and murmured and declaimed. The men of Merthyr and its neighbourhood felt that they have had somewhat too much of this, and that the time for action had arrived. The new Reform Bill gave Merthyr two Members and a constituency of 13,000 electors. They determined Mr. Henry Richard, of London, should be their M.P. They canvassed the electors, and nine thousand at once promised one vote for Mr. Richard. The other candidates were the late sitting Member, Mr. Henry Austin Bruce, Vice-President of the Educational Department of the Privy Council, and Mr. Fothergill, we believe one of the neighbouring ironmasters. It was clear from the first, if there were any value in promises, Mr. Richard's seat was sure, and that to Merthyr would be due the merit of having established the political independence of Wales.

The origin of Mr. Richard's candidature was as follows:—About a year and a half since a meeting was held at Merthyr of certain of the electors, who agreed unanimously to two resolutions, one to the effect that one of the M.P.'s for Merthyr should be a Nonconformist, and another intimating that Mr. Richard "was a fit and proper person to represent the borough as one of its members." A deputation accordingly waited upon him. He gave them no decided answer, but stated that he would come down and address the electors and judge for himself. He fulfilled his promise, and the result was more than the most sanguine could have anticipated. "With the whole mass of our artisan population," writes the local paper, the *Telegraph*, "Mr. Richard is the most popular man of the day." His powerful oratory fell upon willing and enthusiastic auditors. He carried all before him. Merthyr embraced him with all the fervour of a first love. Mr. Richard is a good speaker, his face indicates benevolence, his manners and attainments are beyond the average. For years he has been known as the respected Secretary of the Peace Society; but his success is due to none of these things, but to the fact that he is the representative of the darling and natural ideas of intelligent Welshmen—their nationality and Dissent.

Let us give a brief outline of Mr. Richard's career. His father was the Rev. Ebenezer Richard, a minister of great popularity and influence among the Welsh Calvinistic Methodists. He was born in Cardiganshire, and at the age of eighteen was sent to Highbury College to study for the ministry among the Congregationalists. After spending the usual time at Highbury, Mr. Richard became minister at Marlborough Chapel, Old Kent-road, where he laboured many years with acceptance and with a fair share of success. In 1848 he resigned the pastorate to devote himself exclusively to the Peace Society. For a short time he had endeavoured to unite the two appointments, but he found himself unequal to the task.

Mr. Richard's labours in connexion with the Peace Society have been various. He had to organize the congresses held successively at Brussels, Paris, Frankfort, London, and Edinburgh. In 1856, at the end of the Russian war, when the plenipotentiaries of the great Powers were sitting at Paris to settle the terms of peace, Mr. Richard drew up a memorial which was sent to every one of the crowned heads represented on that occasion, urging the importance of proposing at the conference then sitting "some system of international arbitration which may bring the great interests of nations within the cognizance of certain fixed rules of justice and right." At the same time Mr. Richard accompanied Mr. Joseph Sturge and the late Mr. Charles Hindley, M.P., as a deputation to Paris from the Peace Society, and communicated either by personal interview or by letter with all the plenipotentiaries on the same subject. At their request Lord Clarendon brought the question before his colleagues, and this led to the adoption of the resolution embodied in Protocol 23, in which the plenipotentiaries "do not hesitate to express in the name of their Governments the wish that States between which any serious misunderstandings may arise, should before appealing to arms have recourse to the good offices of a friendly Power." Of this provision Mr. Gladstone has said, "As to the proposal to submit international differences to arbitration, I think that is in itself a great triumph —a powerful engine on behalf of civilization and humanity." And it was to this that Lord Stanley appealed when he mediated recently so successfully between France and Prussia.

The *Morning Star* is partly indebted to Mr. Richard for existence. He was one of the principal co-operators with Mr. Joseph Sturge and Mr. William Rawson for this purpose, and for two or three years, at the request of Mr. Joseph Sturge and Mr. Cobden, acted as editor. Many of the leaders, especially those relating to foreign affairs, were from Mr. Richard's pen. As a writer on behalf of Wales, calumniated by Government Commissioners and Churchmen, who can see nothing good outside their own little system, Mr. Richard has been active and untiring. The notorious Blue-books appeared in 1846, and ever since Mr. Richard has lost no opportunity, whether on the platform or by the press, in vindicating the fair fame of his native land. But recently have been reprinted his letters on the social and political condition of the principality of Wales, which appeared in the *Morning*

Star from February to May last year, for which letters most of the Dissenting bodies in Wales have voted him the heartiest thanks.

Mr. Richard, while defending his countrymen from their slanderers, has felt the need of energetic action in educational matters on their behelf. He was one of the first to originate the movement which led to the establishment of a normal college for Wales at Brecon, whence it was subsequently moved to Swansea. In company with Mr. Edward Baines and Mr. Samuel Morley, he went through Wales on a similar mission, and at a later time he accompanied Mr. Samuel Morley on a tour with a view to provide religious education for the English population of South Wales. As a Nonconformist Mr. Richard has laboured hard to get his countrymen to exert themselves. In 1862, he, accompanied by Mr. Carvell Williams and Mr. Edward Miall, paid a visit to Swansea, to arouse the Welsh Dissenters to the assertion of their political rights: and in 1866 he took an active part in the conferences held in Montgomeryshire, Derbyshire, Merionethshire, and Cardiganshire for that purpose.

It may be further said of Mr. Richard, that more or less he has been connected with the Anti-slavery cause, with the Society for the Abolition of Death Punishment, and that he has acted cordially with Mr. Cobden, Mr. Joseph Sturge, and most of the distinguished philanthropists of England or America.

In 1865 Mr. Richard, whose name had been long kept before his countrymen by the Welsh periodical press, went down to Cardiganshire to contest the representation of that county. He withdrew, fearing that, with three Liberals in the field, a Tory would be returned. This decision was a great mistake. In his retiring address to the electors and people of Cardiganshire, Mr. Richard wrote: "It is evident now that the voice and the hearts of the county were wholly with me. I have received so many proofs from all parts of the country, not merely of approval, but, I will venture to say, of the general enthusiasm felt on my behalf, that I am perfectly sure the people would have carried me triumphantly on their shoulders to Parliament. Unfortunately I did not know all this until it was too late." At Merthyr there was no danger of Mr. Richard making such a mistake. Mr. Richard said of Cardiganshire that the people are sounder and more courageous than many of their leaders, and that there is a grievous want of organization among the Nonconformist and Liberal electors. At Merthyr certainly the organization is effective, and the people and their leaders are alike staunch.

Of the political opinions of such a man as Mr. Richard it is needless to write. Of course he is for the ballot, for the disendowment of the Irish Church, and for a system of unsectarian education. In common with all leading Liberals, he deprecates the rate-paying clauses of the Reform Bill, and is of opinion that there should be a redistribution of seats. Returned for Merthyr, not merely does Welsh Dissent gain a man pre-eminently qualified to speak on its behalf, but peace, the need of our time, when Europe is an armed camp, and industry languishes and pines away in consequence, will see in his proper place, the place where he can do most good, one of her ablest and most persevering advocates.

W. M'ARTHUR, ESQ.

(LAMBETH—LAWRENCE, 15,051 ; M'ARTHUR, 14,553 ; HOWARD, C., 7043.

IT is something to be Sheriff of the City of London and Middlesex. The office is an important and responsible one, and only conferred by the livery upon men of, in the civic sense, very eminent position. Not long since their choice fell upon Alderman Stone and W. M'Arthur, Esq. ; and it is of the latter gentleman that we now propose to write. As a London merchant, with extensive commercial connexions with Australia, as Chairman of the Star Assurance Company, and a Director of the City Bank, the trading community have long been familiar with his name. As a distinguished and liberal supporter in person and in purse of the Wesleyan cause and of the Wesleyan institutions, he has long been popular in the circles of his own zealous and widespread denomination ; and when, at the general election of 1865, he contested Pontefract on Liberal principles, it was felt that he was a man of the right stamp for Parliament, whose return was to be greatly desired by the friends of popular principles in every corner of the land.

Mr. M'Arthur is the son of the late Rev. John M'Arthur, a minister belonging to the Wesleyan body in Ireland. His ancestors originally lived in Argyleshire, in Scotland, but settled in the north of Ireland shortly before the Revolution. Mr. M'Arthur had two brothers, one of whom died prematurely, after a brilliant but brief University career. William, the elder, and the subject of this memoir, was destined for business, and about thirty years ago he settled in that capacity in Londonderry. Though an entire stranger, in a short time he found himself at the head of one of the largest establishments in the city, and a leading member of the Corporation, of which he became an alderman. Differences having arisen between the Corporation and the Irish Society, he was appointed one of a deputation to London, which succeeded in restoring harmony between the two bodies. In the erection of the new bridge over the Foyle in Londonderry, and in the formation of the magnificent line of quays which adorn its banks, he rendered considerable aid. In 1843, just as the gold discoveries had been made in Australia, Mr. M'Arthur's partner and brother went to reside in that colony. He had the sagacity to turn to account this new source of wealth, and, besides attaining in that country high social position, and being nominated by the Government to a seat in the Upper House, he established places of business in Sydney, Melbourne, and Adelaide, all of which have been prosperous in a remarkable degree. One consequence of this rapid increase of their business was the removal in 1857 of Mr. William M'Arthur to London, a movement sincerely regretted by all parties in the town, where, in the language of one of the Londonderry papers, he had been "a member of the Corporation since it was reformed, and not only in the discharge of his duties in connexion with that body, but with other local boards and institutions, he proved himself a most useful citizen." The same journal adds, with regard to Mr. M'Arthur, that "he possessed peculiar aptitude for business, enlarged views, strong common sense, much energy of character, and unimpeachable integrity." No wonder, under these circumstances, that Mr. M'Arthur should have risen to a high position in the City, or that his name should be before the public as that of one well qualified to take an active part in public life. In short, we have every reason to believe that he fully deserves the eulogium pronounced upon him by the well-known Mr. George Moore, of Cheapside, who, in proposing him as a candidate for the office of sheriff, described him "as one of our merchant princes, a man of great energy of character, and of indomitable perseverance and industry;" adding, further, that he "was a philanthropist in the greatest sense of the word. He had given a large part of his worldly means in works of charity and mercy."

In his address to the electors of Pontefract we have an outline of Mr. M'Arthur's political opinions. In 1865, in answer to a requisition forwarded to him by a numerous and influential body of electors, he declared himself "in favour of a moderate and gradual extension of the franchise," and of "any measure calculated to insure a more thorough representation of the intelligence of the kingdom," and also of the abolition of Church-rates. He would have "the strictest economy enforced in every branch of the public service," and he entirely approved "of the principle of non-intervention." In a speech delivered at Pontefract, Mr. M'Arthur explained himself more fully and freely. He expressed his great satisfaction at the fact that Lord Palmerston rather than Lord Derby was in power. He dwelt on the advantages of cheap tea, cheap sugar, cheap newspapers, and commercial intercourse with France, all of which he considered had been secured by Lord Palmerston's Administration. He then proceeded to state we had to thank the Liberals for free-trade, the suppression of slavery, Parliamentary Reform, the repeal of the Test and Corporation Acts, the revision of the penal code, and a large number of other measures which had tended to the amelioration of the condition of the working classes, and the advancement of this great country; and that therefore he was a Liberal, and would be found fighting on the Liberal side. Mr. Disraeli boasts that he has educated his party. It is to the credit of Mr. M'Arthur that he had the good sense to get his education completed before he ventured on the political arena. We all view with reasonable suspicion conversions at the eleventh hour.

As a worthy and active Wesleyan layman, Mr. M'Arthur, in addition to chapel-building and cognate matters, has had specially at heart the advancement of education in connexion with his own denomination. As an Irishman, and son of an Irish minister, his warmest sympathies and his most active exertions have been put forth in support of the New Wesleyan College, Belfast, towards which he and his brother have subscribed as much as 3000*l.*, and the foundation-stone of which was laid by himself, August 24, 1865. This college—the establishment of which marks an era in the history of Irish Methodism—aims to teach the sons of laity and ministry for general purposes, and at the same time to train up a certain number of young men as students for the Christian ministry. While this is done, the alumni will be able to graduate in connexion with the Queen's College, Belfast. The institution is confessedly of great importance to the denomination. It is also regarded by leading minds of different sentiments on questions both of religion and politics, as a most important step in the progress of education in Ireland. In his speech on the occasion referred to, Mr. M'Arthur said—and his language is worth serious consideration at the present moment—"Despite all the cavilling and opposition it had encountered, the national system had been a great success. It had conferred great blessings upon the population at large. He trusted the Government of the country felt too sensibly alive to the interests of the nation ever to interfere with the mixed system of education—a system which had produced such good results." The erection and outfit of the institution cost about 81,000*l.*, and an equal sum was required for endowment. Actually Mr. M'Arthur, in addition to the large sum of money subscribed by himself and brother, spent three months in the United States to plead its many claims on the Wesleyan Church in that prosperous land. But Mr. M'Arthur is by no means wedded to his own denomination. He is a member of the committee of the Bible Society, and of the London City Mission. He is also one of the leading supporters of the Evangelical Alliance, and at its recent meetings for prayer was chairman on one occasion at the City midday gathering.

Lambeth has done well in returning Mr. M'Arthur. We have said enough to show his fitness for the post. We have only one further observation to make: Ireland will for some time to come occupy the attention of Parliament and the nation; and it will be the duty of electors as much as possible to secure the return of warm-hearted Irishmen of undoubted pecuniary position, and sound in the faith as to politics and religion.

CHAPTER VII.

MEN WHO HAVE BEEN M.P.'S.

THE RT. HON. T. MILNER GIBSON.

DID my readers ever travel in the east of England?—a part of the world not suggestive of the fact that the wise men came from the East, but nevertheless a land of honest women and brave men—a land flowing with milk and honey in the shape of strong ale, turkeys, geese, and sausages. In the old coaching days, one of the finest sights in London in the winter time of year was to walk along Whitechapel and to meet the Essex, and Suffolk, and Norfolk coaches, all laden, not with live passengers, but dead stock. There were four horses; there was a coachman—perchance, a guard—but no coach was visible—not the ghost of a passenger—one mass of feathers and skins, of all colours, was the coach, all jumbled and jammed together like an omelet, or one of Turner's pictures. There were turkeys on their way to grace the table of a London alderman; there were pheasants, whose sweet fate was to be consumed by the daintiest of London's fairest daughters; anon out of this mass of fine feathers emerged a goose so corpulent as to remind the gazer of the poet's touching lines—

> "Of all the poultry in the yard,
> The goose I have preferred—
> There is so much of nutriment
> In that weak-minded bird."

Or again, you saw a hare, but yesterday leaping along in lusty life—which had been shot and despatched to a friend in town, who, as he ate it—whether jugged, or hashed, or stewed—whether done into soup, or cooked *à la* Derrynane, or roasted, as is the manner of some, with Devonshire cream—would think, not ungratefully, of the donor and of the pleasant week or two spent, in the bright days of summer, under his hospitable roof. Ah, well! the old coaches are gone, but the east still abounds in good things, and is a land rich in agricultural produce; but the people are not a "fast" people, like those of London and Manchester. It was seldom you heard of Chartism there; and as to Socialism, the people yet shudder at the sound. The landlords are Conservative, the county representatives are Conservative, and a Conservative M.P. seems to be as natural a production of the soil as a Suffolk punch or a prize bullock. In the thickest of this Conservative Paradise is a village called Theberton, in which was the residence of a Major Thomas Milner Gibson, who in the year 1807 had a son born to him.

The father was but little known. I presume he was a country gentleman, and lived after the manner of country gentlemen, when George the Third was king; and, undoubtedly, his son was brought up in his own image, and after his own fashion.

The old divines tell us, "Man proposes and God disposes." You bring up your son to be a miser—he becomes a spendthrift; to be steady, he becomes gay; to be a Dissenter, and he becomes a Puseyite; to revere the memory of Calvin, and he vexes you and confuses himself with Thomas Carlyle. Young Milner Gibson had talent, ambition, and a good estate. Had he been a poor man he would have gone to the bar—been, possibly, Attorney-General to Sir Robert Peel—for Sir Robert was partial to rising talent—and been lost in the confusion which came upon the Conservative party when Lord Derby retired from office. As a country gentleman, Mr. Gibson felt bound to serve his country; and as a country gentleman, to stand by his order. Hence, he began life as a true blue. I remember Sir Thomas Gooch, the *Gaffer* Gooch of one of Macaulay's political ballads, warranting him to be a regular Conservative colt; but it is dangerous to hazard anything where women, wine, and horses are concerned. The promising Conservative colt soon changed its colours, and was found running on the other side. This was in 1839, when Mr. Gibson retired from the representation of immaculate Ipswich, and was defeated on again offering himself to his late constituents. Mr. Gibson's principles were changed—his career was not altered. At Cambridge, where he had been educated, and taken a wrangler's position, he appeared as a candidate, but with little success. It seemed as if the reward of conviction was political annihilation. However, this was not for long. A public-spirited man with money is sure to get into Parliament, if not for one place, why then for another.

In 1841 Manchester needed a representative, and Milner Gibson was returned for the seat, which he held with such honour till Manchester in its frenzy was guilty of the absurdity of stoning its prophets. When the Anti-Corn-Law agitation came, Milner Gibson was one of its most successful orators, and succeeded in maintaining a position second, and only second, to Cobden and Bright. In 1846 the Whigs, anxious to please the people, and having personal objections to Cobden and Bright, made Milner Gibson Vice-President of the Board of Trade, but the Democracy of Manchester grew jealous of the divided affections of their member, and Mr. Gibson resigned the office in 1849. The Corn-Law agitation over, Mr. Gibson, far from used up, sighed for fresh worlds to conquer. At this time the Society for the Repeal of the Taxes on Knowledge was in need of an efficient parliamentary advocate. Mr. Gibson took that responsibility on himself. Session after session, he called the attention of the House to the subject. He prevailed at length upon the Chancellor of the Exchequer to repeal the duty on advertisements. In 1855 he succeeded in abolishing the penny stamp on newspapers; and even when we had still war budgets, Mr. Gibson tried hard for a repeal of the tax on paper. Mr. Gibson certainly has not been rewarded for this as he ought. He was indefatigable in the prosecution of the repeal of the taxes on knowledge, and the Society was nothing without him. It was Milner Gibson, the member for Manchester, who conferred on it respectability and power, who presided at its annual meetings in the metropolis, who got the public to attend them, who put the facts of the case in a telling way before the House of Commons, and by his tact and *bonhommie* secured parliamentary votes, which compelled the Chancellor of the Exchequer to interfere. The advocates of the repeal of the taxes on knowledge painted a glowing picture of the advantages that should ensue when those taxes were repealed. Cheap newspapers were the want of our times. It was because there were no cheap newspapers that the gaols were filled, and that the public-houses did a great business; it was because there were no cheap newspapers that, to the dim and downcast eyes of the people, Knowledge,

> "Her ample page,
> Rich with the spoils of time, did ne'er unroll;"

and it was because Mr. Gibson took up the agitation that it triumphed, in spite of the opposition of the *Times* and the larger section of the press. And yet when the victory was won, I know not whether Mr.

Milner Gibson scarce got thanks; certainly no public meeting assembled to do him honour, and no testimonial was collected in his praise. He had fought and won the battle of the people, and the people said never a word. It is well that the honest statesman labours for something more enduring than their hollow breath. In the increased supply of cheap literature—in the healthy character on the whole of that literature—in the consequent elevation, mental and moral, of the masses—in the stimulus thus given to progress—Mr. Gibson must alone seek his reward. It was the boast of the late Sir Robert Peel that by removing the shackles of trade—that by bidding commerce be free—that by giving to the men and women of this country cheap bread; he should have established his claim to be remembered gratefully long after he himself should have passed away. Lord John Russell has more than once quoted with approbation those well-worn lines in which the statesman is represented as filling the land with plenty, and as reading thanks in the nation's eyes. In a similar manner Mr. Gibson may consider that he has deserved well of his country, for a land lying in ignorance, perishing for lack of knowledge, its mental eye dark and dim, can never become great, or noble, or free. Such as Mr. Gibson may even claim the respect of the most timid Conservatives. No one fears a reading public—a public that does not read may be soon worked up into delirium and madness. At such times the demagogue may be mistaken for a sage, but the reading public sees him to be what he is. The cheap press, like Ithuriel's spear, makes him reveal himself in his true and hideous light.

Let us follow the Ashton M.P. into the House. When he sat with the Manchester party, by the side of Cobden and Bright, he looked little like a Manchester man himself. There was about him far more of the air of the country gentleman and scholar; and you would imagine that he had got there merely for a chat, as his light, gay air by no means harmonized with the serious appearance of his colleagues. Mr. Gibson always looks good-tempered and pleasant, and has been and is now rather a handsome-looking man; and not being blessed with large whiskers, has still rather a young and fresh appearance; but when he became President of the Board of Trade and one of the Cabinet, he certainly did not improve in appearance. On the night when Lord Palmerston moved his celebrated resolutions I thought Mr. Gibson looked peculiarly uncomfortable and disappointed, and I candidly confess no one likes to be balked of victory in the very hour of anticipated triumph. No doubt Mr. Gibson went into the ministry to repeal the Paper duties. A reactionary House of Commons, and an innovating House of Lords, however, decided otherwise at the eleventh hour. With brown curly hair, light complexion, well-shaped features, and blue eyes, Mr. Gibson was as fine a specimen of the Conservative colt as you would wish to see, with the frank and winning manner of the English gentry of the better class. Nothing seemed to put him out; and even the country gentlemen, who regarded him with aversion,—who considered him as a traitor to their cause,—who remembered how he had been born and bred in their camp, and had now gone over to the enemy,—could not find it in their hearts to be very angry with a man who, after all, had been one of themselves. Mr. Gibson's manner is conciliatory. He belongs to the extreme party, without seeming to be extreme. His voice is pleasant and musical. If you differ with him, you don't feel inclined to quarrel with him. Some men in the House are very apt to excite antagonism and to irritate you by the very sound of their voice. We can point to more than one eminent M.P. who makes you feel waspish immediately he is on his legs. It is a pity Mr. Gibson did not speak oftener. Certainly office has a great tendency to make men dumb.

The Cobdenic policy, as illustrated in the person of Mr. Gibson, lost much of its unpopular air. During the Russian war, Mr. Gibson was, comparatively speaking, quiet. He did not prophesy, as Mr. Bright did, that, in a couple of years' time, it would land us in civil war; nor did he, like Mr. Cobden, sit down to write letters republished with glee at St. Petersburg. Even while heading the crusade for the repeal of the taxes on knowledge, he did not, with the latter, hold up trumpery American papers as superior to such papers as the *Times;* nor did he, with Mr. Bright, charge the *Daily News* with ingratitude, because it dared to be independent. Even the *Saturday Review* has dealt gently with Mr. Gibson; and yet, quiet, pleasant-looking as he is, Mr. Gibson can do a great deal of damage. He upset Lord Palmerston's first cabinet. To be sure the latter had his revenge, for he appealed to the country and got Manchester to reject her worthiest representatives. As member for Ashton-under-Lyne, Mr. Gibson reappeared, and when the aged Premier got Manchester to endorse him as a first-rate liberal, Mr. Gibson accepted a seat in the Cabinet. Mr. Gibson has the credit, deservedly, of being one of the best tacticians in the House, but it was the opinion of some who know a little about these things, that in the aged Palmerston he found his match.

At the same time that Mr. Gibson may not share the odium of the leaders of the Manchester party, he may not share their praise. He is a courageous advocate of progress, a flattering representative of Manchester, and a man of great platform power; but he is not, like Bright, a peace advocate on principle; nor could he have sacrificed everything, as Cobden did, to fight the battle of Free Trade. Mr. Gibson's *débût* in the House was fortunate; it was on a subject on which he knew much. Some business connected with the Baltic had been occupying the attention of the House. Mr. Gibson had just been up there in his yacht; consequently he knew more about the subject than any one else, and he told what he knew in a manner at once to win the ear of the House. On other matters, when he has spoken, he has been equally at home. He hits the feeling of the House in his speeches. He does not seem particularly in earnest, or particularly extreme. He is not savagely severe or sublimely eloquent. You do not feel that he is trying to make a great speech, and to be quoted as a second Fox or Burke. Even when he acts the part of the tribune of the people, he has the air of a gentleman, and there is good-nature in his voice, and a merry twinkle in his eye. As long as democracy rejoices in such a representative, patricians need not shrink from it, or old ladies dream of Mirabeau and Robespierre. No noble lord need fear the working classes under the leadership of Mr. Gibson. He, by birth, is a gentleman—was brought up at Cambridge—is the owner of a large landed estate; and if he listens to the manufacturers, and is on good terms with the bugbear of political dissent, and occasionally appears on the platform at St. Martin's Hall, and casts in his lot with the party of Bright, it must be remembered that he at least has, even in the eyes of the Bentincks and Newdegates, a stake in the country, and is of the class who are supposed to be alone qualified for statesmanship, and office, and political rank.

JOHN ARTHUR ROEBUCK.

Are there honest men in the world of politics? and if so, are they the better or the worse for their honesty? These are questions to be asked, and if you will, answered; or, to come to particulars, would John Arthur Roebuck have been more successful, as men reckon success, had he been less honest? The honourable gentleman would reply in the affirmative. The public must form its own opinion. When the great Chatham entered the House of Commons, Walpole exclaimed, "We must muzzle that terrible cornet of horse." The muzzling process is believed to exist at this day. We have seen wonders effected, and we naturally suspect a cause. When Mr. Bernal Osborne, after years of silence and peace, utters his wild shriek of liberty, we naturally come to a conclusion that his seat on the Treasury Bench is insecure. On Irish members the muzzling process is very apparent. Under its soothing influence the roaring patriot aggravates his voice and sings very small indeed. But the man gets his place, and we clap our hands. In success there is manifestly a saving grace. If a man has that we honour him. We stop not to inquire how he has succeeded. If he has betrayed his party, if he has sworn oaths and broken them, if he has said one thing one day and another the next, if he has worn one face on the hustings and another in St. Stephen's, he is honoured nevertheless; just as people flatter the lucky speculator, the successful tradesman, the great millowner, and never stop to inquire by what sharp practice, by what ingenious dishonesty, or gross fraud, the wealth thus venerated has been acquired. In these days it is not the rogues that walk in mud. Ah me! but yesterday, in the slush and rain and cold, I met one born in humble life, but dowered with a beauty for which many a Belgravian lady would sell her soul. Vainly I looked for the loveliness of an earlier day. Care and want had furrowed her brow, and had thinned the luxuriant locks, and had dimmed the lustre of eyes once bright as pearls, and paled the red lips and rosy cheek. In this great city, where sin exists without the sense of shame, she had retained her honesty, but at what a price! *Quid rides?* as a late eminent satirist, with his immense erudition, was wont to say. I felt in that poor creature's presence as if at the shrine of a saint. Thus I do not indicate that Cato is an idiot because he is at the bottom of the poll; because he is alone, poor, neglected; because his struggles have been great and his successes small. A man who will find fault with all parties, will expose officials, will oppose himself to the prejudices and passions of the hour, will blame the narrowness of the Church, and yet at the same time express his abhorrence of the intolerance of dissent, cannot look for popularity. Nay more, if we suspect Cato of occasional injustice, if he himself evinces temper and passion, if he shows a sternness in some quarters where we should expect forbearance, and a forbearance where we should look for sternness, if he is occasionally conveniently dumb or inconveniently fussy, especially if he gets mixed up with a dirty job, like a Galway contract for instance,—if our Cato considers himself master of every subject, if he be always obtruding himself before better men, like Talkative in the "Pilgrim's Progress," exclaiming, "I will talk of things heavenly or things earthly — things moral or things evangelical—things sacred or things profane—things past or things to come—things foreign or things at home—things more essential or things circumstantial,"—perhaps we shall understand how it is Cato is not held in more honour, and shall see that the public are not so much to blame as at first sight may appear.

It is half-past four, and we are standing in the lobby of the House of Commons. A very little man, leaning on a stick, comes tottering towards us. He is shabbily dressed, and seems very, very feeble. Poor man, you piteously exclaim, why are you here in this unhealthy atmosphere—in this fierce arena? Why seek you to wrestle with these athletes when you were better at Malvern, or Scarborough, or some other locality sacred to Hygeia? Such are your natural reflections. They are not, however, those of the subject of them. His feeling evidently is quite otherwise. You can imagine him saying, "I am plain John Arthur Roebuck, friend of the people, advocate of progress, and champion of the rights of man. Out of the way, O ye blind leaders of the blind; are ye not, every mother's son of you, nincompoops, pudding-headed and asinine windbags—shams? Have ye not blundered and placed England on the brink of perdition? I say, go home, and I, John Arthur Roebuck, must save her, or she is lost for ever." It is true that when Mr. Roebuck has had the field to himself he has not been eminently successful. He was Chairman of the Administrative Reform Association; where is it now? He was Chairman of the Western Bank—a bubble that has long been burst. He was Chairman of the Sebastopol Committee; yet how impotent were its conclusions! He was one of the great men of the Galway Steam Packet Company, of the Exchange Bank, and in some quarters a belief was entertained that these were bubbles. Surely a gentler style of criticism, a little less arrogancy of manner, a little less virulence of invective, is becoming to a man whose failures have been so numerous!

Let me describe Mr. Roebuck as I saw him on the night when he made his motion for the appointment of the Sebastopol Committee. Imagine yourself, intelligent reader, in the Speaker's Gallery. Glancing down the gangway, on the Ministerial side, there stands a little man with a hooked nose and a face indicative of weakness and premature decay. The tones of his voice are faint and sickly; his action is feeble. He forgets what he is going to say in a manner painful to witness. He rubs his hand across his forehead, and tries to catch the missing train of thought—but in vain; it is gone from him for ever. The House listens kindly, and cheers, but all in vain. There he stands—he whose winged words were sharper than arrows, whose sting was that of an adder, whose imperious tone, his hand pointing all the while, as if to say, "Thou art the man," drove conscience home to the most careless and made the most phlegmatic writhe, who seemed to scalp his victim, as it were, and the fear of whom was a principle in many a heart—there he stands, with opportunity, the grand thing he had been panting for all his ambitious life, at length his own; the time at length come for which he had prayed since earliest youth—a grand drama, and a grand part to act in it for himself; and oh! the mockery of life, the power gone, and the golden moments lost for ever. The sight was a sad and an affecting one, and when poor Roebuck sat down, for a wonder, for once the House was subdued and hushed and still. Pity for the speaker allayed all hostility. It seemed as if no one cared to create a debate—as if the spectacle of a popular statesman struck down in the moment of what was to have been his triumph was of its kind as sad as that of a gallant army mouldering away beneath administrative imbecility and neglect.

At a public meeting held not very long since at Sheffield, Mr. Roebuck endeavoured to answer the question how it was that he, unconnected with the great parties in the State, not of the great families, undistinguished by wealth, unknown to fame, should have won the approbation and confidence of his countrymen. Warming with his theme he exclaimed—"It is not talent, it is not name, it is not rank, it is not wealth; it is steadfastness in that path which I had marked out for myself in the beginning. I am proud to say that in the year 1832 I published a programme of the opinions I then held. I had prepared myself for a public life, I had then formed my opinions, and I consigned them to paper. I printed them, and to them I now adhere. That which I said in 1833 I say now, and it is my firm and my steadfast adherence to the opinions I then expressed which has now won for me the confidence of my countrymen. Going into Parliament unknown, unsupported, and only recommended by that true friend of the people, Joseph Hume, I determined not to ally myself to either of the great parties then dividing the House of Commons and the kingdom. To that rule I have adhered through life, and no man can now say I am either Whig or Tory." Roebuck, then, may be described as a Radical politician, but of a Radicalism of so singular a character as to induce him to side and seat himself with the Opposition rather than with the supporters of Government. When he makes war he prefers to attack his friends. Gentlemen whose opinions are supposed most to resemble his own he cannot abide. It seems strange now, that he has even acquired the reputation he has; yet there was a time when many competent judges of all the orators of the House delighted chiefly in John Arthur Roebuck, and deemed the skill with which he unmasked a job—the delight with which he brought it before the House—the invective which he directed against all parties connected with it, inimitable. On the whole, now, Mr. Roebuck may be pronounced a failure—that is, other men, less gifted, less honest, less popular, have been more successful. The cause is chiefly in an unhappy temperament; a temperament which makes him always go in an opposite direction to what is required. To get Mr. Roebuck on your side you must beg him to speak against you. Sydney Smith used to say of certain individuals, Mr. S. is a clubable man. Now the House of Commons after all is a club, and Mr. Roebuck is not a clubable man. This is the primary cause. Another is the vanity which makes him insist on playing first fiddle. *Aut Cæsar aut nullus* is his motto.

Again, Mr. Roebuck has exhibited another great fault, he has not trusted in himself. He has shown the vanity, and, I may add, the weakness of a woman. His duel with Mr. Black of the *Morning Chronicle,* his endeavour to get the *Times* censured in the House for a description of the honourable gentleman which every one who heard it confessed to be singularly truthful and exact, his impotent attempt to put Mr. Disraeli down when the latter had but just made his parliamentary *débût,* his vindictive attack, only very recently, on Dr. Mitchell, the ex-Bodmin M.P., who plainly confessed to the House, and in a way which gained for him lasting honour, that it was true that he had agreed to retire from the representation of his borough rather than stay to fight the petition which had been presented with regard to his seat, for the simple reason that he was a poor man comparatively speaking, and had not the money requisite for a parliamentary defence; such things as these deservedly lower Mr. Roebuck's position in the House, and with all right-thinking men all over the country. Were Mr. Roebuck less impulsive, less irritable, less jealous of himself, he would spare his friends and supporters the repetition of such painful scenes. After enjoying the courtesies of the French at Cherbourg, could anything be more execrable than his insulting references to the women renowned all the world over for fascinations, which might even for a moment have soothed Mr. Roebuck into civility and good temper? It is not thus that public men should act, and sure are we that the public man who thus acts must have great talents, great industry, great honesty, to hold up his head in the face of such things. Granting Mr. Roebuck to have done the State some service as a politician and a man of letters, though in this latter capacity he has not greatly shone in his day, it is obvious that his worst foe has been himself, and that if he had, like all truly great men, been above the suggestions of a childish vanity, he would by this time have taken a higher stand. His success must be in himself, in the verdict of his own heart, in the consciousness that he has been true to his mission, that he has not swerved aside for man's smile or frown. Political independence is rare, and is chiefly affected by eccentricities such as the late Colonel Sibthorp, or Mr. Drummond, or Mr. Darby Griffiths. In the case of Mr. Roebuck it is often an obstacle in the path of political progress. Even Mr. Roebuck's pertinacious egotism cannot blind him to the fact that he does not represent public opinion at all.

Mr. Roebuck's references to himself at all times are amusing. We infer, as we glance at his speeches, public education has prospered because it has had Mr. Roebuck's support. On a very recent occasion the severest censure he could pass upon Lord John Russell was, that he had failed to consult Mr. Roebuck. I am the good dog Tearem, says Mr. Roebuck, who guards the lambs who would otherwise be torn to pieces by the ravenous wolf. I am the man, he told the Sheffield people the other day, who says hard things, as if hard-hitting was the *sine qua non* of statesmanship. A man in public life should have no mock modesty; in Mr. Roebuck's case bashfulness has not certainly been carried to excess. An oracle, it was said, warned the Athenians against a man who alone was opposed to the whole city. Phocion claimed the honour of such singularity for himself. When one of his proposals was received with unusual approbation, he turned round to his friends and asked whether he had let anything escape him that was wrong. Bishop Thirlwall tells us, "In his speeches he carefully avoided all rhetorical embellishments, which he had learnt from Plato to consider as a kind of flattery unworthy an honest man, and studied a sententious brevity," which, however, was so enlivened with wit and humour, as often to make a deeper impression than the most elaborate periods. It was even observed by one of his adversaries that Demosthenes was the best orator, but Phocion the most powerful speaker. And Demosthenes himself, it is said, trembled for the effect of his eloquence when Phocion rose after him, and would whisper to his friends, "Here comes the hatchet to my speech." Mr. Roebuck was, and he seemed to pride himself on it, the Phocion of the House of Commons. He must stand alone. He can bear no rival near his throne. He can be as severe on John Bright as Mr. Disraeli, on friends as foes. The right of private judgment, carried to excess, is the vice of modern society, according to Mr. Gladstone's teaching in his "Church and its Relation to the State," and by no one living statesman is this right more rigidly guarded, or occasionally more inconveniently displayed, than by Mr. Roebuck.

His non-success, considered in a worldly point of view, may be in some degree the result of the fact that he has steadfastly set his face against complying with the conditions which insure success. No one ever asked him to play the part of the tribune of the people. The parties in the House are Whig and Tory, and the electors out-of-doors are either the one or the other. It is true the names are rarely heard, but the essential division remains the same. There were Radicals when Mr. Roebuck took his seat for Bath. As he tells us, he has not changed in his opinions since 1832. Well, when he first entered Parliament, there had been the greatest political convulsion known in England since 1688. Democracy, flushed with triumph, like a giant refreshed with wine, trod the land. The privileged classes were in despair, and peers and bishops trembled for their very heads. The reaction had not set in which in so short a time nearly undid all the good that the Bill had effected. The mistake of John Arthur Roebuck was in supposing that it never would—that the Reform Bill had ushered in a new era—that the days of corruption and ignorance and darkness were past—that Parliament was to be a grand reality, and that henceforth the people, enlightened, passionless, high-toned, indignant at all petty meannesses, impatient of all party frauds, were to rule the land. In this estimate, in sorrow and shame be it known, Mr. Roebuck made an egregious mistake. To struggle up from the people, not by pandering to the ruling classes, nor to the prejudice of the mob, nor to the caprices of the peers, is a Herculean task. The great Sir Robert Peel is an admirable illustration of a successful tactician. He sought power, we grant, for public not personal ends: yet how did he acquire that power? By the most unscrupulous pandering to the passions and prejudices of party. What Protestant prejudices—what Tory prejudices—what Protectionist prejudices—received the sanction of his support, and yet what ruin he wrought to the very prejudices he had not feebly advocated, but solemnly and at times sanctimoniously upheld. Still he succeeded, and became England's model statesman. Roebuck has been the reverse of all this, and at the same time he has been unnecessarily arrogant and offensive. He takes Lord Peter as his model. My readers may remember when one of the brothers contended that what he asserted to be good mutton bore a striking resemblance to a slice off a brown loaf—as in reality it was—his lordship replied, "Look ye, gentlemen, to convince you what a couple of blind, positive, ignorant, wilful puppies you are, I will use but this plain argument — it is true good natural mutton as any in Leadenhall Market, and G— confound you both eternally if you offer to believe otherwise." Of this "plain argument" we have somewhat too much in Mr. Roebuck's speeches. He has carried this "plain argument" to an excess. A life spent in unsuccessful invective has soured him. He reminds us of the hero of Tennyson's "Vision of Sin," as he exclaims

> "Unto me my maudlin gall,
> And my mockeries of the world."

MR. BERNAL OSBORNE.

WHY should English gentlemen engage in politics? As a profession, it does not pay. Lord John Russell is not supposed to be immensely wealthy; yet he must have spent, in election contests and for election purposes, quite as much as he has ever received back in the shape of official salary. We all know what serious remonstrances were made by the firm with which Mr. Poulet Thompson was connected, on account of the money he spent with a view to secure himself a seat in Parliament. Theoretically, the system is as bad as it can well be. "I bought you," said an exultant M.P. to a discontented constituency, on one occasion, "and I'll sell you." Such a feeling, of course, naturally rises in the hearts of men who have acquired their parliamentary position by their wealth; and some Radicals will always prove to you, that if a man parts with his cash, unless he be born a fool, he does not do it for nothing. It is too bad such should be the case. We can never expect a reformed House of Commons till we get M.P.'s to be ashamed of the dirty and disgraceful work at election contests. Constituents and M.P.'s are deeply dishonoured by such things. I do not know who are the most to blame—the scoundrels who are dirty enough to bribe, or the scoundrels who are dirty enough to take the bribe. Is it not strange that we get men of honour on either side of the House?

The Osborne family illustrate and confirm this view. Some years back there was a very respectable gentleman M.P. for Rochester and chairman of committees in the House of Commons. In the discharge of his duties in this latter capacity he received the respectable allowance of 1200*l.* a year; but, in order to secure that sum, he was reported to have spent in election contests a sum amounting to 60,000*l.* This gentleman was the father of the late M.P. for Nottingham. A description of the former will almost suit the latter. Mr. Grant thus describes Mr. Bernal:—"His face is round, and his features are intelligent and agreeable; his complexion indicates an ample stock of health; he has a fine forehead; his hair is of a dark brown colour; he is of Jewish description; he is a commanding person, and in the prime of life." The resemblance may be carried still further. Mr. Grant says of the father, that "he speaks very seldom, and never at any length on any question of commanding importance." The son, also, in common with the father, illustrates the fallacy involved in the idea that the House of Commons is a place for common people. Both found that parliamentary existence, as a rule, requires a very considerable property qualification. Some people will tell you the latter is abolished. It is not, nor ever will be. The more democratic is a constituency, the more essential a requisite will it be for its representative to be a man of wealth. What could a poor M.P. do in Westminster, or Finsbury, or Marylebone, or the Tower Hamlets? If by a miracle he were to be returned, depend upon it his constituency would soon tire of him. I write this with full knowledge of the fact that the House of Commons forbids bribery at elections, and that the returns of expenses certified by the auditor appointed for the purpose are ridiculously small. It is really wonderful, considering all things, how we get such good members of Parliament as we do; and that we do get them at all is, we fear, in a very small degree the fault of the electors, but chiefly the result of that *esprit de corps* which exists amongst English gentlemen, and which is ever found in an assembly of patriots. It is not knowingly that the House of Commons is a party to anything dirty or mean. When they truckled to the Lords, and suffered the latter to continue the paper tax which they had rejected, they did so because there was not spirit enough in the country to back them, if they had resisted the dictation of the Lords. One Reform Bill after another languished and died for a similar reason.

But to return to the gay — the graceful — the chivalrous Bernal Osborne, for many years the saucy boy — the *enfant terrible* — of the House of Commons. He is the chartered libertine of the Liberal party. He is popular in the House, and popular out of doors. We owe him much for the liveliness he has given many a dull debate. His speeches are always reported at considerable length, and—if we may believe the reporters, and I see no reason to doubt them—they always elicit a great deal of laughter. He makes much fun out of Mr. Newdegate; and nothing pleased him better than to see Mr. Spooner shake his grey and reverend head. Occasionally he flew at higher game, and was only too happy if he could catch Mr. Disraeli napping. He has plenty of fun—the fun of a good constitution and of animal spirits, and that fun he infuses into his speeches. Occasionally he is very happy in his remarks; thus, in his speech on the Derby-Disraeli Reform Bill of 1859, he protested against such "political millinery." "The franchise," he contended, "would be completely at the mercy of a scolding landlady or smoky chimney." He intimated to Mr. Disraeli that he had a heavy omnibus of country gentlemen to pull up the hill. Mr. Osborne is also great in interruptions, and pretty often raises a laugh. Thus, when Mr. Heywood was gravely arguing in favour of the retention of the Crystal Palace in Hyde Park, on the ground that gentlemen had no place of amusement at the West-end, Mr. Osborne's question, "Where is Cremorne?" was greatly to the amusement of a House always disposed to laugh, even when hard at work. The wit in which Mr. Osborne deals is not difficult of achievement. Sydney Smith writes—"It is argued that wit is a sort of inexplicable visitation, that it comes and goes with the rapidity of lightning, and that it is quite as unattainable as beauty or just proportion. I am so much of a contrary way of thinking, that I am convinced a man might sit down as systematically and as successfully to the study of wit as he might to the study of mathematics; and I would answer for it that, by giving up only six hours a day to learning wit, he should come on prodigiously before midsummer, so that his friends should hardly know him again." Parliamentary wit, it is clear, is often studied and far-fetched. Mr. Wilberforce said of Sheridan, the general impression was, that he came to the House of Commons with his flashes prepared and ready to let off. Mr. Osborne, we fancy, resembles Sheridan in this respect. He is not a frequent debater. It is seldom he attempts to catch the Speaker's eye. So long as he is in office, he generally contents himself with a silent vote. Out of office he is vehement; or if the ministry with which he is connected be in danger, he exerts himself, and makes one or two telling speeches. While M.P. for Dover, and at the Admiralty, he made no complaints; but no sooner was he turned out of Dover, and a Conservative in his place, than his righteous soul was grieved beyond all endurance at the corrupt administration at the Admiralty. Such a state of affairs was intolerable, and not to be borne; but Mr. Osborne once more at his old place, and he sleeps quietly, only waking up at quarter-day. It is as a parliamentary wit, rather than as a statesman, or debater, or able administrator, that Mr. Osborne's reputation is made. Now, wit in the House of Commons, or in any large assembly, is of the lowest possible character. For instance, how childish is a joke of some facetious judge on the bench, when it appears in print, and yet with what shouts of laughter was it received! The cause of this is twofold: in the first place, in a business assembly, when men's minds have long been on the stretch, the faintest excuse for a smile is welcomed as a grateful relief and change; in the second place, there is a contagious principle in jokes as well as in fevers. A man is acted on by others. You laugh when you see others around you laughing. Go to a crowded theatre or public meeting. There is a mass of human bodies piled up in front of you, so you can neither see nor hear actor or speaker, wherever and whoever he may be; yet you hear every one around you laughing, and you do the same. The wits of the House of Commons are not very witty men; but they are successful in raising laughter for the reasons already mentioned. The ready wit of a good, sound, physical constitution is invaluable in a man who is in a position to be a little independent and impudent. In a poor man, of course, it would not be tolerated an instant; but Mr. Osborne is not poor, and hence he successfully elicits the loud laugh that speaks the vacant mind. Besides, an impudent man is always a successful one. There is no standing up against impudence. Sir Peter Laurie cannot put it down. It acts on us as the poet says vice acts on us—"We are first shocked; then endure; then embrace." The Marylebone vestry were in arms against

Mr. Osborne because he called them a lot of political tinkers—we should like to have seen the expression of Mr. Osborne's face as he seriously assured them that "thinkers" was the word he used.

Mr. Osborne's career may be very easily told. He began life in the army. He then became a Liberal M.P. in favour of the ballot and free trade. In 1852 he was appointed Secretary for the Admiralty. He sat in Parliament as M.P. for Wycombe from 1841 to 1847, when he was returned for Middlesex. His connexion with the Admiralty helped to return him for Dover. Being, however, ultimately driven out of that borough, when the Tories had the command of the Admiralty influence, he retired into private life. To Liskeard was the merit due of having restored him to the public service. Liskeard and its representative, however, in time fell out, and for too short a while Nottingham rejoiced in Mr. Bernal Osborne as one of her representatives.

EDWARD MIALL, ESQ.

A LITTLE while ago the writer was spending the night on the North Sea while the wind was blowing a gale, and when it was far pleasanter to be at home in bed. Finding that the ship was making but little progress he made towards the engine-room to know the cause. "Why," said the engineer, in answer to his inquiries, "the captain says we must wait for the daylight before we make the harbour." In that answer was the whole secret of political success. For instance, Mr. Miall has learned to wait for the daylight, and now, we trust, he has floated into the harbour. The lesson is hard to learn. It is so much more agreeable, especially if you be a philosopher, to stick to your theory and to see it win.

In the old Scandinavian theology the world was a living animal. The geologists who tell us its backbone is made of granite confirm the idea. Analogy suggests a similar arrangement in the moral world, at any rate so far as regards a backbone of fundamental principles. There they are lying deep down in the eternal fitness of things. Above them there may be quicksands and rubbish, and *débris* of all kinds, but without you build on a principle you build in vain. About thirty years ago there was great danger of the Dissenting public forgetting this. That public was not a very logical body. Its dissent was more practical than theoretical. The chapel filled because at the church nothing better than a barren morality was preached, and because in the week the preacher often lived at variance with that; but in his heart of hearts, especially in respectable circles, the Dissenter venerated the national establishment, and fervently longed for the day when the sporting, hunting, drinking, swearing parson of his time should be superseded by clergymen of the school of which the late Mr. Simeon, of Cambridge, was the head. Toleration was the boon for which the Dissenter craved, and he was thankful for it. If a clergyman went so far as to shake hands with the humble pastor of the meeting-house, and to stand on the same platform with him on special occasions, such as Bible Society anniversaries, good deacons wept for joy, and in many quarters it was believed that the Millennium had come. A few, a very few, took higher ground. In that grand declaration, "My kingdom is not of this world," they had learnt that God's truth needed not the magistrate—that it flourished only as it touched men's hearts and modified their lives, that it was paralysed rather than strengthened by State patronage and support.

This truth had become very dear and precious to a young, spare minister of the Congregational denomination preaching at Leicester in a large chapel, and amongst a people of more than average culture. He had been born at Portsea somewhere about the year 1809. In his youth he had originally turned his attention to scholastic duties; subsequently he became a student at Wymondley College, Herts, and then settled, as the phrase is, at Ware, in the same county. From Ware he had moved to Leicester. It seemed to him the time had come for the Christian Church to learn the secret of its strength—to cease to trust in Parliament or Acts of Parliament. As the Church Establishment was founded on the very opposite theory—on the superiority of the compulsory over the voluntary principle, it was against that his righteous indignation was aroused. He gave up the pulpit; he left Leicester; he came to London. He founded, with the aid of many friends and sympathisers, a newspaper to show what wrong was done to God and man by State Churchism and priestcraft. The name of the paper was the *Nonconformist*—of its founder Edward Miall. He made some enemies, but more friends. Boldness always captivates the young, and they rallied round him. The young men of 1840 are the preachers and teachers and the masters of to-day; and thus to the world Mr. Miall stands out as the clearest advocate and ablest exponent of modern Dissent. That such a man should have no place in the representative assembly of the nation is a serious mistake; and it was to the credit of Bradford—alas, in vain—that it fixed upon such a one as the unanimous, or nearly so, choice of her Liberalism and Dissent.

Mr. Miall first contested Southwark, but it was Rochdale that had the merit of first returning him to Parliament. He lost his seat when so many of the chiefs of the popular party lost theirs, at the time of the Chinese war, and since then he has unsuccessfully contested Tavistock. In Parliament, in spite of a voice not very strong, and of a mannerism somewhat stiff and angular, he made considerable way. His position as the mouthpiece of the large Dissenting public was at once recognised and respected. Nor has his Parliamentary experience been lost upon him. To the theorist everything is straightforward and clear and beautiful. You grant the premises and the conclusion must follow. The abstract philosopher in his study, and with his pipe, has a faith that can move mountains: put such a man in the House of Commons, set him practically to work, and he learns there is another logic quite as strong as that of the abstract philosopher, making no allowance for disturbing causes, and evolving renovated worlds out of the depths of his inner consciousness, and that is the inexorable logic of events. The passionless *doctrinaire* plays chess in utter ignorance of his adversary's moves, and he often blunders as much as the most impulsive and unreasoning of platform orators. The philosopher Square was but an indifferent character after all, though, to quote Fielding, "he measured all actions by the unalterable rule of right and the eternal fitness of things." In politics, as at sea, however correctly you steer by the compass, you must, to be safe, wait for the daylight. With what care and labour did Mr. Miall, in his earlier editorial years, devote himself to the subject of manhood suffrage! yet we have just passed through a great Parliamentary Reform settlement without the name being ever uttered, or in a whisper so feeble as to be scarce audible! How very plainly and forcibly has Mr. Miall shown the mischievous effect of the State interfering in education; yet now the nation is unanimous in its demand that the first thing to be done by the new House of Commons is to provide a general system of national education, and Mr. Miall tells the people of Bradford that he will now devote his "best energies to shaping the practical measures which are intended to give effect to the will of the people in this matter." Then, again, there was the Anti-State-Church Association, of which Mr. Miall was the life and soul. What refreshing distinctness there was in the title! how—to a Dissenter—rigid and uncompromising, how bold and manly the programme; no quibbling about Dissenters' grievances, no pettifogging petitioning about Church-rates, no milk-and-water attempts to ameliorate what had better be abolished; the evil was not in the effects of the system, but in the system itself—the un-Christian alliance of the Church and State. Attack the State Church, level that to the ground, and Dissenters' grievances and Church-rates will disappear. And now the Anti-State Church Association is a society with a name so long and roundabout that I may not trust myself to quote it from memory, and its chief practical work is opposition to Church-rates. Daylight has come, and Mr. Miall has learnt from it how more safely and usefully to steer his course. The very men who were most strongly opposed to him are now on his side.

Many of Mr. Miall's writings have been reprinted from the *Nonconformist*, and have met with a favourable reception at the hands of the public. As a writer he is distinguished by clearness and power, and his topics are almost as much now as in his pulpit days more or less religious. The *Nonconformist* is decidedly a religious paper, and was the first to give the improved tone intellectually to the religious press of the country which is the characteristic of our age. In purely secular pursuits we hear little of Mr. Miall. It is understood that he writes a weekly leader for one of the most widely-circulated of our weekly contemporaries, and as one of the commissioners appointed to inquire into the state of education in England he discharged his duties in a way claiming public regard. He is stouter than he was, he has a bushier beard than was his wont, he does not dress in black as it is to be presumed he did when preaching at Leicester, but as much now as then his earnest religiousness is evident in all he says or does. He is a man you feel you may depend upon; not a Bohemian *littérateur*, or a man of many-sided crotchets, but one spurning all ignoble ways, holding to truth and duty as the pole-star of life, mild in demeanour, inflexible in purpose, not elated when crowned with success, not cowed when covered with defeat.

RIGHT HON. EDWARD HORSMAN.

That was a happy idea of Mr. Bright's in which he described certain discontented M.P.'s as living in a kind of political Cave Adullam. There are in the House a set of people whom it is impossible to please, for whom Reformers go too fast and Conservatives too slow—in whom the critical faculty is in excess—who can see faults more clearly than merits—who can originate nothing and support nothing. Of this class the Parliamentary lead belongs by right to Mr. Horsman, whose promising career seems to have been stopped by a sudden blight, and whose young affections now run to waste, and "water but the desert."

In 1836 a young member took his seat as M.P. for Cockermouth. The impulse given by the Reform movement in many quarters was dying out. A reaction fatal to the Whigs had commenced. The Reform Parliament had long been dissolved; and Sir Robert Peel had gained a hundred additional Members, and for a few months had retained office till driven away from it by a combination of Whigs and followers of Daniel O'Connell. Lord John Russell had returned to office, but not to power. He had the Court against him, the great landlords against him. In the Upper House Government measures were mutilated or thrown out, just as it seemed good to the Duke of Wellington or Lord Lyndhurst, the masters of the situation there; and in the House of Commons those able speakers and administrators, Sir James Graham and Lord Stanley, had not only deserted Lord Russell's ranks, but had become bitter opponents. The Duke of Richmond and the Earl of Ripon had also withdrawn from the Administration. Thus shattered and shorn of their strength, the Whigs at this time feebly engaged in a hopeless struggle. It is true that they had done much. They had carried Parliamentary Reform; they had relieved the Roman Catholics of Ireland by legislating on the tithe question; they had reformed the principal abuses of the municipal system; India and China had been thrown open to free trade, and slavery had been abolished in our colonies; but now they were resting on their oars and babbling of finality, as if there could be such a thing in a world where evil is eternal and ever young,—where, stamped out here, it springs up there,—where, cut down in the day, in the night it renews its hateful life. Between the two stools of Conservative fear and Radical alienation, the Whig Cabinet was in daily danger of falling down. They needed an external impulse and an infusion of fresh blood. With this view Cockermouth sent as her representative Mr. Horsman. His programme was satisfactory. On his banner he inscribed, "An efficient Church Reform, vote by ballot, and the removal of all the taxes on knowledge." Here was a Radical bill of fare. What more could the hungriest of them require?

For a while, with all the zeal of a first love, Mr. Horsman played his part, and Cockermouth had reason to be proud of her M.P. The Church was not in good odour then; for the abuses connected with Church property were simply infamous, and required reform. Here were bishops, and deans, and chapters, rolling in wealth, while working clergymen were starving, and ignorance and heathenism were spreading all around. If men pointed to a scandalous abuse, to a flagrant instance of episcopal nepotism, or to some dirty transaction that savoured more of filthy lucre than of the spirit of Christ, they were called infidels and Radicals, and the cry of "The Church in danger!" was raised. At length, Commissioners were appointed to take care of Church property, and lo! a greater scandal was the result. These holy men thought more of themselves than of spiritual destitution. Souls could wait, they argued, but bishops' palaces could not; and so the Bishop of Oxford had 6500*l.* for beautifying his palace at Cuddesdon, and the Bishop of Bath and Wells 4000*l.* for melon-pits and conservatories, and others more, out of the funds set apart for the building of new churches and the augmentation of small livings. Most mercilessly were these proceedings dragged to light and condemned in Parliament by Mr. Horsman. This ardent reformer was a terrible thorn in the sides of bishops and ecclesiastical dignitaries like the late reverend and noble Francis North, Earl of Guildford, who, as rector of St. Mary's, Southampton, received 3000*l.* a year, while he paid his curate 80*l.* The late Bishop of London was especially singled out for attack by Mr. Horsman. This venerable man kept insisting that his income was diminishing, in spite of the enormously increased value of what was known as the Bishop of London's estate in Paddington,—an estate estimated as certain to produce 100,000*l.* a year. Mr. Horsman asked "how was it that, after the erection of such an extent of handsome and apparently profitable buildings, covering an extent of 400 acres, the right reverend prelate having signed about 2000 leases, and those not let upon fines, but upon a steady and permanent rent, increasing as the buildings themselves increased,— how happens it, I ask, that in the case of episcopal estates the ordinary rules of cause and effect are completely reversed, and a town property becomes less valuable the more it is built upon, and that when a large tract of land is turned from a waste into a city, and its value calculated by the square foot instead of the square acre, the income should fall as the rental increases? I cannot explain it. It is impossible to doubt the fidelity of an episcopal return. All I can say is, What an idea does it give of episcopal management!" Such speeches were unpleasant; the more so because they were unanswerable. But they did an immense amount of good. They strengthened the Church in spite of itself. In 1850 the Ecclesiastical Commission was reconstructed. Waste and mismanagement of Church funds are now the exception. Prior to 1863, benefices with 10,000 inhabitants had been endowed up to 300*l.* a year. In 1864 the Commissioners augmented to the same amount benefices with 8000 souls; and then they did the same for districts which had between 6000 and 8000 inhabitants. They then proceeded to endow in a similar manner the income of every benefice in public patronage the population of which is not less than 5000. Mr. Horsman and the Whigs were in reality the true friends of the Church.

We have said Mr. Horsman entered Parliament in 1836. In 1841 he became a Lord of the Treasury, and in 1856 was Chief Secretary for Ireland. This appears to have been the turning-point in his career. He resigned his office in 1857, because, according to his own account, he had nothing to do, or, as others say, because he contrived to offend most of the Irish M.P.'s with whom he came in contact. Since that time more than one Liberal administration has been formed, and on the Treasury Benches have been seated M.P.'s with neither Mr. Horsman's abilities, experience, nor Parliamentary position. Such a state of things Mr. Horsman does not approve of. Stroud then returned him as a Liberal, yet he found fault with all the measures proposed by the Liberals. Gradually he has been receding from his party. The leading measures of that party since Mr. Horsman's retirement have been Mr. Gladstone's budgets, the French Treaty, and the Franchise Bill. All these measures have been the subject of his studied invective and hostile criticism. Surely he is very unfortunate in his Parliamentary position! He is a man of first-rate abilities—he is an admirable speaker, but he is independent and unpopular. "It is folly," said Mr. Wellesley Pole to Plumer Ward, "to attempt to be a power in the House of Commons without a party." Of this folly Mr. Horsman is guilty.

Mr. Horsman, when he spoke, generally secured a seat below the gangway on the Liberal side on the front bench. Personally, he is a fine-looking man, tall, thin, and gentlemanly—his hair is dark, and his whiskers are streaked with gray (he was born as far back as 1807), and his face does not denote good temper; but his style is polished—his command of language extensive—his voice clear and his delivery striking and impressive. I should think his speeches are carefully and conscientiously prepared. He speaks like a man who respects himself and his audience. You may differ from Mr. Horsman, you may think him unduly critical and captious; but you can hear him. The House looks upon him as one of its leading orators, and the Conservatives, at any rate, applaud his speeches. Indeed, it is to them Mr. Horsman must mainly trust; the neutral party of which he aims to be the head, as yet has no existence. The head is there, but the tail has yet to come. Neutrality in politics is an impossibility; you must either advance or recede. Nations, like individuals, can never stand still.

Little more need be said of Mr. Horsman, save that he was educated at Rugby, that he was called to the Scottish bar in 1832, and that he married in 1841, Charlotte, daughter of the late J. C. Ramsden, Esq., M.P. We would acknowledge that he has done the

State some service. Gratitude is graceful; and Liberal and Dissenting Stroud, in supporting Mr. Horsman, showed that constituents are not forgetful, and are slow to take offence. There was exhibited towards him a generous forbearance, to which, however, Mr. Horsman found at length there was an unmistakeable limit. It is well to be an orator, but deeds are better than words; even household voters have sense enough to know that. Another thing also is clear to them now—that is at the best but a doubtful liberality which expends itself in obstructing, and as far as possible defeating, the only possible existing Liberal Administration. The British public will never cordially take to Reformers who vote against Reform; to clergymen who write "Essays and Reviews;" to bishops who demonstrate that our old Hebrew Bible is not to be trusted.

WILLIAM S. LINDSAY, ESQ.

A good man of business need not necessarily be a bad politician. In England trade and commerce have been looked upon almost as ignoble; only a landed proprietor could be a true gentleman, and contained the raw material out of which might be formed the accomplished orator or the heaven-born statesman. This idea has been latterly somewhat rudely shattered by the severe logic of facts, but it is a fallacy which exists still in a mild form, especially in agricultural districts. Hence is it that even in our time the regular red tapists are very much annoyed at a gigantic innovation introduced when Lord Palmerston had become Premier. They were angry that a man of business should have been sent to Paris to negotiate a commercial treaty, and they were still more angry when an extensive shipowner was reported to have gone to America to try and get better terms from the American Government for our shipping than hitherto they had been able to do. This complaint might be well founded if our distinguished and noble diplomatists were well acquainted with commercial affairs. As notoriously they are not, there can be no harm on special occasions in calling in the aid of men well acquainted with particular subjects. Surely Mr. Cobden knew something about the manufactures of Lancashire and Yorkshire, and Mr. Lindsay ought to know something about ships. Our great statesmen may cram for a specific object, but knowledge so acquired is of very doubtful value. The success of the late much-lamented Mr. Wilson was chiefly owing to the fact that he was practically, not theoretically, a man of business. For a similar reason Lord Cowley was glad enough to call in the aid of Mr. Cobden, and Mr. Lindsay set sail for the United States.

A few years since the name of Mr. Lindsay was put very prominently before the public. There was a time when the Administrative Reform Association was very popular, and was not Mr. Lindsay one of its greatest men? There was a time when emigration was in vogue, and did not Mr. Lindsay's ships form the bridge by which the ocean was passed, and El Dorado, as some idly dreamt, won? And when the ruined British shipowners—the men who amassed fabulous wealth by the trade they denounced as irretrievably ruined—were moving heaven and earth for a return, in some form or other, of Protection, they could find no language bad enough or harsh enough for Mr. Lindsay, because he would not join them in what he deemed their mistaken course. It was almost amusing, at the City meeting held a few years ago, after Mr. Lindsay had tried to get a word in on behalf of Free Trade, to hear Duncan Dunbar recal the word "friend" he had applied to Mr. Lindsay ("a man who could utter such sentiments as Mr. Lindsay had, he," Mr. Dunbar, "could never, never call his friend"). One was reminded of the famous scene in the House of Commons, when the aged Burke renounced for ever the friendship of his pupil and admirer, Fox.

In the year 1816, in a humble station of life, Mr. Lindsay was born at Ayr—that town dear to all admirers of Burns for its

"Honest men and bonnie lasses."

At six, the future ship-owner was left an orphan; and, when only fifteen years of age, he commenced his career, leaving home with only three shillings and sixpence in his pocket, to push his fortunes as a sea boy. He worked his passage to Liverpool by trimming coals in the coal-hole of a steamer. Arrived in that great commercial emporium, he found himself friendless and destitute, and seven long days passed before he was able to find employment. Let those who tell us that the poor man has no chance in this country—that, be he industrious, moral, and intelligent, he can never rise—that capital is a hard task-master, and holds its victims in worse than American slavery—learn, then, that during this time young Lindsay experienced the most abject poverty—that he was reduced to the necessity of sleeping in the sheds and streets of Liverpool, after eating nothing but what he begged for! At length he was fortunate enough to be engaged as cabin-boy on board a West India-man. Frightful were his hardships even then; but his heart never failed him, and in three years he rose to be second mate. The following year he was first mate, and in his nineteenth year became captain of the *Olive Branch*. By this time he had had enough of the sea. He had suffered one shipwreck; had had both legs and one arm broken; had been cut down by a sabre stroke in a hostile encounter in the Persian Gulf. So we are not surprised to find Mr. Lindsay in 1841 agent for the Castle Eden Coal Company. In 1845 he removed to London, and laid the foundation of that extensive business which made him a competent authority on all matters connected with his craft, and which entitled him to rank with the merchant princes of the metropolis.

Mr. Lindsay, in the midst of his upward struggle from poverty to wealth, sedulously sought his own mental improvement. Instead of wasting his spare evening hours in dissipation and idleness, or even harmless recreation, he diligently sought to make up for the defects of his early education, and to acquire that knowledge which in his case emphatically became power. The result was he soon acquired popularity as a writer, especially by his important work on "Our Navigation and Mercantile Laws." His next step was to get into Parliament. He contested Newport, Monmouthshire, in April, and Dartmouth in July, 1852. In March, 1854, after a severe struggle, by a majority of seventeen, he was returned for Tynemouth. In 1857 he was re-elected without opposition, and of Tynemouth he continued the representative till disabled by ill health. In every sense of the word he was a free trader. At the City meeting already referred to, he claimed the right to address the meeting in opposition to the resolution, as he could not allow it to go forth that the distress of the shipping interest was attributable to the existing system of maritime commerce, or the repeal of the navigation laws. The resolution and the memorial presented to the Crown were fallacious. He was favourable to reciprocity; but not enforced reciprocity, because that was protection in its worst form. It would revive the war of classes and the system of commerce which prevailed in the time of Cromwell. Mr. Lindsay's opponents may be right, but the extent of our shipping under free trade points to an opposite conclusion.

In size, Mr. Lindsay resembles Mr. Cobden, nor is he unlike him in shape; but he has a redder face, darker hair, and his voice is of that rich Doric of which a little is quite enough. Pure Scotch is very pleasant to read in the *Noctes Ambrosianæ*, but one soon tires of it in the House of Commons. It is very probable Mr. Lindsay would have remained an obscure man in that illustrious assembly, had not the Crimean war broken out, and our great heads of departments completely broken down. Mr. Lindsay was fortunate in finding that the weakest part of the whole affair was precisely that which he knew most about. Accordingly he exposed Government blunders in many ways, and became all at once a notoriety. He was known to speak as one having authority. Had he not originally been a cabin-boy, and now had he not at his command a fleet almost as extensive as that belonging to the Lords of the Admiralty! Heads of departments trembled, for they knew Mr. Lindsay understood his own business; whereas, they could make neither head nor tail of theirs. The *Times* admitted Mr. Lindsay to be an authority, and the House of Commons, always ready to hear a man when he has something to say, listened when he spoke; strangers stared over the gallery, to the great disgust of the doorkeepers, who in vain bawled out, "Keep your seats, gentlemen!" when Mr. Lindsay was on his legs. In the lobby he was pointed at as the man who was to save the State; and when Old Drury opened its wide doors for the administrative reformers, and Mr. Lindsay was the attraction of the night, the multitudes who flocked in showed how easily and completely Mr. Lindsay had achieved an extensive fame. Yet Mr. Lindsay was no orator—no statesman—no scholar, with wise saws and modern instances. Burke would have turned from him with disgust, and Sheridan would have swallowed a bottle of wine in the attempt to elaborate, with regard to him, what he would have endeavoured to pass in society as some extempore jokes. A temporary emergency gave to Mr. Lindsay a temporary importance; he said the right thing at the right time; he had to perform the very easy task of picking holes in a very rotten coat, and he performed it easily. More than this he never attempted. As it is, he has been fortunate in life, more than most men, and need not be ungrateful or rail at the gods if he have not the privilege of being called to the Privy Council or of dying a Cabinet Minister.

Nor is this to be regretted. A man is happier without the responsibilities of office. Still I like to point out to the illustrious stranger as imperial senators men who talk provincial English; I like to say, Sir, thirty years back that man was a ragged boy; he was lucky; he got on the right track; he made a fortune, and the people of this country, out of their deference to wealth combined with talent, chose him as a representative.

Let me here demonstrate the evanescent nature of reputations. Except when ship-owners are clamorous, Mr. Lindsay is forgotten.

> "Oh no, we never mention him,
> His name is never heard."

His life devoted to commerce, his intellect sharpened, yet did not make him a statesman. The shipping question over, he sank into the usual track of ordinary M.P.'s; in an assembly of educated gentlemen, of logical reasoners, of trained rhetoricians, he was on general subjects easily distanced, and, by his own confession, was easily duped into voting for the Derby Reform Bill, in the belief that it was to have been all that the most ardent reformer could desire. It is not wealth—not success in life—not a lucky speculation, that can compensate for the liberal views and opinions, which, it is true, education does not invariably supply, but which rarely exist without it. In an assembly which ought to be as eminent for its genius and talent and statesmanship as it is now lamentably the reverse, we want something more even than practical men.

THE RT. HON. JAMES WHITESIDE.*

I CANNOT understand the use of long sermons, or long speeches. I suppose the House of Commons can. For instance, let us take the Kars debate. Lord Palmerston confessed—what every one knew—that Lord

* Since made an Irish judge.

Stratford de Redcliffe was very much to blame; that he is an obstinate, irascible old gentleman, with a laudable hatred to Russia, and an intense love of bullying; that he fancied he had 7000*l.* a year for the sake of playing the Bashaw on a grand scale; and that it was high time he were ordered home. Why, then, for three nights did people keep on reiterating this, or making long speeches to which no one listened, and repeating points of which every one was convinced? One reason—and the chief one—was this: the House is an old-fashioned assembly, and acts according to precedent. People made long speeches, and got very red in the face, and indulged in pompous declamation, and were always plunging the country into a crisis in the days of Pitt and Fox, so why should not Britons do so now? are they not Britons? and "Britons never, never, never will be slaves." Unfortunately M.P.'s forget the days of Pitt and Fox were the days of the slow coaches, when a man was a week or a fortnight going from Edinburgh to London, and made his will first. These are the days of Hansoms and electric telegraphs—of the steam-ship and the railway, and the thoughts that shake mankind.

Again, this is as much a lawyer-ridden as it is a priest-ridden country. What the curate—starched, lean, and leaden-eyed—is to the weak-minded females of Putney and Hampstead, the lawyers are to the rest of the House of Commons—a terror by night and a plague by day. Unfortunately for the country, almost all our places are given to barristers, and therefore the barristers must make speeches, good, bad, often—chiefly—indifferent, or they will not get Government places. As they have tongues to sell, they must let the Government have a taste of their quality; so the House wastes its time, and the strongest constitutions give way. Mr. John Bright was seriously hurt by his parliamentary attendance; Mr. Blackett, one of the most promising young men in the House, not long since died ere his prime, thoroughly worn out. Will the House never subside into short speeches and common sense? I fear not, so long as the constituencies return gentlemen of the long robe. I read somewhere a tale of a French opera performer who visited Constantinople, and had the honour of performing before the ruler of the Ottomans. With Oriental gravity, the Sultan looked and smiled, and made no sign. The Frenchman exerted himself to the utmost; his pirouetting was extraordinary, indeed terrific, if not almost sublime. The performance over, the Sultan beckoned the performer. The latter drew near, expecting as the reward of his unparalleled agility, the shawls of Cashmere, the silks of Persia, the jewels of Golconda, possibly the revenues of a province. Gravely smoking his chibouque, said the Sultan, "I have seen So-and-so and So-and-so (naming one operatic star after another), but I have never yet seen any one who perspired as much as you." The tale may be mythical, nevertheless it has a true flavour. The Sultan is the

British House of Commons; the French operatic performer is Mr. Whiteside. I should imagine, when he speaks, no one perspires so much as the member for the University of Dublin. I am sure he ought to do so, for he is the longest and loudest speaker in the House. Lord Palmerston never said a wittier thing than when, in the Kars debate, he assured the hon. member that all who saw his speech would consider it as highly creditable to his physical powers.

As a party man Mr. Whiteside is very useful. Occasionally he makes a blunder, as he did in that Kars debate, which, after engrossing three nights, ended in smoke, and rather aided than damaged the Government; but I imagine there are few more useful or ready gentlemen on his side of the House. Somehow or other, an Irishman seems naturally a thorn in the sides of the Saxon; and in Ireland party spirit exists in a degree of which we on this side of the Irish Channel can form no idea. In a parliamentary *mêlée*, no one is so indispensable as an Irishman; he lays about him thoroughly; with him, evidently the affair is no child's play; he has an enviable command of very expressive adjectives, rendered still more expressive by means of his brogue, which, however educated he may be, he finds it impossible utterly to shake off; and, as I fear there is a great deal of jobbery in Irish politics, he has very often on his side the advantage which every man has when he happens to be in the right. This fervour is natural and to the manner born.

Ireland is famed for faction fights, and a party is but a faction on a larger scale. How fierce and fanatic Irishmen can be we have seen exemplified in the conduct of the Orangemen to the Prince of Wales while in Canada, and in such meetings as that of the Religious Propagation Society at Down, when the Bishop was almost kicked out of the chair and the rector of the parish seated in his place. It is in this fervour that we must seek the cause of the success of Irishmen in parliament. Sheridan and Burke, in the palmy days of parliamentary eloquence, are splendid specimens of this; nor must we forget Canning or Grattan, Sheil, or O'Connell, or Plunket, all names indicative of great oratorical power, and of men who achieved great parliamentary success. An Irish writer tells us that "the fighting age in Ireland is from sixteen to sixty," and I may add that this is true as far as the House of Commons is concerned. It is true we have no Irishmen so young as sixteen, but we have them older than sixty, and the most ancient of these scents a battle from afar, and rushes to it as the war-horse of the Book of Job.

Dod tells me that James Whiteside, son of the late Rev. William Whiteside, and brother of the Rev. Dr. Whiteside, Vicar of Scarborough, was born at Delgany, county of Wicklow, 1806; educated at the University of Dublin, where he graduated M.A. with honours, and the London University College law classes, where he took honours. He was called to the bar in Ireland in 1830, and is a Queen's Counsel; was Solicitor-General for Ireland from March till December, 1852; author of works on Italy and Ancient Rome; a Conservative in favour of a grant to the Church Education Society—rather an obscure definition of a man's political opinions; first returned for Enniskillen, April, 1851. But I must point him out in the House of Commons. You will see him on the first bench of the Opposition, sitting somewhat near the end furthest from the Speaker. Of course he is bald. In England no man attains distinction until he has reached an age when time begins to tell upon the face or figure. Our young poets are middle-aged, and our rising novelists are compelled to resort to wigs. We have young-looking statesmen, but then they are lords. We English are wonderfully afraid of talent in political life. As much as possible we fence round place and power, and put up "No admittance except to the aristocracy;" and when a man with brains does force his way in, it is generally when he has become almost worn out in the struggle. The only exception is that in favour of lawyers; as the chances are that a lawyer, from the force of habit, becomes attached to some party or other, and thus gets a start which, if he be clever, he will be sure not to lose. Mr. Whiteside won his laurels by his defence of O'Connell, and, on the strength of that defence, at first seemed rather inclined—if I may be allowed such a phrase—to ride the high horse. Latterly, however, he has assumed less, and gained a respectable position. There was a time when lawyers were the champions of popular right, and the dread of all who assumed a despotic power. "Who," says Mr. Townsend, "took the lead in those memorable discussions which established the freedom of his Majesty's poor Commons, and confirmed a wavering House in their resolution, but Sir Edward Coke, Selden, and Lyttleton? Who but these great constitutional lawyers managed the memorable conference with the Lords which preceded the Bill of Rights? Who drew up that Magna Charta but Sergeant Glanville, and Pym, and Hyde? At the Restoration, the cautious wisdom of Sir Matthew Hale would have fettered the King with conditions that might have saved his reign from alternating between anarchy and despotism. Whose voice more loud than that of Maynard, Sawyer, Somers, and Williams in denouncing the tyranny of James?—whose suggestions so valuable in establishing the happy Revolution? Henry IV. on one occasion called a parliament from which he excluded lawyers; old Coke tells us, 'The prohibition that no apprentice or man following the law shall be chosen, made the parliament fruitless, and never a good law passed thereat, and called the Lack-learning Parliament.'" Mr. Whiteside does not belong exactly to this class. He is undoubtedly too much of a party man, and out of his party he will never rise. The most nefarious characters—of course, I speak politically—in this country are the Irish Orangemen; men whose advent in the Green Isle was a result of victory, whose continuance there has been a curse; who cared not that the nation rotted away—that the people grew up in heathenism, that the land was ravaged with civil war, so long as they grew rampant on the patronage and privilege doled out to their class. It is not in Ireland as it was; emigration, cholera, the potato famine, the Encumbered Estates Court, the growth of common sense in the English Cabinet where Ireland is concerned, have somewhat diminished the extent and the frightful consequences of what was called Protestant ascendancy in the Sister Isle; but the habit of thought engendered by that fierce partisanship still lives, and in the person of the Right Hon. James Whiteside still too often finds utterance also, in what should be the most enlightened assembly in the world.

As an orator Mr. Whiteside seems to have chiefly studied Demosthenes' advice as to action, and literally to have adopted it. It is all action with him. He has his countrymen's great command of language, which is the command, as Whately remarks, of a rider over his horse when it is running away with him. His language is not pregnant with meaning, so as to afford delight and instruction when the occasion which called it into existence has passed away; nor is it sharp and well defined, so as to hit hard home; nor does he descend to plain, unadorned sense like

Cobden, or rise into a sublime personality like Disraeli. He has more the appearance of a lawyer strutting his hour upon the stage, seeking to make mountains of hills, to invest the most obscure incidents with the most important consequences, to keep the truth of the question altogether out of sight, and to be reckless of everything so that he succeeds in making out a case. I fear Mr. Whiteside forgets the advice of a celebrated countryman. "When I told Curran," says Moore, "of the superabundant floridness of the speech, he said to me, 'My dear Tom, it will never do for a man to turn painter merely upon the strength of having a pot of colours, unless he knows how to lay them on.'"

JOHN STUART MILL, ESQ.

In his preface to his speeches on Reform, lately published, Mr. Lowe tells us there are three ways of treating political subjects, the theological, the metaphysical, and the inductive or experimental. The doctrine of the divine right of kings is an instance of the first kind of treatment; the argument so much relied on at Reform meetings in favour of extended suffrage, and the writings of James and John Mill, are examples of the second; and discussions of the House of Commons on almost every other subject except Reform, and the arguments against it, are examples of the third. This classification is correct, and of the class to which he belongs Mr. Mill is the distinguished head. *A priori*, it was not in one of the official class that you would have expected such a phenomenon. "On the whole," wrote poor Haydon, after he had been painting the Reform Ministers in 1842, "public men shrunk from discussion. They are so occupied with the fate of nations and their political relations, that truth even, on other points, seems unworthy investigation. Physical inquiry they detest, matters of taste they shun, religion they consider only as an engine of State; and I do not think much extension of knowledge on general principles is to be acquired by intercourse with them. They are interesting from their rank and occupation, but a habit of having such mighty interests hanging on their decision generates a contempt for abstract deduction, and an indisposition to enter into matters of literature, arts, and morals." It is true Mr. Mill was not a public man in the same sense as Lords Grey, or Brougham, or Palmerston; but, like them, he was in office, and at the East India House, as well as elsewhere, circumlocution reigned supreme.

It is said circumstances make the man. In Mr. Mill's case it was clear that he was doomed to be the greatest philosopher of the day. His father, Mr. James Mill, says a writer in the *Westminster Review*, "was hardly less effective in conversation than by his pen. His colloquial fertility on philosophical subjects, his power of discussing himself and stimulating others to discuss, his ready responsive inspirations through all the shifts and windings of a sort of Platonic dialect—all these accomplishments were to those who knew him even more impressive than what he composed for the press. When to this we add a strenuous character, earnest convictions, and single-minded devotion to truth, with an utter disdain of mere paradox, it may be conceived that such a man exercised powerful intellectual ascendancy over younger minds. Several of those who enjoyed his society—men now at or past the maturity of life, and some of them in distinguished positions, remember and attest with gratitude such ascendancy in their own cases. . . . . When a father such as we have described, declining to send his son either to school or college, constituted himself schoolmaster from the beginning, and performed that duty with laborious solicitude—when, besides full infusion of modern knowledge, the forcing process applied by the Platonic Socrates to the youthful Theætetus, was administered by Mr. James Mill continuously, and from an earlier age, to a youthful mind not less pregnant than that of Theætetus—it would be surprising if the son thus trained had not reached even a higher eminence than his father." The fruit borne by Mr. John Stuart Mill has been worthy of the culture bestowed, and, adds the writer of the article in question, the "Examination of Sir William Hamilton's Philosophy," "is at once his latest and his ripest product." Martinus Scriblerus we know failed to teach his son logic. He could never get him to risc to the abstract idea of a Lord Mayor. The unfortunate youth never could conceive of one apart from his fur cap and gold chain. Mr. James Mill had more success.

Trained by his father in the school of abstract philosophy, the speculations connected therewith have absorbed in the son the attention of a life. In the regions in which Mr. Mill has gained his laurels we may not attempt to follow. As a writer in the *Westminster Review,* and as an original thinker, Mr. Mill had long become distinguished ere he left the seclusion of the study for the bustle and rough work of the political arena. Perhaps it was his "Political Economy" that made his name universally familiar. We had all heard of the fairy tales of science, but certainly it was not in the department of it connected with statistics and the pursuit of wealth that we anticipated any such revelations. Mr. Mill's work appeared, however, and so clear was the style, so logical the arrangement, so generous was the living spirit of humanity by which it was inspired, that people began to wonder however they could have considered the speculations of political economy dull and devoid of interest. Other works succeeded, such as that "On Liberty," "Considerations on Representative Government," dealing equally with abstract principles, and equally warm and human in their treatment of them. The general public avoided, it may be, his great work on "Logic," his "Dissertations and Discussions," his "Examination of Sir William Hamilton's Philosophy;" they were left to the scholar and the divine, but his other writings, as we have said, gained for him popularity and power. He became the head of a party; the young and the enthusiastic rallied round him; Westminster, in a noble burst of enthusiasm, made him her M.P., and immediately after, the students of a Scotch University, in a similar fit of enthusiasm, conferred their Rectorship on him. In neither case was the confidence of his friends misplaced. We have rarely read an abler address than that which Mr. Mill delivered at St. Andrew's. His success in the House of Commons justified the hopes of his friends. It did more. It taught the sceptics and the sneerers, that in debate a philosopher can be a man, as ready and as self-possessed as a practical man. At his first rising Mr. Mill had missed the right pitch for his voice, and his "stupid party" anticipated his failure. On the second occasion he was better heard, and their discomfiture was so much the more complete. The traditions of the House tell us, to succeed in it a man must enter it young. Mr. Mill, born in 1806, was bald and middle-aged, yet at once he got the chatty conversational style in which the House rejoices, and succeeded in convincing some and amusing all. It is a rare triumph at the same time to be witty as well as wise.

Philosophers, you may depend upon it, are much alike all the world over. The orator for the million, be he a Spurgeon or a Daniel O'Connell, is bound to be fat and fleshy. The abstract thinker is of a different temperament and frame. Mr. Mill is of a light complexion—is long and thin; his clear blue eye is deep sunk, as if its gaze had been rather internal than external. He has a brisk, genial appearance, and is always neatly and scrupulously dressed in black. His appearance is different from that of any other member. His is not the horsey look of some, nor has he the business air of others, still less does he affect the style of a man of fashion. Altogether, he seems out of his element on his seat on the third row below the gangway on the Opposition side. The men around seem of a coarser and less refined nature. There is a *genus loci* connected with the House, of hard drinkers, mighty sportsmen, big blusterers, eager partisans. You would never expect to find a philosopher there, yet there is Mr. Mill; and there is not a more constant attendant, or one more able or willing to take his part in the debates when the opportunity occurs. Those acquainted with Mr. Mill's writings will be prepared to find in him a fearlessness in the application of his opinions which is perfectly refreshing. He has a scorn of dulness which renders him impervious to its attack. It is not the unpopularity of a conclusion that will force him to shrink from embracing it. He follows where reason leads the way. Satisfied of his logic, it is nothing to him that timid men forsake him as Churchmen shrink from heresy. It is said of Satan on his voyage in search of our earth—

> "At last his sail-broad vans
> He spreads for flight, and in the surging smoke
> Uplifted spurns the ground; thence many a league,
> As in a cloudy chair ascending, rides
> Audacious."

And thus Mr. Mill careers along in the world of thought, armed at all points, ready to hear as well as to talk, and defend as well as attack, a match for the hardest and direst and most self-possessed on the hostile benches before him.

CHAPTER VIII.

MEMBERS WHO HAVE BECOME PEERS.

LORD JOHN RUSSELL.*

IN 1811 Professor Playfair wrote to Miss Berry, "I shall request to be permitted to introduce Lord John Russell to you. He is one of the most promising young men I ever saw." In 1813 this "promising young man" was returned to parliament as M.P. for Tavistock, and became one of England's foremost men. Had he been a very unpromising young man he would have been M.P. for Tavistock all the same. Lord John Russell won his laurels as a political reformer, yet in his early youth he was not a very ardent one. In 1819 Sir Francis Burdett—the leader of the then Radical party—made his annual motion on the question of Parliamentary Reform. In the course of the debate on it, Lord John said, "I agree in the propriety of disfranchising such boroughs as are notoriously corrupt, and I will give my consent to any measure that will restrict the duration of Parliament to three years. I cannot, how-

* Raised to the peerage as Earl Russell in 1861.

ever, pledge myself to support a measure that goes the length of proposing an inquiry into the general state of representation, because such an inquiry is calculated to throw a slur upon the representation of the country, and to fill the minds of the people with vague and indefinite alarms." His lordship at the end of the year unfolded his Reform Bill. "I come now," he said, "to the resolutions which I shall have the honour to propose; the two first declare that when a borough is accused of gross and notorious bribery and corruption, it shall cease to send members to Parliament, and that a great town or county shall enjoy the rights it has forfeited. On these heads I have nothing to add. The third declares that it is the duty of this House to consider of further means to detect and prevent corruption in the election of members of Parliament. . . . . The last resolution declares the opinion of the House that the borough of Grampound ought to be disfranchised." Of course his lordship was in a miserable minority. In a few years after, the proposer of this milk-and-water scheme, Lord John Russell, was at the head of a victorious Reform party—a party that wrested Reform from a frightened aristocracy and a reluctant monarch; and there was a general impression gone forth that a grateful nation would elect him dictator for life. Since then he has been said more than once to have politically extinguished himself—a phrase used by thoughtless writers, who forget that you cannot extinguish a certain amount of territory in a territorial system of government. At the present time his lordship is not decidedly unpopular. As Secretary for Foreign Affairs, coming after the Earl of Malmesbury, and representing English sympathy with the cause of Italian nationality, he not long since had a fair chance of becoming, in some quarters, a popular man again.

How has Lord John Russell sunk so low? The inquiry is not uninteresting. In the first place, we think the essential aristocratic nature of the man has something to do with it. To be genial is to be popular. Lord John Russell cannot be genial. There is an icy tone in his voice and glitter in his eye; you may work for him—you may write for him—you may canvass for him—you may shout his praises till you are hoarse—and from his lordship you get civil acknowledgment, scarcely that. It is true his lordship is a liberal statesman, but in much the same manner as the Spartan Ephor, who, when charged by his wife with having abandoned half the privileges of his children, replied that he had done so in order that he might preserve for them the other half. Lord John Russell was born a political reformer—just as he is a Protestant. It would never do for the inmates of Woburn Abbey to be catholicized, and no name is so sacred to the Whigs as that of Russell. Then again, his lordship has made grievous blunders—has alienated his friends and given encouragement to his foes. Then again, the days of strong government, and of the sway of individuals, as regards the

Whigs, is gone. We have leaders, but where are the led? We have officers, but where are the rank and file? Pitt had a majority to his mind. The way in which the country gentlemen, and rotten borough proprietors and representatives, followed that jolly old model Whig, Sir Robert Walpole, into the lobby of the House of Commons, was enough to remind a certain gentleman who shall be nameless,

> "How Noah and his creeping things
> Went up into the Ark."

Sir Robert Peel, like a Colossus, bestrode the Protectionist Squires, whom he changed into Free-traders; but these men belong to the past. Men have lost confidence in the judgment and tactics and wisdom of those whom they were wont to call their leaders. The individual allegiance to party of which our fathers boasted, exists no longer. Every man does that which is right in his own eyes. It was not so when his lordship served his political apprenticeship. Then, as the scion of the great Whig Duke, Lord John Russell had a right to expect public patronage and support, and he got it. The stage was clear; all that was requisite was a certain amount of industry. Everywhere the fable of the tortoise and the hare is realized, but nowhere more so than in the House of Commons. To a friend entering Parliament, Wilberforce said, "Attend to business, and do not seek occasions of display. If you have a turn for speaking, the proper time will come. Let speaking take care of itself. I never go out of the way to speak, but make myself acquainted with the business, and then if the debate passes my door, I step out and join it." We have a similar advice from a still greater man. When Sir George Murray attempted to excuse himself from taking office under the Duke of Wellington, on account of his inexperience in public speaking, "Pho, pho," said the Duke, "do as I do—say what you think, and don't quote Latin." In accordance with the advice of these men, did Lord John Russell commence his political career. Had he acted more closely in accordance with it, he would have been more successful. But when a second-rate man attempts the part of a first-rate man, we all know what must be the result. It is not then difficult to account for the occasional decline in popularity of Lord John Russell. It is a slander on the public to impute it to the fickleness of the people. The people are prone to idolatry, and a lord on the liberal side is irresistible. Any electioneering agent will tell you it is almost impossible to beat such a man. Lord John Russell especially has little reason to complain; the public have borne with him in the most patient manner; they have picked him out of the mud; they have washed him, and put clean things on him; they have patted him on the head, and bidden him be a good boy and try again. They have repeated these interesting processes over and over again: they have forgiven him seven times, and seem about to do so seventy times seven; yet Lord John is rarely popular. Indeed, it may be almost hinted that the whole career of England's constitutional and heroic statesman has been a mistake. Lord John is by birth the son of one duke and the brother of another. In his youth he associated with the Edinburgh Reviewers, and learnt the *quantum sufficit* of Liberal slang. He has been an unfortunate man through life —always hard up—always out of luck. He wrote a novel that did not sell—a history that no one would read. His philosophy was equally worthless, and his poetry—he wrote a drama—was (the word is harsh, but we really can find no other so fitting)—his poetry was positively damned. Thus abhorred by gods and men, he became a politician, and had a finger in that dainty dish, the Reform Bill, by which the people of England were most confoundedly deceived. The only thing that can be said of him positively is, as it may be said of the Great Bedford Flat, he has the questionable merit of being connected with the Bedford family. He belongs to the people as Johnson's friend Campbell belonged to the Church. "Campbell," said Johnson, "is a good man, a very good man. I fear he has not been inside of a church for many years, but he never passes one without taking his hat off. That shows, at least, that he has good principles." Lord John omits no opportunity of professing proper attachment to the people, whilst the whole course of his political life makes that profession doubtful. He serves them in the same way as that in which Scrub serves the ladies in the farce when commissioned by them to obtain information as to the stranger they had seen at church. He tells them he has a whole packet of news. "In the first place," says he, "I inquired who the gentleman was? They told me he was a stranger. Secondly, I asked what the gentleman was? They answered and said, that they never saw him before. Thirdly, I inquired what countryman he was? They replied, 'twas more than they knew. Fourthly, I demanded whence he came? Their answer was, they could not tell. And fifthly, I asked whither he went? and they replied, they knew nothing of the matter." To the people, thus clamorous to reform, Lord John gives as much welcome intelligence as Scrub did to the ladies. He has a whole packet of reform and retrenchment, if they will but wait; but it it is not meant for use. It is never ready when it is wanted. He is a Whig, a Reformer, a friend of the people, an advocate of progress. He does not deny but that further reforms might be made—he is very indignant at being suspected of finality; yet somehow or other, it did happen that every attempt made in that direction met with the most unscrupulous opposition of Lord John and the party whom he represented. He did not think much of Mr. Cobden's plea for retrenchment, and arbitration instead of war. He had but a poor opinion of the ballot, he scornfully eschewed household suffrage, and the five points he could not abide. In the Palmerston administration his presence in the Cabinet was said to be a guarantee for carrying a Reform Bill. As usual, Lord

John is much too late. He would be a party to no reform when Hume and the rest were urging him to move with the times, and till quite recently he was placidly advising the people, often duped and disappointed by promises of a Reform Bill, their wisest plan was to Rest and be Thankful.

Again, through a long parliamentary life, Lord John has been little and spiteful, and troublesome in opposition. In his diary, Tom Moore wrote of his lordship, that "he was mild and sensible" on a particular occasion, but sometimes his lordship has been neither the one nor the other. Moore regretted that Lord John Russell "showed so little to advantage in society from his extreme taciturnity, and still more from his apparent coldness and indifference to what was said to him." This coolness and indifference, combined with no small opinion of himself, has often led his lordship into conduct which has made him very unpopular. When in this state, and expelled from office, he has not had strength of mind sufficient to lead him calmly to wait till the nation has called him back to the helm of state, but he has tried all sorts of contemptible manœuvres. Never can we forget the appropriation clause which he carried to unseat Sir Robert Peel, and then abandoned when in power. Lord John called "the repeal of the corn laws mischievous, absurd, impracticable, and unnecessary;" yet his Edinburgh letter in favour of their abolition was hastily written and published when he found that his great rival, Sir

Robert Peel, was about to take steps in the direction of Free Trade. In his opposition to the budget of Sir Robert Peel, it is questionable whether the force of meanness could further go. Then what a mischievous attempt, on his lordship's part, to acquire popularity was the Durham Letter, and how fatal the rebound. Lord John's "spirited letter" certainly led the nation to open its eyes. That a Minister who had long been suspected of designing to endow the Roman Catholic Church should have written such a letter, was very surprising; but that after writing that letter he should have cooled down; that after roaring like a lion he should have aggravated his voice till it was little better than a whisper, was more surprising still. The old adage of "much cry and little wool" was never more ludicrously realized. In the name of the prophet, exclaimed his lordship, with pompous strut and voice,— In the name of the prophet—figs! The contrast between his letter and his legislation—between his speech and his bill—was as wide as that between Philip drunk and Philip sober; or as that between

> "Sappho at her toilet's greasy task,
> With Sappho fragrant at an evening mask."

If Popery were what Lord John said in his speech it was—a curse in every country in which it exists; and if legislation can grapple with it,—then the bill was delusive and a mockery. Lord John, in his speech, complained of synodical action. The bill left that untouched. The greatest condemnation of Lord

John's bill was Lord John's speech. Disraeli could say nothing stronger against it than what his lordship himself implied. The truth was, to gain a little transient popularity, or to draw off public attention from the growing cry for further Financial and Parliamentary Reform, the First Minister of the Crown stooped to a line of conduct of which the veriest demagogue might have been ashamed. An intense anti-Catholic feeling was aroused. From almost every county and town—from almost every sect and class—petitions went forth expressing burning indignation at the foolish aggression of the Pope. To whatever an Englishman is indifferent, he is not to the growth of the power which in time past lit up the fires of Smithfield, or the *auto da fé's* of Goa and Madrid, or which, even at the present day, condemns to the degradation of the gaol the lover of his country and his kind. Under the influence of that feeling, men steeped in everlasting infamy—such as Titus Oates, or Sacheverell, or Lord George Gordon—have strutted on the stage the heroes of an hour. A wise Minister would have paused ere that feeling was rashly excited. A wise Minister would have considered his power of controlling the storm ere he had bidden it ride forth. A wise Minister, before he put himself in collision with a system, the influence of which exists in every land, would have kept for himself a way of coming out of the strife victorious. Lord John Russell signally failed in doing this. All that he did by his bill was to proclaim a weakness it had been easy to conceal, and to put in bolder relief the magnitude of Papal pretences and the littleness of Ministerial legislation. His letter was a sham. He but touched upon the surface of the evil, and that in a manner not difficult to evade. In all its intensity, the evil remained the same. "With our pleasant vices we make the whips with which we scourge ourselves." That Ecclesiastical Titles Bill sealed Lord John's career as Premier. To retain office he had to descend from that lofty position. Under the Aberdeen Administration he committed a similar mistake. A public system had broken down; a magnificent army had wasted away. By many an English fireside was it told how in that winter there had been, far away, a tragedy done unequalled in the worst days of official mismanagement, as criminal as any of the Walcheren and other forlorn efforts of the past. From one end of England to the other, wherever man met man, whether in the haunts of fashion or of business, whether at home or abroad, there were curses uttered, deep and loud, against the men responsible for these disasters. Parliament met; it was known that the first thing required would be the appointment of the Sebastopol Committee. Of course that was a vote of censure on the existing administration; but instead of calmly awaiting the vote, and endeavouring to defend himself and his colleagues, Lord John had the littleness to abandon his post, and to cast stones at the men with whom he had sat at the council board. Again, in his haste to appear before the world, he rushed to Vienna, there still further to be duped and rendered ridiculous. That his lordship, as he grows older, does not grow wiser, is clear from his having had recourse to his old tactics up to the time of his leaving the Lower House. Reform was a matter of such vital importance that it could not be trusted in the hands of the Derby Cabinet; only Lord John Russell could deal with such a delicate subject. Lord John moved his memorable resolutions. Lords Palmerston and Russell forgot their ancient feuds and swore eternal friendship; the liberal rank and file followed suit; the Derby administration was rejected; and as a practical result, reform was delayed till Lord Derby came into office again.

It may be asked, is his lordship's oratory of so fascinating a character as for a time to render the House of Commons blind to his many faults? By no means. Look at him marching into the lobby—frigid, dwarfed, and self-complacent. For such a man there can be no real enthusiasm on the part of those who know him. See him in the House—always equally cold and chilling, and civil to all around. Follow him to the platform and the hustings, he is the same repellant, unattractive Whig. But he has lived for the House of Commons, and the House is not ungrateful. To Lord John also is due the merit of having led the House efficiently in time past. In this respect his tact was only equalled by that of his great rival, Sir Robert Peel; and in knowledge of forms and precedents by many he was considered the superior of that distinguished man. There was really something grand in the aspect of the House under his leadership. It was a remarkable instance of the triumph of mind over matter. In a crowded House, at the close of a heated debate, you would see the smallest man in that great assembly advance to the table, and the noise of the House, and the murmur of many voices, was hushed and still; the Opposition became attentive; strangers would lean forward their heads; peers and diplomatists would hearken. Seemingly careless and slovenly, the speech would be found to contain the right amount of liberalism to go down with the back benches; parts would be elaborately polished, and sparkle with a quiet irony which the audience would not be slow to appreciate, nor reluctant to apply.

Lord John has much to contend with. His outward form is frail and weakly; his countenance sicklied over with the effects of solitary communing; his figure shrunk below the ordinary dimensions of humanity; his general air that of a meditative invalid. But within that feeble body is a spirit that knows not how to cower, an undaunted heart, an aspiring soul. His voice is weak, his accent drawling and provincial, his elocution broken, stammering, and uncertain, save in a few lucky moments, when his tongue seems unloosed, when he becomes logical, eloquent, and terse. Then is his right hand convulsively clenched, his head proudly thrown back, the outline of his face becomes rigid, and his dwarfed figure expands as if he were a giant. Lord John is sometimes very happy, as when, in his letter to the electors of Stroud, he declared that "the whisper of a faction shall not prevail against the voice of a nation;" or when, in answer to Sir Francis Burdett, who charged him with the cant of patriotism, he told the baronet there was also such a thing as the recant of patriotism. One of Lord John's most celebrated speeches is that known as the Aladdin Lamp Speech, delivered by his lordship in 1819, and which Sir Robert Peel read to the House during the debate on the Reform Bill, in 1831. "Old Sarum," said Lord John, "existed when Somers and the great men of the revolution established our government. Rutland sent as many members as Yorkshire, when Hampden lost his life in defence of the constitution. Are we then to conclude that Montesquieu praised a corrupt oligarchy? That Somers and the great men of that day expelled a king in order to set up a many-headed tyranny? That Hampden sacrificed his life for the interests of a borough-mongering faction? That the principles of the construction of this house are pure and worthy? If we should change the principles of our constitution, we should commit the folly of the servant in the story of Aladdin, who was deceived by the cry of "New lamps for old!' Our lamp is covered with dust and rubbish, but it has a magical power; it has raised up a smiling land, not bestrode with overgrown palaces, but covered with modest dwellings, every one of which contains a freeman enjoying equal protection with the proudest subject in the land. It has called into life all the busy creations of commercial prosperity. Nor, when men were to defend and illustrate their country, have such men been deficient. When the fate of the nation depended on the line of policy which she should adopt, there were orators of the highest degree placing in the strongest light the arguments for peace or war. When we decided upon war, we had nerves to gain us laurels in the field and wield our thunders on the sea. When again we returned to peace—the questions of internal policy, of education of the poor, of criminal law, found men ready to devote the most splendid of abilities to the well-being of the community. And shall we change an instrument, that has produced effects so wonderful, for a burnished and tinsel toy of modern manufacture? No; small as the remaining treasure of the constitution is, I cannot consent to throw it into the wheel for the chance of obtaining a prize in the lottery of revolution." Let me add, that in debate Lord John is always a gentleman; not merely are his sentences and phrases indicative of polish and refinement, but he is always courteous, never flippant, like Lord Palmerston, nor savage, like Mr. Disraeli.

His lordship had a seat in the House of Commons as far back as 1813; but he shows few signs of age. He is one of England's chiefs; and by his lofty bearing, and the sparkle in his eye, you would fancy he is quite aware of the fact. Reaumur, in his book on "England," describes his lordship: "A little man, with a refined and intelligent though not imposing air." A malicious Quarterly Reviewer, in a voluntary translation of the same passage, rendered it, "A little, sharp, cunning-looking man, with nothing of an imposing presence." I think both are wrong. Lord John Russell looks the aristocrat as much as any man I have seen. Up in the Strangers' Gallery, however, you lose this appearance, on account of the distance at which you are placed from his lordship. It is true he is seated on the Treasury Bench: but he sits with his chin buried in his bosom, his head buried in his hat, and all that you can really see, as he sits cross-legged, and with his arms across his breast, are his diminutive extremities. See, he rises to address the House. Slowly he lifts off his hat, advances to the table, crosses his arms, and, in a brogue somewhat provincial, and not very musical, says "Mr. Speaker." All at once the Babel of conversation, the shuffling, coughing, laughing, and talking, is a little hushed. He commences; it is an important question he has to answer, or an important declaration he has to make, and you may hear a pin drop. You hear a weak voice hammering and stammering at every four or five sentences, those sentences often most slovenly and inelegant in construction, and, at first, you wonder how a man, without figure, voice, delivery, or fluency, could become the leading orator of the House of Commons; but, as he goes on—as he courteously replies to one, and administers a sly sarcasm to another—as his little frame dilates, and his eye sparkles—as he warms, and the House with him, you will feel that the little man has more in him than at first appeared. Read the speech next morning, and you will find how closely to the point it was—how exactly calculated to the occasion—how it suited the atmosphere of the House, and then you must remember how cool and unruffled was the speaker, and what tact he displayed. In these latter respects Lord John has greatly shone, and has evinced a smartness of which you would not suspect him as you listen to his drawling tones, and witness his slovenly delivery.

In one of his numerous works, Lord John Russell says that the House of Commons, while it admires a man of genius, always gives its confidence to a man of character. It is on his character that Lord John takes his stand. Character, as we all know, is one of the most delusive phrases in the English language; one man may steal a sheep, while another may not look over a wall. Half the scoundrels that are tried at the Old Bailey are, like Redpath, and Sir John Paul, and others, men of good character. A good character is the *dernier ressort* of a man who has little or nothing else to recommend him. And Lord John Russell certainly has made no little capital out of his character, and that of the great family to whose history he adds another very interesting page. Herein is Lord John Russell's speciality. He takes his stand upon his character. He had a good character twenty or thirty years ago, and he reaps the benefit of it at this moment. "So long as your father sticks to that ugly wife of his, and goes regularly to church," said Erskine to the Prince of Wales, "he will always be popular;" and Lord John has gained much of his popularity in a similar way. What a man he is for public meetings! How familiar are Exeter Hall, and the Freemasons' Tavern, and the City of London Tavern, with his name. How amusing is that account Mrs. Stowe gives of her visit to his lordship at Pembroke Lodge. "We were received," she writes, "in the drawing-room by the young ladies. Two charming little boys came in, and a few moments after their father, Lord John. I had been much pleased with finding on the centre table a beautiful edition of the revered friend of my childhood, Dr. Watts's Songs, finely illustrated. I remarked to Lord John that it was the face of an old friend. He said it was presented to his little boys by their godfather, Sir George Grey. And when, taking one of these little boys on his knee, he asked him if he could repeat me one of his hymns, the whole thing seemed so New England-like that I began to feel myself quite at home."

"Private vices," says Mandeville, "are frequently public benefits." Is not the converse true, and are not private virtues public mischiefs? "George the Third's constancy to his wife and his shoulder of mutton," wrote Albany Fonblanque, in the palmy days of the *Examiner*, "his taste for regularity and simplicity, enabled him to plunge us into wasting, unjust, and unnecessary wars. Had he kept various concubines, and dined off French dishes at nine o'clock, the people would have had a lively perception of the depravity of his politics, and an intimate persuasion of their wrongs."

I confess that, to myself, Lord John Russell seems more an historical than a real flesh and blood at this day existing man. His was a name dear to the nation, and always received with delight, when the men and women of to-day played with dolls and marbles, and feasted on indigestible pastry. I remember well the almost idolatrous veneration with which he was worshipped by reformers, and that large and influential class, the Protestant Dissenters, whose unrighteous shackles, by means of the abolition of the Test and Corporation Acts, he had been the means of removing. In that era, Lord John was deemed the champion of what was much talked of then, civil and religious liberty all the world over.

> "We have changed (for worse or better?)
> Since the time of Charlemagne."

And I have lived to see the House of Commons grow restive under his leadership, his followers diminished, and the country, if not weary of, at any rate very indifferent to the man. I fear gratitude can never be a permanent state of the mind, unless, as in O'Connell's acceptation of the term, a sense of thankfulness for favours to come; or rather, that the law of humanity is, that when a man has done his work and taken his wages, he should trouble us no more. It is not the individual that makes revolutions. The age makes them, and merely honours an individual as an agent. We should have had Parliamentary Reform had Lord John Russell never lived; and the Test and Corporation Acts, and the Slave Trade, would have been swept away in a similar manner. These changes are made when the time for them has arrived. The statesman who carries them is in reality carried by them. He is merely the servant of the public, and translates into legislative enactment the wants, and wishes, and convictions of the age. Had Lord John Russell realized this truth, he would never have lost himself by talking of finality, as if in this world of eternal change finality could be predicated of any one thing. *Mors janua vitæ,* death is the gate to life, is true in politics; reform is a never-ending process. The old Whig view is different. It is the man who covers the land with plenty—who removes evil—who admits the *profanum vulgus* to a limited suffrage, and who reaps his reward in the blessings of ages yet to come. But to any man who looks at the core of things, who seeks to know the causes of what may seem revolutionary changes, and who remembers the influence of an oligarchy, it is clear that if Lord John had never lived, some other scion of the noble house of Bedford would have done that which he has done, and if of equal industry and devotion to public life, would have formed as material a part of a Liberal cabinet. The conclusion, if not flattering to his lordship, is very much so to his lordship's order, and especially to his family, indicating, as it does, the rigidity and fixedness of what is called a popular system of government.

Tennyson makes Ulysses say,

> "Old age hath yet his honour and his toil."

Similar language might be put into the mouth of Lord John Russell. He is full of what may be termed House of Commons knowledge. In his youth he measured with Fox, and inherited the traditions of the Rockingham Whigs. If his lordship has been ambitious, his has been no mean or contemptible ambition. His aspirations have all been of an ancient and heroic mould. He carries us back to the great days of Parliamentary eloquence. His principles were formed, and his habits acquired, and his style fashioned, on principles and persons now no longer known. He has still around him some of the lustre acquired by contact with the immortals. Mournfully he may exclaim, as he reviews his diminished prestige and fading power,

> "Much have I seen and known; cities of men,
> And manners, climates, councils, governments,
> Myself not least, but honoured of them all,
> And drunk delight of battle with my peers,
> Far on the ringing plains of windy Troy."

In the decline of his lordship's reputation there is

reason for national regret. When he trips and falls, the feeling created is one of sorrow and vexation. Lord Sydenham declared that his lordship was "the noblest man he had ever the good fortune to know;" and though the old hosts he led to victory, the statesmen who were proud to call themselves his followers—the public speakers and active politicians in our chief towns and cities, who stood by his side on many a platform, are gone never to return, we wistfully gaze still on the pluck and ambition and varied fortunes of his lordship. The nation cannot but sympathize in his lordship's decline and fall. There was a time when manners and fashions were more courtly and dignified than at present; when gentlemen wore wigs and knee-breeches; when ladies did not dance the polka; when fathers and sons addressed each other in the most distressingly respectful language. Lord John, in political life, retains something of this grand air, which always tells, just as what the actors say about a man who lays hands on a woman is a brute, is approved by the gods, who return home and whop their wives with a double gusto after cheering so virtuous a sentiment. In his character of a Roman Senator Lord John is always successful. The strangers in the Gallery are always delighted, and no wonder, for then the little figure draws itself up to its full height; the eye glistens; the husky voice becomes animated and tremulous with emotion; his lordship looks boldly round on admiring back benches, defiantly to the well-filled ranks of Opposition in front, and you would swear that he was at least six feet high.

SIR BULWER LYTTON.*

WHAT wonders can be wrought by time, and patience, and energy! Like faith, they can remove mountains. In what walk of life has not Sir Edward Bulwer Lytton succeeded? who writes better novels? who has published more popular poems? who has penned smarter essays, or delivered more eloquent speeches? Without being a genius, by steady industry he has outstripped genius itself. It is true his position has been very favourable to success. He has never been a poor author. He has always been able to dine his critics. From the first he has mixed in what is called good society, and such as he never toil for fame in vain. There are some people who maintain that virtue is always rewarded, even in this life. Be that as it may, a gentleman of talent, and learning, and wealth can never fail as politieian or writer. The late Mr. Henry Drummond, who abused everybody and everything, whose speeches always pointed in one direction while his votes went in another, was a success as wit and statesman, because he was a partner in the banking-house in Charing-cross. For the same reason Mr. Sam Rogers got the public to buy so many editions of his "Pleasures of Memory." For the

* Raised to the peerage as Lord Lytton in 1866.

same reason, going back still further, were the verses of the Hon. William Robert Spencer—now rescued from oblivion merely by his being pilloried in the rejected addresses—in demand. We may go back still further. Swift's song, by a person of quality, indicates how, even in the Augustan age, the position of the writer was a very important consideration. But the subject of this sketch has done more than merely achieve the success always achieved by his class. His pluck, and perseverance, and brilliant qualities would have made him a marked man had he been born in a garret, in a kitchen bred. We like to sympathize with success, especially when that success is won by one of the "upper ten thousand." A good man struggling with adversity may be a sight dear to the gods, but certainly not to the British public. That august body is apt to vote such a one a bore, and infinitely prefers the contemplation of a good man residing on his own unencumbered estate, and well endowed with this world's goods.

It is the night of a great debate. The men out of office are trying to drive out the men who are in; and everything betokens that a crisis is at hand. The whippers-in in the lobby are counting up their men; the telegraph boys are hard at work; the Irish patriots have had things made pleasant, and popular M.P.'s are quietly being sold; a few fierce patriots from Finsbury or Marylebone are gazing wildly at the gas and the door-keepers, while treachery is being done before their very eyes. The strangers in the Gallery are vastly excited, and wonder how it is the leading characters should look as weary as actors on any other stage. It is early yet, and the House is very full. The first speech of the adjourned debate has scarce commenced when a tall, ghostly figure glides on to the Opposition bench, and places himself by the side of Mr. Disraeli—nearest to the Strangers' Gallery. His eye glistens like that of the ancient mariner, and his hand is almost as skinny. All the flesh on his face seems to have run into hair; and his aquiline nose is as much a feature as was that of *the* Duke, or as is that of my Lord Brougham. He stoops forward, places his elbow on his side, makes an ear-trumpet of his hand, and turns his face to the speaker for the time being, as if unwilling to lose a single word. Perhaps he may take a note or two; rejoice, if he does, for that is a sure sign that he will speak next; and, if he does, you will have, indeed, a treat. As a dramatist, the man before you has won fitting fame; as a novelist, the world is familiar with his name. The voice of woman, quivering with emotion, has sung his choicest songs. The hard man of the world, the scholar in his cloister, the idler in Belgravian drawing-rooms, have alike to be grateful to him for many hours of real joy; and therefore is it that not in vain does the author of "The Caxtons," and "My Novel," and "The Pilgrim of the Rhine," rise to catch the Speaker's eye. Sir Bulwer Lytton does not often address the House; when he does, his speeches are carefully prepared, and have the questionable reputation of reading well. He is artificial throughout. His voice is most studiously modulated; his action, which is exuberant, is the same; his moustache, and dress, and deportment have an equally elaborate air. Though a wealthy baronet and a leading statesman, there is something of the author of "Pelham" hangs about him; yet all that art and knowledge can do for him has been done. If reciting an essay were debating, Sir Bulwer Lytton would achieve no mean place in the annals of parliamentary eloquence; but he lacks the true secret of oratorical success—the genius for speaking, which nothing can buy—which no art can give, no industry secure—for the absence of which nothing can compensate—and the presence of which makes low-born, half-educated men principalities and powers. You see at once that the orator is on stilts; but he has a name, his composition is perfect, and he is, besides, immensely rich; so cheer after cheer greets him as he delivers, one after another, his well-prepared thrusts. Vivian Gray tells us—"In this country, to achieve distinction, a man must have a genius, or a million, or blood." Sir Bulwer is favoured by the gods, and has all three, and now the tall and once handsome baronet would win yet another triumph—he would be a statesman as well as a novelist—he would act a part in history as well as imagine one—he would live in Downing-street as well as in Paternoster-row.

Sir Edward George Earle Lytton Bulwer Lytton was born at Heydon Hall, Norfolk, in 1805, and was educated at Trinity College, Cambridge, where he gained the Chancellor's prize medal for the best English poem. He sat for St. Ives in 1831, and for Lincoln from 1832 to 1841, and was then supposed to be an advanced Liberal, and eager for the repeal of the taxes on knowledge, on which question he founded an annual motion, and which, on one occasion, it is supposed he would have carried, as there was a large majority in his favour, but Mr. Spring Rice appealed to him, and the motion was consequently withdrawn. At that time also he was in favour of the ballot, but now a large landowner, and seeing its utter inefficacy in France and America, he can no longer defend that theory. Altogether, he has very much altered his opinions, in common, I believe, with the rest of the British public, since he first started in life as a public man, and edited that respectable but long-defunct publication the *Monthly Chronicle*. He now concurs with the general policy espoused by Lord Derby—would readjust the income-tax and mitigate the duty on malt and tea. Yet the Whigs made Sir Bulwer a baronet. Sir Bulwer's maiden speech was by no means over-effective; but Sir Bulwer is a man not easily daunted, and he tried again. He obtained a committee to inquire into the laws affecting the drama, and introduced and carried a bill to grant stage copyrights to written dramas. One of his best speeches was that for the immediate emancipation of the West Indian slaves. O'Connell described it as one of the most vigorous efforts of impassioned reasoning he had ever heard in that House, and the speech was printed at the request and expense of the delegates from the societies in favour of immediate emancipation. Some of his political pamphlets, especially one called the "Crisis," have been very effective. On Lord Melbourne's resumption of the reins of power, it led to the offer of a place as one of the Lords of the Admiralty, an offer which Sir Bulwer very wisely declined. Of the "Letters to John Bull" I can only add that they plead for protection, and that the cause was already lost ere the baronet ventured into the field. On this question, however, he was consistent, as, so early as 1839, we find him resisting the repeal of the Corn Laws; and when he returned to public life, the old bonds of party had been in some degree broken up. He pronounced himself in favour of a fair trial to Lord Derby's Government, and shortly after his return to Parliament, delivered his sentiments to this effect in a speech applauded by Disraeli as one of the most masterly ever given to the House. He spoke again once in the session of 1853, upon his own motion against the enactment of the income-tax on its former footing; and when the Aberdeen Administration drifted into war, and broke down beneath the unaccustomed load, more than once was the voice of the baronet heard uttering what all England thought and felt. In 1858 the member for Hertfordshire—for in 1852 Sir Bulwer achieved that honour—became Secretary for the Colonies, and retained that office till the Derby administration fell, owing to the laudable desire of Lords Palmerston and Russell to present the people of England with a full and efficient measure of Parliamentary Reform. Altogether the literary baronet is a great catch for the county party; with an intellect equal to that of Disraeli, and a name how much more English and racy of the soil!

As an orator, he carries us back to old times. The last time I heard Sir Bulwer Lytton reminded me of the last time I heard Macaulay. In more senses than one they resembled each other. They both laboured under physical disadvantages; they were both prepared speakers rather than debaters; and they both sustained similar relations to their party. It is the fashion of the baronet—as it was of the peer—to speak early in the evening; and what a rush was there to hear them! how the House filled! how the Gallery opposite the Speaker filled! how keen was the enjoyment of the audience, and how sincere and enthusiastic the applause! The occasion to which I more particularly allude was the adjourned debate on the second reading of the Reform Bill. Sir Bulwer Lytton spoke for nearly two hours, and certainly never did the hon. baronet make a more effective speech. Unfortunately he is very deaf, and as he cannot tell when he is audible or not, at times he elevates his voice—which is very clear and shrill—and at times he drops it so much as to be utterly inaudible; and then he has such vehement and forcible gesticulation, as frequently to excite the apprehension quite as much as the admiration of the hearer. His spare, wiry, weird appearance; his thin outstretched arms; his figure, one moment thrown back to the eminent danger of the spine, and anon reaching as far as possible forward, in an opposite direction, seems scarcely English, and one feels as if witnessing the feats of some foreign professor of legerdemain, who has made the round of the principal Courts of Europe, and has condescended, for pecuniary reasons, to abide awhile in the more aristocratic regions of the metropolis. But this feeling soon vanishes as the accomplished rhetorician proceeds to invest even the commonplaces of party with an original and classic air. One great merit Sir Bulwer Lytton has, and that is, he is never dull. As a rule, M.P.'s are dreadfully dull. Dulness—if I may judge by what I hear and see every day, especially in the Church and in the Senate-house—is much appreciated by the English public. We seem quietly to assume that a dull man is never either a rogue or a fool. In vain we take the taxes off knowledge, and teach people to read and write:

> "Still her old empire to restore she tries,
> For, born a goddess, Dulness never dies."

One word as to Sir Bulwer Lytton's Parliamentary position. The House of Commons every day becomes a more plebeian assembly. One cannot be surprised at this, for its saving virtue is, that it is the People's House; and of course every day we are told that it is less and less an assembly of orators. This is a very old complaint; Wilberforce made it in 1809, when Canning and Brougham were in the House. As soon as the Reformed Parliament met, all the rejected M.P.'s and anti-Reformers said the same. The truth is, the House meets for business, and the leaders and most successful men talk about business, and M.P.'s, no matter how distinguished they may be for their talents, who forget this and seek to shine by mere eloquence, must assuredly fail. Now, Sir Bulwer Lytton belongs to the old school, and does the oratorical on the grand scale, while Disraeli and Lord Palmerston speak for power, and are indifferent as to display. Sir Bulwer seems to consider himself merely "as a living apparition, sent to be a moment's ornament;" and hence it is that he has never taken first rank in an assembly which is jealous as a mistress of a divided homage.

CHAPTER IX.

DECEASED MEMBERS.

LORD PALMERSTON.

THIS is a great, free, self-governed country. I must believe it, for I read it in the newspapers every day. The aristocracy tell us this when they condescend to adorn our public dinners; and popular lecturers at Mechanics' Institutions and Athenæums repeat it. Our Constitution is the growth of ages, and has attained a perfection of which Hobbes despaired and of which Locke never dreamt. It is the envy of surrounding nations, says Mr. Horsman in our day,—just as George III. did in his—when Pitt and an unreformed Parliament added £200,000,000 to the national debt. The franchise, we are told, is a trust; that trust is placed in the most trustworthy hands. (Cato was the original ten-pound householder.) Our elections are the envy of surrounding nations. There is at them a studious abstinence from beer; no one is solicited for a vote. The great manufacturer, or railway contractor, or the neighbouring peer, always retire to the Continent when an election takes place, in order that the honest voter may act in accordance with the dictates of his conscience. The religious feel that it is a solemn event, and sermons appropriate to the occasion are preached in chapel and church alike. The ablest men of the community, irrespective of their wealth or want of it, are selected as candidates. On the day of nomination, in the plain garb of citizens—without music or flags, or demonstrations of party feeling—they appear upon the hustings. Their speeches, in unadorned but plain language, comment upon the men and movements of the day. They declare the principles upon which they act, and upon which they deem the Government of Great Britain and its imperial dependencies should be carried on. These speeches, with the exception of a few immaculate boroughs, such as Yarmouth and Totnes, or Gloucester and Wakefield, or Berwick-upon-Tweed, are listened to by an audience fresh from the perusal of Bacon, Bentham, and Mill. A show of hands then takes place. The best man has invariably the majority, the others immediately retire, and the constituents, satisfied that they have done their duty, return home; the representative, in his turn, becomes a constituent in another assembly, where he meets some six hundred similarly-minded gentlemen. They select from themselves, in order to form a cabinet, the ablest and wisest. These invariably are peers, or sons of peers. They, again, select the ablest and wisest as their head. He was, till the

Crimean war tarnished, and the Schleswig-Holstein war destroyed our European reputation, the first man in the universe, and remotest regions learned to bless his name. Happily, in our day the system has arrived at a blessed fruition, and we have as Premier the Right Honourable Viscount Palmerston, G.C.B., a veteran official long before the present generation bewailed or rejoiced in long clothes.

So much for theory, now for actual fact. Is it not singular that statesmanship as a rule is the only thing monopolized in this country by a class, and that class one which has invariably broken down when it has come into contact with men without grandfathers? From the days of the Huntingdon brewer—not forgetting him who was emphatically "the Great Commoner"—to those of Gladstone and Disraeli, our chief orators and statesmen have sprung from the middle ranks. If Fox belonged to the aristocracy, he confessed that he owed his noblest aspirations to Burke, the latter himself one of the wisest of men, yet who never was admitted a member of the Cabinet, whose chiefs he honoured by his service. If England's rulers accepted the services of Canning, they could prey upon his genius and prematurely exhaust his life. We saw the Earl of Derby honoured with the Garter on his retirement from the Premiership in 1859, while the man without whom his party could not have remained a day in office retired to Hughenden Manor undecorated and without reward. There may be great advantages attending this state of things, but an evident disadvantage is, that this system compels us to accept a kind of Hobson's choice. Hence, when Lord John Russell is sent for, and confesses that he cannot carry on the Queen's Government, and Lord Derby has confessed the same—if Lord Palmerston does not condescend to be our saviour, we are plunged into the horrors of a parliamentary dead-lock. This was the reason of Palmerston's premiership. He was Premier just as men are villains by necessity and fools by a divine thrusting on. We read in Luther's "Table Talk," "Maximilian one day burst into a great laugh. On being asked the cause, 'Truly,' he said, 'I laughed to think that God should have trusted the spiritual government of the world to a drunken priest like Pope Julius, and the government of the empire to a chamois-hunter like me.'" We have it in evidence that an idea of this kind used to flash through Lord Althorp's honest brain. In his retirement at Broadlands, Lord Palmerston may indulge in a similar laugh. If we may judge from a public life of unusual extent, the last thing he aspired to was the Premiership. It was offered him, and he could not well refuse it. No man has less gone out of his way to attract or retain the admiration of the people than Lord Palmerston. When he upset Lord John Russell—and, in the language of the turf, began to make a good running—the novelty of the idea was quite refreshing. Palmerston Premier! the thought was absurd. Who were his followers? who would march through Coventry with such a ragged regiment? What ability, save that of consistently sticking to office, had he ever shown? The clever men of a past age—Wilberforce, Plumer Ward, Dean Milner, Canning, and others—it is true, always spoke and wrote of Palmerston as a man of great promise. In the House of Commons, the general opinion was that Palmerston was a man possibly to be laughed at for his juvenile airs, but certainly not to be despised; but the outside multitude—"the people, the only source of political power"—had no other idea of Palmerston than that he was always in office, that he was one of the best horsemen in Europe, and that he bore a *soubriquet* supposed to indicate an amorous temperament and personal charms. Even writing so recently as 1837, Mr. James Grant, in his "Random Recollections," could say, "Of Lord Palmerston, Foreign Secretary and Member for Tiverton, I have but little to say. The situation he fills in the Cabinet gives him a certain degree of prominence in the eyes of the country, which he certainly does not possess in Parliament. His talents are by no means of a high order. Assuredly they would never, by their own natural energy, have raised him to a distinguished position in the councils of his Sovereign, in which a variety of accidental circumstances have placed him. He is an indifferent speaker." In 1839, another critic speaks of him as too aristocratical for the present day. This monstrous criticism was accepted at the time as honest and fair.

How little can writers know of those of whom they write! Since 1837, Palmerston's career has been a continued triumph: he put on the armour just as other men are putting it off. As a sexagenarian he descended into the political arena, and exhibited all the ardour and vivacity of a youth. Men were first astonished, then enraptured. All England swore by Lord Palmerston. Even the professors of the refined science of cookery —the disciples of Ude, Carême, Soyer—caught the enthusiasm, and a Palmerston sauce became *en vogue*. In the four quarters of the globe the name of Palmerston was a tower of strength. There was rejoicing at Vienna when Palmerston fell in 1851. In the troubled years of 1848-9 a German popular couplet intimated that if the devil had a son, that favoured mortal was our facetious Premier. "*Suda Palmerston seechas*" (Hither Palmerston, forthwith!) we are told, was during the Crimean war the cry with which the Cossack of the Ukraine stilled his steed when restive, or urged it on when weary. Nay, more, at dinners at Damascus Mr. Disraeli makes an Eastern emir pettishly exclaim, "I cannot endure this eternal chatter about Palmerston: are there no other statesmen in the world besides Palmerston?" Even on the other side the Atlantic his influence is felt. I read in an American paper that the truly culpable act of Brown and his deluded followers at Harper's Ferry was all owing to Lord Palmerston.

Well, all this abuse is a confession of Palmerston's power, and that is a compliment to the English nation, for the Palmerston policy in the eyes of the world represents English policy, and we love the man who makes all the world talk of what England will do and dare. But in the man himself there is something else which creates and maintains his popularity. In the first place, nature has been bountiful to his lordship, and has given him length of days; this is a greater advantage in statesmanship than at first sight it appears. A man many years engaged in political affairs learns much—gets an insight into men and parties—quotes precedents and becomes an authority. As he sees his contemporaries and rivals one by one snatched away by death, there is a clearer stage for himself. Promotion often in politics goes by seniority. We all spoke of the late Marquis of Lansdowne, for instance, as a political Nestor, yet, if we look back to his younger days, when he first started in public life, we do not find that he made a very great impression; then, again, in many of the fierce party fights of the last generation, Lord Palmerston was called on to take but a secondary part, his department having been more foreign than home politics. He has thus rarely come into collision with the passions and prejudices of any powerful class; thus it is that he has had, more than once, we believe, in ministerial crises, advances made to him by the leaders of the Conservative party; and thus it is that he often receives a large share of Conservative support. Then, again, there is a thoroughness in his way of doing business, which we all like. Let him be Home Secretary, let him be Foreign Minister, let him be Premier, he does everything thoroughly and to the best of his power. "When Lord Grenville was in the height of his power," writes Horace Walpole, "I one day said to him, 'My lord, as you are going to the king, do ask him to make poor Clive one of the council.' He replied, 'What is it to me who is a judge or who a bishop? It is my business to make kings and emperors, and to maintain the balance of power in Europe.'" Now, Lord Palmerston would never have made such a silly answer. When he is at work we soon find out. Whether for work or play, no man can beat his lordship. Is the House of Commons determined to waste its time in idle debates, to abandon its privileges, to promise everything out-of-doors and do nothing in-doors—Lord Palmerston fools them to their heart's content. And then there is a *bonhommie* about his lordship which is popular; a good-tempered, jolly man can never be unpopular. This was the secret of Lord North's success, and of that of a still greater man before him, Sir Robert Walpole. It must be confessed my lord has something to laugh at. What must he think of popular M.P.'s who charge him with treason, and yet dare not vote against him for fear of damaging the shop?

It cannot be that such a one is the nonentity so flippantly portrayed by Mr. Grant; the captain of shams described by Mr. Bright; or the arch-traitor sold to Russia, as Mr. Urquhart will be happy to tell you any day. Years ago, the writer, meeting with one of the numerous agitators with which the metropolis abounds, requested the enthusiast referred to to explain his movements. "Oh," said he, "we are going to impeach Palmerston!" We suggested the desirability of losing no time if such a course were resolved on. "Oh!" said our informant, "Palmerston will live ten years longer: Russia calculates that he will do so too." Palmerston lived on, but who was guilty of the folly of talking of impeaching him?

Voltaire says, men succeed less by their talents than their character. As an instance, he compares Mazarin and De Retz. In quoting a passage in a letter to the Bishop of Llandaff, the late Lord Dudley said, "Walpole and Bolingbroke make a similar pair in the next century. Castlereagh and Canning are remarkable examples of the truth of the maxim which our days have furnished." The list might have been extended so as to embrace the career of Lord Palmerston. Undoubtedly the noble lord's talents are of a high order. "We are all proud of him!" said Sir Robert Peel, and the words were caught up and re-echoed all over the land; but it is the character he has acquired that has placed him where he is. It would be the height of absurdity to deny Lord Palmerston the possession of great talent. He has made brilliant speeches; his pro-Catholic orations were republished; and the way in which he put down Julian Harney at Tiverton tickled every midriff in Great Britain. His five-hours' speech in vindication of himself in the House of Commons was a masterpiece. A Conservative member, walking home that night, said to a literary member of Parliament, "I have heard Canning, and Plunket, and Brougham in their best days, and I never heard anything to beat that speech." Yet our Premier has never scaled the heights of oratory; has never attained to the utterance of new and brilliant truths; genius has never thrown around him her robe of dazzling light; he has been a dexterous debater, skilful at fence, nothing more. Palmerston is but a man of the time, while Pitt and Fox, Burke and Canning, were men for all times. He even ranks below Sir Robert Peel, whose speeches are still quoted, and occasionally read. He leaves on you the impression that he is adroit; that he is liberal in profession where Austria and Italy are concerned; that he is grand at bullying little states; and that it is true of him what the first Napoleon said of Providence, that it was always on the side that had the strongest legions. Glance at his lordship's administrative career, and this is manifest. Toryism was popular, and Palmerston began life as a Tory; Reform was popular, and he turned Reformer; war with Russia was popular in 1855, and he became a furious war-minister. In some quarters, more recently, people were talking of a further parliamentary reform, and an extension of the suffrage, and Lord Palmerston, who resigned office rather than accede to anything of the kind, condescended to introduce a comprehensive and satisfactory measure of reform, which comprehensive and satisfactory measure was withdrawn quite as readily as it was introduced. This readiness to swim with the stream is a great thing in a statesman. Indeed, in spite of what men may say to the contrary, it is a virtue, if the stream flows in a right direction. But this is not the sole secret of the Premier's popularity. There is another and more potent cause. An anecdote will best illustrate our meaning.

Once upon a time two gentlemen went to dine at a noble mansion; on their departure, according to the fashion of the age, the servants were ranged in the hall, waiting with extended palm the expected honorarium. The guest who first departed was seen to produce a smile on every countenance as he passed. His friend interrogated him as to the cause, "I gave them nothing," was the reply. "I merely tickled their hands." In a precisely similar manner has Palmerston tickled Englishmen. Undeniably, John Bull is very vain—not of himself, like a Frenchman, but of his nation. The Chinese slave, writing to the Lord of the Sun and the Brother of the Moon of the encounter at Peiho, says, "The barbarians attacked us with their usual insolence and audacity." We have a similar way of speaking of foreigners. "It is a grand country this," exclaims the enthusiastic but grumbling Briton, while he abuses its laws, its customs, its institutions, and its climate. Our aged Premier has spent nearly half a century in repeating this cry for the edification of foreign courts. England has been the model which he has asked France, Spain, Portugal, Austria, Russia, to say nothing of countless smaller principalities and powers—no matter the difference of religion, of custom, and of race—to imitate and admire. If, occasionally, the parties thus addressed have shown a little irritation; if, occasionally, an indiscreet Italian, or Polish, or Hungarian patriot, has in consequence appealed to the sword, believing that England's arm will uphold him in his application of English principles; the fault, of course, is not the noble Viscount's, and the English nation hugs itself into the belief, that the dislike and suspicion of foreign courts and peoples (for the singularity of the Palmerston, or rather the English foreign policy, is, that whilst it is too democratic for foreign courts, it is too aristocratic for foreign peoples) is the measure of their respect and fear. Hence the national enthusiasm for Palmerston has placed him on the very topmost pinnacle. Abroad the cry has been, "Palmerston and Constitutionalism!" at home, "Palmerston and the Vindication of the National Honour!" John Bull, even now, when an adventurer and the son of an adventurer, with an audacity almost sublime, has climbed up the steep ascent of empire, and with his armed legions bids all Europe tremble, flatters himself that England sustains to the modern, the relation Rome sustained to the ancient world. Under the broad sun of heaven he sees no more exalted personage than himself; he insists upon his rights in the remotest corner of the globe: in the presence of the Pope, whom he deems little better than one of the wicked, under the shadow of the gigantic despot who holds France in his mailed hand, before Austrian Kaiser, Russian Czar, Yankee backwoodsman, or astonished citizen of Timbuctoo, he exclaims, "*Civis Romanus sum!*" In his own opinion, it is his proud prerogative wherever he wanders to break all laws, to violate all customs, to pour contempt on all prejudices, and to run all risks. Now, in such circumstances, Palmerston always backs his countrymen, even when, like Sir John Bowring, they rush wildly into war; and this mischievous John Bullism we all appreciate and admire. Again: under Palmerston's direction, we called Belgium into existence, settled the succession in Spain and Portugal, drove away from Syria Mehemet Ali, made Greece a kingdom, and blockaded the African coast to put down slavery. People who do not examine matters very closely think it a fine thing to read what an English fleet has been doing at the Tagus, or on the Douro, or on the coast of Africa; or how an English minister has lectured the Bourbons and Hapsburgs, or insulted the representatives of the great republic of the West, or succeeded in lowering the flag of France. That Palmerston has not precipitated the nation into war, argues not so much his discretion as his luck; but the nation that does not see the danger, admires the spirit, and forgets how Palmerston suffered Poland to be blotted out, disdained to assist Hungary, betrayed Sicily, hastened to congratulate Napoleon for erecting an iron despotism on the ruins of a republic, and twice since he was Premier was brow-beaten and bullied by the late idiot King of Naples. But perhaps the great secret of the popularity of the Palmerston foreign policy is its utter unintelligibility. Non-interference in what does not concern us is clearly our duty; Lord Palmerston accepts this, yet he interferes. We are not in a position to go lecturing, yet Palmerston is never happy unless so employed. The Palmerston foreign policy—in reality very much like that of Lord Aberdeen, for since the time of Canning the policy of the Foreign Office has differed but little—has this good about it, that it must weary people of sense of secret diplomacy. The world will move on, its dark places will be made light, its crooked places will be made straight; but if we may judge from the past, not by the manœuvres of diplomacy or the protocols of Lord Palmerston. In his home policy the noble Viscount has been more successful in producing practical results. Here again he has gone at once to the national heart. An Englishman must be comfortable, or he cannot live. The two great ills of life are a smoky chimney and a scolding wife. By Act of Parliament, Lord Palmerston has forbidden the one and has enabled the wretched victim to free himself of the other. This latter Act must always remain a proof of the noble Premier's earnest activity and perseverance. Night after night he and his Attorney-General, Sir Richard Bethell, had to fight the battle alone; a man of feebler will than Lord Palmerston would have given way. When Palmerston became Home Secretary there was another sore evil under the sun: in all our crowded towns population had planted itself most densely in the neighbourhood of the churchyard; the result was, the living were poisoned by the dead. Some of the clergy, fearful of losing their vested interests, opposed the removal of this fearful nuisance, but Lord Palmerston shut up the churchyards as burial-places, and humanity gained the day. His few months at the Home Office were very beneficial to himself, and paved the way for his Premiership. The English public had a nearer view of their pet Foreign Minister; no public duty appeared to come amiss to him; he was weighed in the balance, nor was he found wanting. In 1855, when the Aberdeen cabinet fell, when Lord John Russell had covered himself with odium by his desertion of the sinking ship, all eyes were directed to Lord Palmerston. He was the only possible Premier, and would have remained so had not the Conservatives caught him tripping on the Foreign Conspiracy Bill, and, with the aid of Milner Gibson, defeated a measure which otherwise most probably would have had their support. It must be also confessed, Palmerston required a rebuff. Like Jeshurun of old, he waxed fat and kicked;

there was something approaching to insolence in his treatment of the House of Commons.

Lord Palmerston's chief merit is his cheerful honesty. He has made no pretensions to virtue. The *Record* intimated that he was the man of God because he made low Churchmen bishops, but Lord Palmerston himself never laid claim to so sacred a character. He has paid remarkably little deference to an enlightened British public. The lover must blame not his mistress, but himself, when he finds the idol of his fancy plain and commonplace. Beery readers of newspapers must not complain that their model statesman once resigned office rather than give them votes. The British public dearly love a lord that will take the chair at Exeter Hall. Lord Palmerston began life as Cupid—does not think children tainted with original sin—dared to tell the Scottish clergy that they had better wash than fast to keep off the cholera—was never on the platform at Exeter Hall: yet is he popular. With the exception of once presiding at the distribution of prizes at the University College, London, and a visit to Manchester, he studiously avoided the arts by which small men become great. The last American traveller who has published a book on us, Mr. Field, writes: "An American can hardly believe his senses when he sees the abasement of soul which seizes the middle classes in the presence of a lord. They look up to him as a superior being, with a reverence approaching to awe." There is some truth in this: it is to the credit of Lord

Palmerston that he has traded as little on this feeling as it was possible for any man to do.

Come and see Palmerston the Statesman. That is he—that old gentleman in the middle of the Treasury bench of the House of Commons, with hat pulled down tightly over his eyes, arms across his breast, and one leg thrown over the other. Is not he in a capital state of preservation, with nothing to hurt him but now and then a twinge of his old enemy, the gout—a souvenir of jollier years? A wonderful old man, truly; still erect on horseback as ever youthful knight wending his way to lady's bower. Dr. Johnson said of dancing dogs, "the wonder is, not that they dance so well, but that they dance at all;" so with Lord Palmerston, the wonder is, not that he rules the country so well, but that he does it at all, when most men would be in a state of idiotic decay. It says something for the goodness of his lordship's constitution—something for the light character of his labours as a statesman of half a century, and something for the Romsey air and his lordship's medical attendants. But mark! he is on his legs, with all the briskness of a four-year-old. His pertness is quite juvenile. How neat and effective is his retort, and yet how little there is in it! Disraeli said Sir Robert Peel played on the House as an old fiddle, Palmerston does the same. His birth, his office, his experience—all make him feel at home in it; and when he sits down there is a laugh, and the questioner, somehow or other, feels he has done something very foolish, though he scarce knows what. Your expectations are heightened. Very naturally you imagine that, as the evening passes on, and the excitement deepens, his lordship, in a corresponding manner, will become earnest, and passionate, and overpowering. Wait a little while, and you will find out your mistake. There is the same pertness and levity; the same eagerness to evade the question by a joke; the same skilful dodging; the same artful adaptation of his speech, not to the conscience or convictions of the public, but to the prejudices, and knowledge, and interests of the House. No one so disappoints the eager stranger as Lord Palmerston. His hollow feeble voice—his intolerable haw-hawing—his air of hauteur and flippancy, all combine to dispel the illusion which, in a manner most wonderful, his lordship has contrived to gather around his name.

> "Life is a jest, and all things show it;
> I thought so once, and now I know it,"

will be an appropriate epitaph wherewith to deck the marble monument that the grateful nation shall erect when death shall have torn the wily Premier from the doctor's care. Lord Palmerston never speaks long: he is down almost as soon as he is up, he seldom rises above the level of after-dinner oratory, and as you watch his lordship out of the House at one A.M., at the close of a debate which has tried his lordship's mettle and damaged the handiwork of his lordship's valet, the shambling old gentleman, leaning on a friendly arm, does not seem quite the prodigy in your eyes which the admirably made-up nobleman did, who stepped out of his carriage just as you reached Westminster Hall.

Nevertheless, it must be remembered that for half a century Lord Palmerston was a leading statesman, and during the latter half of that time *the* leading statesman of his age. As Foreign Minister for a generation at least, by his subtle intellect and resolute will, he dominated over Europe. Greece and Belgium were his handiwork; he cherished constitutional government in Spain, and Portugal, and the Italian peninsula. France under his influence became our cordial ally.

SIR JAMES GRAHAM.

THE life of Sir Thomas Fowell Buxton is one that deserves to be studied by candidates for Parliamentary renown. In a letter to the late J. J. Gurney, Sir Thomas says, the debate on the Manchester Riots "convinced me that I have the opportunity of being a competitor on the greatest arena that ever existed, but it also taught me that success in such a theatre is only for those who devote their lives to it." Sir Thomas declined to make the requisite sacrifice. Sir J. Graham has paid the price, and takes a foremost rank in any gallery of modern statesmen. He has devoted his whole life to the House of Commons, and he is a fair specimen of a House of Commons orator. "The speaking," wrote Sir Thomas, "required, is of a very peculiar kind. The House loves *good sense and joking* and nothing else, and the object of its utter aversion is that species of eloquence which may be called Philippian. There are not three men from whom a fine simile or sentiment would be tolerated; all attempts of the kind are punished with general laughter." This was written before Parliamentary Reform was won, but the description is still applicable. Parliamentary speaking has not altered in the least, and Sir James Graham, who won his laurels in the old days of corruption, is still a skilful debater in the greatest arena that ever existed.

"Vidth and visdom grows together" was the remark of no less acute an observer of human nature than the respected parient of the immortal Samiwel Veller. In the case of Sir James Graham this truth is strongly exemplified. In a work published in 1839, entitled "St. Stephen's; or, Pencillings of Politicians," I find a chapter devoted to a brace of turncoats. One of them is Sir Francis Burdett—he has long ceased to interest mankind; another is Lord Stanley—as Lord Derby, he is now the leader of the Conservatives; and the third is Sir James Graham who is quoted as an example of "the wretched stuff which poor human nature submits to admire and wonder at." No man has been more odious in the eye of the British people. When Sir James, as Secretary of State for the Home

Department, laid before the House of Commons the outline of his Factory Education Bill, the Dissenters raised such a storm that the hon. baronet was soon compelled to give way. When Mr. Thomas Duncombe proved that he had opened Mazzini's letters, the ferment and outcry were greater still. At his head was hurled a torrent of abuse; anti-Graham wafers were advertised, and met with an extensive sale. One could scarce believe that Sir James was the same individual who had made radical speeches of the most violent character, who had a hand in drawing up the Reform Bill, and who, as Secretary to the Admiralty, had effected unexampled savings. And now, as you look below the gangway on the ministerial side, and see the gigantic form of Sir James, it cannot but occur to you that in that illustrious assembly there is not another man apparently so wise and wide.

Good fortune was very favourable to Sir James Graham. She made him one of the strongest men in the House of Commons, and one of the wealthiest; and by reason of those two qualities was he from the first a man of mark. To hear a wealthy baronet talking radicalism forty years ago, was a curious novelty; and by reason of his immense physical capacity did he live down his unpopularity, his political inconsistency, his recklessness on the platform and the hustings, his bitter partisanship, inside St. Stephen's or out. His patriarchal appearance quite touched the heart of the stranger in the gallery. If there be truth in physiognomy, Sir James could not have been the atrocious criminal at one time his enemies affirmed. In his youth he must have been a very fine-looking man. He had a portly frame and a most benign presence. Very few, says Mr. Doubleday, surpass him in power of expression and the talent of commanding and enforcing attention. It was singular to watch him in a parliamentary fight. Sir James Graham had always a meek smile upon his face, and as he turned to listen to the orator for the time, who poured out upon him the vials of his wrath, he seemed to say, "Oh, go on, my good fellow, you are not hurting me, but you are injuring yourself." There he sat, a great mountain of a man, with a calm placid face, which apparently no storm could ruffle or disturb, and with a frame that would make its possessor conspicuous wherever men assembled.

Perhaps, respected reader, you are a stranger to the House, and of an excitable temperament. Perhaps you belong to that large class who cannot control their feelings. As the orator grows frantic, you do the same. As his bile rises, so does yours. You turn the lightning of your eye on the apostate knight of Netherby, the opener of Mazzini's letters, the betrayer of the brothers Bandiera—even in his green old age the slanderer of Layard—and you wonder the earth does not open and swallow him up, as it did Dathan and Abiram of old. Wait a little while. The age of miracles is gone; and yet I will show you a miracle. The orator sits down. Sir James is in no hurry to reply. Slowly he lifts up his big body and rises to speak. At any rate, you say, the House will hoot him—it does nothing so rude, it receives him with cordial cheers. Well, then, Sir James himself will speak with the faltering accents of conscious guilt—on the contrary, he is perfectly unembarrassed. Well, then, his defence will be impotent and lame; it will convince no one and disgust all—the real fact is nothing of the kind. It comes out slowly and calmly, as if the orator felt its truth. Letters are read, but all in the calmest and most deliberate manner, which show how very right was Sir James, and how very wrong the wicked man by whom he was attacked. You never heard such a candid speaker in your life. He looks as if he would not do a naughty thing for the world. What a depth of untold tenderness there is in that man's bosom! How kindly he speaks of every one! What innocent simplicity lurks in his face! As he stands, slightly stooping, his arms behind his back, his voice seemingly broken with emotion, you fancy never was there a more injured person; and when he indignantly asks if it is to be supposed that he would forfeit the reputation of a life? when he declares that his character is at stake, that at his time of life—so soon to pass away from among men—it was monstrous to suppose that he would do anything so paltry and mean as that with which he was charged, your warmest sympathies are aroused for the injured baronet, and you become indignant as you remember how he has been the helpless victim of party slander, of personal pique, or lying tongues.

His juvenility was, I imagine, another reason of Sir James's success. He was a boy, and remained so to the end of the chapter. I know he was born in 1792, that he has been in and out of office times innumerable, that he has sat on all sides of the House, advocated all sorts of measures, and coalesced with all parties; but the enthusiasm with which he did all this was youthful. He was an artless, simple, unsophisticated youth, devoted to politics. He accepted office because he delighted in activity. He has done some very mischievous and disgraceful things for the same reason; actually, in some instances—as when he denounced Lord John Russell's Ecclesiastical Titles Bill—he has evinced a sagacity for which few gave him credit, and which fewer still appreciated at the time; but to the last he was in a state of development—his principles not yet fully formed, his judgment not fully ripe; but still, from his position, from his abilities, from his cleverness as a debater, from his wide experience, from his intimacy with the great chiefs departed—a man with great influence in the House of Commons, one of the half-dozen whose speeches were looked forward to in every great political crisis. We all know Sir Robert Peel had a high opinion of Sir James, and Sir Robert's opinions had, and still have, immense weight in the House of Commons. In truth, in the

House of Commons a man is judged independently of the opinions formed of him out of doors. Hence no juvenile indiscretion on the part of Sir James permanently affected the high position he took in that assembly when he first entered it, and which he ever since retained.

Sir James is emphatically a man of the times, and for the times. As a politician he was always in a somewhat chrysalis state. He, it is clear, cut himself off from the Derby party. For the same reason he could never be very closely allied with Lord John Russell. Sir Robert Peel was his Magnus Apollo. He was his most faithful, most sympathetic, most useful and devoted friend, and deprived of his leader, Sir James's course was somewhat desultory. His main fault has been this, that as a hard-working, busy party-fighter, he has never studied polities as a science, never been above the tumult and turmoil of party—never risen into the superior elevation of the political philosopher—never got a glimpse of abstract principles. He has contented himself with politics in the concrete; he has wrestled with parties and persons as we can imagine one of his ancestors fought in the jolly old moss-trooping times. Sir James's faults and official blunders have been those of his class. La Fontaine tells us of a motherly crab, who exclaimed against the obliquity of her daughter's gait, and asked her if she could not walk steady. The young crab very reasonably pleaded the similarity of her parent's manner of stepping, and asked whether she could be expected to walk differently from the rest of her family. Sir James is like the rest of his family. Letters had been opened by previous Secretaries of State, and when he opened Mazzini's letters he was neither worse nor better than others. If he laid about him pretty freely, it is the manner of all faction and party fighters to do so; and if he occasionally exhibited intense ignorance of the middle-class public—as shown in his Factory Education Bill—why, country baronets with thirty thousand a year have but little chance of understanding the shopkeepers and Dissenters of our borough towns. An amusing instance of this Sir James displayed on one occasion. In the course of a speech in favour of voluntary education, Sir James quoted Mr. Baines, of Leeds—not then what he now is, a member of the House—as "a man of talent, though a Dissenter;" as if a man's talents depended on his profession of religion. A middle-class man would have known that genius and talent are of no church. Yet, in the House of Commons, so ignorant are the leading men in it, necessarily such a phrase passes muster, and Sir James no doubt thought he paid Mr. Baines a high compliment.

Sir James's deeds will remain to vindicate his claims to respect. On the whole he has been on the side of progress. During the Reform agitation he did much to insure the passing of that measure; and the aid he gave to Sir Robert Peel in fighting the great battle of commercial freedom was of the most invaluable character. As one of the faithful band of "paid janissaries" and "renegades," as they were termed by Lord George Bentinck, Sir James stood by his leader manfully, and fought with a courage the memory of which yet remains; and when, by means of a combination of Protectionists and Whigs, Lord John Russell was placed in office, Sir James helped to preserve the ministry in their free-trade career. As regards ecclesiastical questions, he has ever been consistent. He left the Whigs on account of their Appropriation schemes, and he was ever faithful to the church by law established in these realms.

W. JOHNSON FOX.

THERE is a virtue in our English constitution that, however aristocratic it may be, it is not exclusive; here a low-born man may rise. It is true, at first he has a hard time of it, but it is equally true that, if he have talents—and sense enough to use them—he can climb up into a position of equality with the highest and the noblest in the land. When the Ten Hours' Bill was before the House of Commons, the late Mr. Joseph Brotherton, then M.P. for Salford, alluded to the period of his life when he was a factory boy, and detailed the hardships and wrongs to which he was subjected, and the resolution that he had formed—to improve the condition of the factory hands, should he ever have the power. At the conclusion of his speech, Sir James Graham rose up, and declared amid the plaudits of the assembly, that he did not know before that Mr. Brotherton had sprung from so humble an origin, but that it made him more proud than ever of the House of Commons, to think that a man rising from that condition should be able to sit side by side and on equal terms with the hereditary gentry of the land. A barber's grandson we have known to become Lord Chancellor; a linen-draper's son, in our time, has been an archbishop. Privates rise from the ranks, and some of our naval heroes had names not supposed to indicate good family. A successful commercial career has also lifted a man into the privileged circles of the Upper Ten Thousand. Still, the cases are few in which a man without wealth or aristocratic connexion has been chosen by the English people to represent them in their own house. Even when a class has been strong enough to send a man to St. Stephen's to look after their own peculiar interests, his career has not been flattering nor his success great. The West Indian proprietors did not do themselves much good by returning Peter Borthwick. Feargus O'Connor got into Parliament, and Chartism immediately died out. The Tower Hamlets had little to pride themselves on in the success of Mr. George Thompson—a man whose orations out of doors, in connection with the Anti-Slavery Agitation, were as brilliant as they were effective. Mr. Henry Vincent, though he stood for Ipswich, never got into the House of Commons at all. But occasionally we have an illustration of the fact that learning is better than house or land, and this has been illustrated in the person of Mr. Fox—whose father was a very small farmer in Suffolk, whose connexions were of the humblest character, who himself worked as a lad in a Norwich factory, and who long represented one of our most democratic boroughs—that of Oldham. Mr. Fox's position was creditable alike to himself and his constituents. Practically, it was an argument in favour of the extension of the franchise which was not lost on a thinking public.

Years and years back, in the thinly-populated district of Homerton, there was an Academy—belonging to that most respectable body of dissenters then called Independents, now Congregationalists—presided over by that learned and pious divine, the laté Dr. Pye Smith, whose "Scripture Testimony to the Messiah" is still an authority in theological circles. To this Academy the youthful Fox was sent, at the suggestion of a congregation worshipping in a very ancient building—yet, I believe, existing in Norwich—who had witnessed the talents of the youthful disciple, and deemed that he might become a teacher and preacher among themselves. Mr. Fox passed through his academical career successfully, and was settled, as the phrase is, as a minister somewhere in Hampshire. So far the result was favourable, and the Norwich people prided themselves on their sagacity. The time now arrived when they were to be disappointed. In those days Neology had not made its appearance, but Unitarianism had; and by the orthodox it was regarded as just as bad. To borrow a simile from Dryden's "Hind and Panther," Reynard ravaged the garden, and pulled up and destroyed fruit and flower. One of the buds thus rudely torn away was William Johnson Fox. Possibly he was of a disputatious turn; possibly he was led away by that celebrated William Taylor, the correspondent of Southey, who first made German literature known to the English, and who conferred on the old cathedral city in which he lived a literary reputation which Norwich has ever since done its best to retain; possibly Fox had never been very orthodox. However, the time came when he publicly abandoned the denomination to which he belonged, and became a Unitarian minister. Ultimately he settled down in South-place, Finsbury-square, London. His Sunday morning orations were a great success; he gathered around him many of the wits of London—Dickens, and Douglas Jerrold, and Macready were among his auditors; he edited a magazine now defunct, wrote in the *Morning Chronicle* and other papers; and as lecturer, and wit, and man of letters, took high rank in London life.

Nor is this to be wondered at. A man of wide reading, ready memory, with a strong sense of humour, and inclining to the liberal and popular view of things, if able to talk at all, may be sure not to talk in vain. The times also were propitious. When Mr. Fox commenced public life, people had not become indifferent to politics, and struggled fiercely against the optimist conclusion—

"Whatever is, is right."

The men with whom he lived had seen Sidmouth cover the land with a network of spies and informers; had seen the Habeas Corpus Act suspended; had heard of the massacre at Peterloo; had applauded while Hone badgered Ellenborough to death; and had sympathized with Hunt when in his cell for calling the Prince of Wales an Adonis of fifty. They had been taught by Godwin as he wrote of political justice; by Owen's "New Moral World;" by Shelley, as he passionately inveighed against the society which had robbed him of his children, and had driven him an outcast from his ancestral home. They had seen Sir Samuel Romilly in vain pleading that a poor wretch should not be hung for stealing goods of the value of five shillings; and their newspapers had told them how bishops and royal dukes had swelled the majority in the British senate in favour of the accursed slave trade. Hints that reached them of doings at the Brighton Pavilion—of the disgusting revelations of Mrs. Clarke—of the great trial at Westminster Hall, when the character of an English Queen was at stake, had made the middle and lower classes view with infinite alarm the aristocracy and all connected with them. Reform had to be won, and the Corn Laws destroyed. In those days a powerful writer and eloquent orator could do much, and Mr. Fox laboured at his vocation, and not in vain. His Anti-Corn-Law speeches were of the noblest order of eloquence, and had a most powerful effect. It seems to me we have no such orators now; that we have fallen on evil days; that duty has lost her charms, and that right or wrong are viewed by men now with an equally impartial eye.

But it is time I point him out. You are in the Speaker's Gallery. As you look towards the ministerial side, about half-way down, you will see at the end of the fourth bench the subject of the present sketch. You cannot mistake him; there is not such another figure in the House. There are fat men in the House, there are short men; but there are none who so combine fatness and shortness as does Johnson Fox. There are very many serious, reverend-looking gentlemen in the House; but there are none so serious and reverend-looking as Fox, who not only wears a Puritan hat, but who wears it with a Puritan air, and whom you might easily imagine side by side with Praise-God-Barebones, or Hew-Agag-in-pieces-before-the-Lord. The upper part of the face is that of the divine, the lower part that of the alderman. There is a rare world of speculation in that eye, and of good cheer in that double chin. How out of that pile of flesh there can come forth a clear, articulate sound, and some considerable amount of superior thought, is to me a mystery, or would be did I not see upon the shortest and fattest possible body the largest possible head, still adorned by thick masses of grey hair, parted in the middle and hanging down on each side—altogether a face resembling very much that of John Bunyan. Mr. Fox's collar is down—no collar could stand up round such a chin—and an old-fashioned suit of black completes his *tout ensemble.* If his hat is on, you feel inclined to adopt the slang of the streets, and respectfully to ask the honourable gentleman, "Who is his hatter?" for it is low and broad-brimmed, and of a style that never would have won the smile of a Count d'Orsay. The resemblance, then, is complete; and if you could believe there were Puritans in these degenerate days, when Christians think they can make the best of both worlds, when actually one of our popular teachers tells us, that it is a sign of respectability to have an account at a bank—if, I repeat, in such times as these you can imagine that the men whose quaint words, and gloomy creeds, and self-sacrificing lives were heroic and marvellous then, and are heroic and marvellous still—are still existent, you would swear that chief among them was William Johnson Fox.

But Mr. Fox is on his legs. What a clear, musical, yet somewhat melancholy and mannered voice he has—how studied yet how natural is his air—how effective is his humour, and how marvellous his power of constructing climaxes! At any rate, there is nothing of the demagogue about him. There is no screaming, no vulgarity, no disgusting vehemence of matter or manner; but he gives you the idea of gentleness, and thought, and power. You tell me he is monotonous. Well, so he is. He stands in the same position invariably, and speaks with the same tone. When you have heard him once you need not hear him again. Look at him; his head is slightly on one side, his left arm, crossing his breast, supports his right elbow, and as he declaims, the fore-finger on his right hand emphatically rises and falls. Mr. Fox was a speaker, not a debater. His style of speaking has been born elsewhere than on those benches, and may be read and understood as well out of the House as in it—as well next year as this. Mr. Fox was the pulpit orator in the House of Commons. His speaking was that of a man who has, all his life, had a little perch to himself, in which he can teach, and from which he can lay down the law; and Mr. Fox was as much in it in St. Stephen's as when standing in South-place, Finsbury-square. Well might George Stephenson once say to Sir Robert Peel, "Why, of all the powers above and under the earth, there seems to me to be no power so great as the gift of the gab."

RICHARD COBDEN, M.P.

For a few years previous to the Crimean war, when the public in general believed that white-robed peace had taken up an eternal residence among the sons of men, the name of Richard Cobden was one everywhere received with respect. Sir Robert Peel had testified to the power of his "unadorned eloquence." The exasperation of rosy-checked country squires, not gifted with great oratorical powers, had subsided almost into a calm as they found that the alteration of the Corn-Laws had impaired neither their influence nor their wealth. The manufacturing interests had, in a substantial manner, by a subscription of 80,000*l.*, testified their value of Mr. Cobden's services. The hero of the Anti-Corn-Law League, the opponent of the Taxes on Knowledge, the champion of the ballot, the Coryphæus of the Peace party, the *decus et tutamen* of the Freehold Land Societies, had only to show himself to his countrymen to be regaled with the most vehement applause. In Exeter Hall, in St. Martin's Hall, at the Freemasons' Tavern, at the City of London Tavern, at the Free Trade Hall in Manchester, or the Town Hall in Birmingham—in short, in all the haunts and homes of popular agitation, honours were plentifully showered on the man who had commenced his political career as an obscure Manchester cotton dealer; who, by his wonderful tact, had won from a hostile senate the triumph of Free Trade, and whose very name was received on the continent as the embodiment—politically speaking—of English thought and feeling. A plain citizen never achieved a higher pinnacle of greatness. A revolution, in its consequences even at this distance of time not to be over-estimated, and as yet but partially developed, had been effected mainly by his agency. In old Rome, when Tiberius Gracchus headed a movement against the landed aristocracy, the result was a sudden and bloody death. In modern England the popular tribune meets with a happier fate. But this popularity was too great to last. When the Russian war broke out, Mr. Cobden's protest against it lowered him in the estimation of the mob. His conduct in the Chinese affair—when an old ally, Sir John Bowring, was condemned unheard—rendered him still more unpopular; and the clever appeal of Lord Palmerston to the country for awhile sent Mr. Cobden, politically speaking, to Coventry. It is a long lane that knows no turning. If Englishmen are ungrateful it is only for a season. When the passions and prejudices of the hour had passed, men of all opinions felt that, Cobden not in Parliament, that assembly was deprived of some portion of its lustre. To the honour of Rochdale be it said, it was the borough that, at the earliest opportunity, returned Mr. Cobden to his proper place; and when the latter returned from America, where he had been sojourning a while, it was to find that not only was he once more an M.P., but that a seat in the Cabinet waited his acceptance. Still more, he lived to see it a matter of national regret that he did not join the Cabinet, and add right honourable to his name. In the case of Mr. Cobden we have a clear illustration of the axiom that it is the age that makes the man. When Cobden entered on public life, commerce was in need of a mouthpiece to assert her importance and to demand her rights. English country gentlemen had governed the country in accordance with the fancied interests of English country gentlemen. How to keep up the rent was the problem to be solved. That the time would ever arrive when the farmers would be scientific, and have a fair command of capital, and be enabled to pay higher rents and make more money under a system that did not prohibit the introduction of foreign corn, never entered into the heads of the landed class. England was growing to be the workshop of the world. From the backwoods of Canada, from distant Chicago, from the banks of the Danube, from the vast corn districts of Southern Russia, there came a voice saying, "Give us your manufactures and take our corn. So will your poor have work, so will your hungry be fed, so shall commerce more effectually bind us in the golden cords of peace." In Manchester, in Birmingham, in Sheffield and Leeds, where men live by the production of mechanism and manufacture, this truth was clearly and painfully felt. But it was only till within the last few years that the political existence of Manchester, and Birmingham, and Sheffield, and Leeds, had been admitted by our governing classes. Huskisson was beginning to see the truth in these matters, but the sudden termination of his lamented life left the commercial classes almost friendless and alone in the Senate. The landlords ruled the roast, and administered the game laws, and believed with Malthus that society had a tendency to advance beyond the means of subsistence, and stood aghast at the ever-increasing mass of pauperism, a terror by night and by day in their midst. The pious recommended resignation, the intelligent began to inquire how it was that life was such a curse, that here there was abundance, there starvation. They found that our Corn-laws produced much of this mischief; that the time had come for England to burst her chains and take tremendous strides, or to be for ever fallen. At this crisis Richard Cobden arose. He had been a Manchester manufacturer; he was now to be the utterance of the wants and wishes of the age. The best years of his life he devoted to that work, and the splendid testimonial subscribed to him by the people of England at the termination of the Anti-Corn-Law agitation was but a poor equivalent for the pecuniary losses he had sustained by renouncing a successful mercantile career. Even a subsequent pecuniary subscription, on the occasion of his losses by his American investments, was but a small per centage on the profits made by the subscribers under Free Trade.

Is it not time that we begin to understand history? The one great fact taught by wars, and rebellions, and revolutions of all kinds; by the decline and fall of Rome, by the collapse of French monarchies, by the growth of English freedom, by the spread of Anglo-Saxon institutions in America and Australia; is, that by fair means or foul, every twenty-four hours a man must dine. Men are led by their passions rather than their principles. Understand this, and the past ceases to be a mighty maze without a plan. Understand this, and history is no longer a riddle. Understand this, and the curtain is drawn up and you see living men. Our statesmen and historians use fine phrases, but they have no meaning, and merely darken and perplex. For instance, who besides a professed statesman, or partisan writer, or Edinburgh Reviewer, ever cared a straw about the balance of power in Europe? Men are not moved by such phantoms. Yet, if you read history, you would think that millions of men have died, and millions of money have been squandered about an unmeaning phrase. The simple fact was, that in France people got hungry, and did not know how to satisfy their hunger without upsetting a monarchy. From the peace of 1815 to 1830 we had bad harvests and distress, and the result was a Reform Bill; a few years later the potato crop failed in Ireland, and we had Free Trade. Life is too short and people are too busy to go to war for the grand reasons given by the historian or embodied in state papers. In ordinary life the hottest politician is a plain, plodding tradesman, taking care of the pence, and civil to his customers. In the same manner the ordinary life of a nation is devoted to its material interests. If it be otherwise, there is something wrong. Perhaps Mr. Cobden understood this truth better than any man living. His perception of it was the secret of his success and the pole-star of his life. In developing this idea, he made sad havoc of old notions and party cries. An M.P. present in the House when Canning made that famous speech about calling the New World into existence, to redress the balance of the old, said: "While he was speaking, Mr. Canning seemed actually to have increased in stature, his attitude was majestic, his chest heaved and expanded, his nostril dilated; a noble pride slightly curled his lip, age and sickness were forgotten and dissolved in the ardour of youthful genius." Cobden would never—could never—have produced such an effect. Had he been in Canning's situation, had he held the reins of power, his eye would have sparkled, and his breast would have expanded, and his whole frame would have quivered with emotion; not that he had called into existence some half-dozen of the most accursed governments under the sun (for such Canning's emancipated colonies turned out), but that he had won for the toiling masses of his countrymen a right to earn their daily bread. Undoubtedly that is the primary need. Without that right achieved, no nation can be prosperous, or renowned, or great. It is not in utter poverty that the Graces love to dwell. Where the struggle for existence is bitter and all-absorbing, there is no morality, no intelligence, no civilization worthy of the name, and man is but little better than a brute. A nation may fight to revenge the wrongs of oppressed nationalities, but ere it does this, it must have done its duty to itself.

Among the middle classes nine men out of ten told you what a pity it was that Mr. Cobden had lost himself by his peace crotchets. It is true he said many things, and some of them possibly not wise ones. A man who has made as many speeches as Mr. Cobden did is pretty sure occasionally to fall into blunders. In the heat and excitement of great struggles, things are said which turn out to be utter folly, yet the speakers of them are not set down as fools. The Duke of Wellington said it would be madness in him to think of being prime minister, yet directly after he attained that exalted rank. You could almost always tell when Sir Robert Peel was about to turn by the solemnity and vehemence with which he asserted he was not. Did not Sir Robert Inglis prophesy that ten years after the Reform Bill was carried, the House of Peers and the State Church would be destroyed, and England would be turned into a republic? Did not he say he would be afraid to trust the Bible to the people unless it was in the hands of the clergy of the Church of England? And yet the man who could thus doubt the truth and power of the Bible, and could thus insanely prophesy, was, to the very last, representative of an English University. Lord Eldon upheld the most disgraceful and sanguinary criminal code in

Europe, and for years he was worshipped as the wisest of mankind. Many of our leading statesmen took an active part in opposing the Corn-laws, and predicted the most disastrous results. We do not sneer at them, but Mr. Cobden and the champions of industrial rights are taunted everlastingly when they blunder, as if no other men did the same. For them and them alone there are no waters of Lethe. Surely this is hard measure. Public opinion in this country is led by the aristocracy, and they, of course, very naturally look upon the Cobden class with more or less disfavour, but the disfavour of the Manchester school is to be attributed to a deeper source. Old Hobbes tells us man naturally is in a state of war. The Manchester school ignore this primary fact, and thus run counter to the universal instincts of our race. War is a folly, a crime, a curse, but men have always fought nevertheless; and now, when all Europe resounds with the measured tread of armed men, more distant than ever seems the day when the war-drum shall throb no longer,

> "And the battle flag be furl'd
> In the parliament of man, in the federation of the world."

Now Mr. Cobden's Peace speeches have not merely been falsified, but have been distasteful as well. Thus, when in a speech at Wrexham, in 1850, Mr. Cobden said he would rather cut down the expenditure for military establishments to ten millions, and run every danger from France or any other quarter, than risk the danger of attempting to keep up the present standard of taxation and expenditure, common sense told us that the real question is one of national safety, and not of expense. If our war expenditure in time past had been greater we should have saved money now, as it is clear that our neglect in this respect has stimulated in other quarters increased activity. Mr. Cobden, in the same speech, said he believed there never was an instance known in the history of the world of as many as 50,000 men being transported across the salt waters within 12 months—an assertion which was proved fallacious very shortly after. In the same way he argued against a French invasion, because the French Emperor treated him personally with the utmost distinction, and because he and his family happened to have a comfortable domicile in Paris. Knowing the immense material advantage to England and France of peace, he could see nothing in the immense naval preparations of that country—nothing in such fortifications as Cherbourg —nothing in the invective, which under the license of the government was launched forth in French Journals against perfidious Albion. "The pacific genius of the house of Pelham was not unknown to France, and fell in very conveniently with their plan of extensive empire," writes Horace Walpole, in his "Memoirs of the Reign of George II." Was not the passage applicable to Mr. Cobden? The Peace party and Mr. Cobden, in the same way, undoubtedly had much to do with that miserable Crimean war. The late Czar, I have no doubt, imagined that Mr. Cobden and the Peace party represented England, and that under no circumstances whatever would she go to war. The late Czar saw an old ally at the head of affairs. He saw Mr. Cobden, the mouth-piece of thousands, representing all war as absurd. He saw Peace Congresses perambulating the land, and he knew that the prime movers of them, the Quakers, were men who if smitten on one cheek, would meekly turn the other, and await the blow. He saw that we had allowed him to trample Hungary under-foot—that we had been silent when Poland was blotted from the map of nations—that wildly and viciously Protestant as we were, we had allowed the Pope to be re-seated on his tottering throne by the aid of French bayonets; and might he not well think that so reckless had we become of our ancient prestige—so absorbed had we grown in the pursuit of wealth—so permeated had we been by Manchester oratory and Peace tracts, that scarcely the dictates of self-preservation—certainly not the claims of humanity or the obligations of treaties, or the considerations of an enlightened public policy, or the cause of an effete race whose very existence in Europe was an anomaly—would induce us again ever to draw the sword? The Peace party themselves helped to create this confusion. Everybody wished them well, and soldiers and sailors were at a discount. Most of them, simple-minded, good-meaning folk, fell very naturally into the error of mistaking their select assemblies of neat Quakeresses and verdant youths for the people of England. When Mr. Bradshaw, of the "Guides," died,—a decent man I doubt not, but not known to the nation in any capacity whatever beyond that of his trade,—I myself heard Joseph Sturge at a public meeting at Edinburgh exclaim that there were more tears shed when the nation heard of the death of Mr. Bradshaw than when the hero of Waterloo died. Now in England we simply laugh at such an assertion. But in Russia they could not see its absurdity. And the Czar having seen that in one agitation Mr. Cobden had represented the will of the nation, fell into the very easy error of supposing that on the question of Peace, as well as that of Free Trade, Mr. Cobden was similarly backed. Still more may be urged against Mr. Cobden. The war having once begun—Quaker Sturge having travelled to St. Petersburg, bearing the olive branch in vain—he should have remembered that he was an Englishman, and having lifted up his warning voice and finding it disregarded, should have waited till the nation had recovered from its war-fit. Mr. Cobden, it may be said, helped to prolong the Russian war in the same manner as the Jacobites in 1696 helped to prolong the war with Louis the Great. Macaulay tells us Louis was inclined for peace. After the failure of the Assassination Plot he had made up his mind to the necessity of recognising William Prince of Orange as king of England, and had authorized Callières to make a declaration to that effect, but the Jacobites in

London wrote to the Jacobites in St. Germain's such tales of the distresses of the country—of its exhaustion and the unpopularity of the Prince, that to the great joy of the non-jurors Callières became high and arrogant, and denied that William was anything more than a pretender to the throne.

Mr. Cobden was strong enough to have said, "I, in common with the wise and good of the British nation, have blundered, and find the Millennium of peace further off than I dreamed."

All men deprecate war. It is not to be believed for an instant that the men in drab are the only friends to peace. As sincerely and passionately as Mr. Cobden did himself, we believe, do our leading statesmen long for peace; for illustration of this we have only to look to the Ashburton capitulation, as Lord Palmerston termed it, and the cession of the Ionian Islands to Greece: but we cannot shut our eyes to the fact that the course of events has placed us in the foremost files of time—that we may not stand in despicable isolation, printing calicoes and jingling guineas, while the strong are trampling on the weak, and robbery is being attempted at our very doors. Sure are we that when the nation shall have stooped to take so mean a view of its vocation, its glory will have departed, and the period will have arrived when the famous picture of Macaulay shall be realized, and the stranger from New Zealand, standing on London Bridge, and contemplating the ivied ruins of St. Paul's, shall mark the traces of a greatness that has passed away. The spirit that animates the nation in a righteous war is a noble one. Humanity has shone brightest at such periods. It would require the most profound ignorance of history for a man to assert that the contests which gave the victories of Marathon and Salamis to the Greeks—that roused up in the Middle Ages the followers of the Crescent and the Cross—that triumphed at Waterloo—that crushed the Indian revolt—were among the least illustrious events that occupy and adorn the annals of the world. Our most pacific periods of history have not been our most brilliant ones. About eighty years since, our statesmen were very pacific. Our national income was unequal to our peace establishment; our navy was a "visionary fabric;" our troops were not sufficient to be of any service; Frederic the Great had civilly declined the overtures of Mr. Fox; we had attempted to patch up an ignominious peace; yet a War Minister came into office, and never did the nation achieve a wider reputation, or wield a more irresistible power.

Mr. Cobden, like Mr. Bright, underrated the influence of the landed aristocracy, and he was too willing to believe that the public is an enlightened body, acting solely from a sense of its own interests. The truth is, that the public, whether of France or England, is very often the dupe of its passions and fancies, and that in England, whatever may be done occasionally by dwellers in cities, the real power is in the hands of the land-owners. He and Mr. Bright also took it for granted that we had a party in this country who wish to go to war merely for the sake of war.

"What do you think of Cobden?" said the writer to a large Norfolk farmer, after the former had been delivering an address in the fine old hall of the county town. "Why," said he, "I believe if Cobden had held up a sheet of white paper and told us it was black, we should all have sworn the same thing." This answer may be accepted as a fair description of Cobden as a speaker. By his appearance he disarmed all prejudices. You saw a man of middle size, very plainly dressed, rather fresh coloured, with brown hair slightly streaked with grey, and with arched eyebrows, which gave him a very shrewd appearance. There was a harshness in his voice, but that went off after he had spoken a sentence or two, and there was such an ease about the man, such a clever adaptation of himself to his audience—you felt so much at home with him, he had so thoroughly the air of one arguing alone and familiarly with yourself—that it was almost impossible, at any rate while he was speaking, not to range yourself on his side. His unaffected good nature, his natural pleasantry, were irresistible. In the House of Commons he was much the same as on the platform, equally clear, equally unaffected, equally at home. There he stood on the right of the Speaker below the gangway, slightly stooping, as if from physical languor, alternately pointing with the fore-finger of his right hand to some honourable gentleman on the Opposition benches, with whom, if you could only see and not hear, you would suppose he was carrying on a very animated conversation. Occasionally the left hand was brought into play, and by means of sundry taps administered to it by his right, Mr. Cobden denoted that he had made some very effective observations. Mr. Cobden did not attempt eloquence—did not quote the classics—was very seldom witty—but gave you the idea of a plain man talking upon business in a business-like way. You listened to him in vain for the magic play of fancy—for rhetoric "rich with barbaric pearl and gold"—for a philosophy that shall live when speaker and hearer shall have passed away. He made no attempt at display; never did you hear a more natural speaker, and we may add, fairer reasoner. Charles Fox's test of a speech is eminently applicable to Mr. Cobden. "Does it read well? if so it was a bad speech." As spoken his speeches were always a success. Mr. Cobden satisfied himself with arguing the questions of the present moment with the facts of the present; all his references, all his hits and his speeches, abounded with them; all his arguments were gathered from the experience of the day; to the men of to-morrow he left the task of doing to-morrow's work. Indeed, before his decease there were symptoms occasionally discernible indicating that Mr. Cobden was more ready to seek repose than to buckle on the armour for fresh fights.

In one thing he was to the last, however, as earnest as ever. In the cause of Free-trade, and the vast interests involved in the idea, he neither tired nor fainted. For the recent changes in the commercial policy of France—for the pledge it gives us of peace—for the plenty it will give to manufacturing millions on each side the Channel—for all the blessings, social, intellectual, moral, it will scatter the wide world over—let the English nation tender grateful thanks to Richard Cobden.

MR. THOMAS S. DUNCOMBE.

No account of parliamentary orators would be complete or satisfactory that did not include the name of Mr. Duncombe. It is true he belongs to the past rather than to the present; but he was the pet of the people at one time, did good service in his day, and represented a class of men becoming rare. The gay young aristocrats who went in for popular applause, have been a numerous class. When we think of them, the names of Alcibiades, Count Mirabeau, and Charles James Fox, instinctively recur to our minds. They had a love of liberty which they carried out to the fullest extent. They were the wonder and admiration of their contemporaries. How intense was their contempt of money, how ardent was their pursuit of pleasure, and how complete was their devotion to the cause of the people! Men smiled on them, and women too. In this soberer age of ours, we can scarce understand their ways, or do justice to their character. Mr. Duncombe was almost the last of his class. A rising statesman now must work hard to win his laurels. He must lecture at Mechanics' Institutions, he must attend at the sitting of the Social Congress, he must be always at his place in Parliament, and, if he appears on the platform of Exeter Hall, so much the better. It may be that we have gained in honesty, but I am not quite so sure of that. There are whited sepulchres now as there were when the Gospel story was first published to the world.

Middle-aged or rather elderly gentlemen will tell you that young Thomas Duncombe, then M.P. for Hertford, was one of the handsomest and gayest men about town some thirty or forty years ago. Whatever are their politics, they will all confess how dashing was his appearance, how sparkling was his eye, how musical his voice, and how gentlemanly his breeding. I take up a series of parliamentary portraits by a Conservative writer. He says, "If the shade of Beau Brummell had revisited the earth to nominate his presiding genius in the departments of fashion in the senate, his choice must have fallen on the honourable member, for in person Duncombe is the *beau ideal* of a gentleman; dresses well, and always in keeping, as far as fashion goes, with its most approved modes; never seen with less than brilliantly-polished and well-fitting boot, a smart, somewhat d'Orsay hat, beautiful lavender or straw-coloured kid gloves, and a turn-out, by way of equipage, worthy of an aristocrat of the highest order. If a line be pardoned in favour of his personal attractions, we might venture to observe, in conclusion, that if the days of chivalry were returned, and a dashing cavalier selected from some gay troubadours to pay homage to the shrine of his ladye love, few knights would stand more prominent in the ranks than the popular M.P. for Finsbury." Mr. James Grant, in his "Random Recollections," gives an equally agreeable character of Mr. Duncombe. He was then a favourite in the House and a favourite out of doors. Of course, much was due to his singularly attractive personal appearance. Few could be angry with such a well-bred, agreeable man of the world. However extreme might be his opinions, however uncompromising his speeches, however he might tease and irritate officials (for when Mr. Duncombe was an ardent politician there were thousands of Chartists in the country—men who believed in Feargus O'Connor and the *Northern Star*, of whom Mr. Duncombe was the mouth-piece), somehow or other men did not get angry when the Finsbury M.P. was on his legs. There was always a merry twinkle in his eye, as if he were in fun, and then his manner was so easy, his voice so pleasant, his tact so admirable, that his bitterest enemies could not find it in their hearts to be angry. It was seldom that he made long and laboured speeches; his *forte* was rather in asking questions, in presenting ultra-Radical petitions, and in making statements relative to aggrieved (more especially Finsbury) individuals; and this he did to perfection. No man in the House had a happier knack of making a clear, intelligible statement in a manner simple and unaffected, and of occasionally relieving it with a little touch of humour; and when he took up the case of Mazzini, and convicted Sir James Graham of opening letters sent through the Post Office, he achieved a triumph of which almost every man, woman, and child in the British dominions was proud. The old poet tells us of a certain individual, that

> "If to his share some trifling errors fall,
> Look in his face, and you'll forget them all."

Duncombe could stand this test better than any man in the House; and yet he was not merely a Liberal but an ultra-Radical, when merely to be Radical was to be low, and ungentlemanly, and little better than one of the wicked. How came Mr. Duncombe connected with such a set? the question is interesting. Sheridan said Lord Holland (Tom Moore is our authority) was an annual parliament and universal suffrage man, but it seemed rather as a waggery that he adopted it. "There is nothing like it, he would say; it is the most convenient thing in the world. When people come to you with plans of reform, your answer is ready, Don't talk to me of your minor details. I am for annual parliaments and universal suffrage; nothing short of that." Did Duncombe act in this manner? The thought is uncharitable, yet some burning and shining lights of the popular party have been open to the charge. We are told Wilkes was indignant when taken for a Wilkesite. Men often act from mixed motives, and even patriots are imperfect. Mr. Duncombe could, however, do what few men could—point to an independent career of many years. There was a time when the sweets of office would have been acceptable; yet he remained unshackled by its trammels, nor did he, even to please the very large religious public of Finsbury, in any way identify himself with their proceedings. I never heard even of his being at a Ragged School meeting, or subscribing a farthing for the reforming young females. This is something, when we remember how old sinners by such means die in the odour of sanctity,—when we remember that not long since a Solicitor-General laid the foundation of a Primitive Methodist Chapel, and the wonderful Wolverhampton speech of Sir Richard Bethell (now Lord Westbury). But I have been speaking of Mr. Duncombe as he was in the hot days of Reform. The gay Tom Duncombe of the fashionable world of late had grown sedate and elderly, kept good hours, and took great care of his health. You did not see him in the House after midnight, and it was seldom that he spoke after the dinner-hour. The agile frame was almost a skeleton; age dimmed those eyes once so full of fire and light; the jet-black hair was gone, and in its place we had a wig; the pleasing, cheery voice sounded hollow and reedy; yes, there, behind the Treasury benches—that pale, tall, thin, elderly gentleman in black—was all that remained of that universal favourite, Tom Duncombe. However, even to the last there was still about him something of the old style. In that hour devoted to notices of motion and questioning of Ministers before the orders of the day are read, Mr. Duncombe often spoke, and almost as effectively as of yore—often, as of old, by his ready wit, provoking laughter. When he said "'Tis impudence and money make the peer," every one wondered that he was not prosecuted for libel. We, in these latter days, have reason to be thankful to men who, like Duncombe, aided in the great struggle of the past. Religiously, and commercially, and politically free, the last thirty years have been years of wonderful progress, of softening of party hates, of abandonment of prejudice, of rooting out of error, of exploding absurdities and injustices and ancient wrongs.

Mr. Duncombe's political career was a long one. His parliamentary existence began in 1824, when he sat for Hertford, which place he continued to represent till 1832, when he was ejected by Lord Ingestre, the honour of which was not long enjoyed, as a petition against Lord Ingestre's return, by the friends of Mr. Duncombe, had the effect of unseating the noble lord. In 1834 the retirement of the Right Hon. Robert Grant caused a vacancy for Finsbury, and agreeably to the powerful requisition of its electors, Mr. Thomas Duncombe, according to his own words, "was translated, as the bishop says, to its see." By descent Mr. Thomas Slingsby Duncombe was the last of a staunch line of Tory ancestry. His father was a brother of Lord Faversham, and his mother was the daughter of a High Churchman, Dr. Hinchcliffe, Bishop of Peterborough. His connexions were not of the class from which advocates of the Charter have sprung, though possibly his birth and breeding may have tended to make him more acceptable to Finsbury constituencies. Dod briefly sums up the gentleman's political creed as follows:—"A Radical reformer, is in favour of triennial parliaments and the ballot." Said I not rightly, Mr. Duncombe belongs to the past rather than the present? What elections now are decided with reference to triennial parliaments and the ballot? I question if a declaration of attachment to either of them now would secure a single vote. We have got beyond these formulas. We are now more social and religious reformers. The years have brought to us

"A higher height—a deeper deep."

HENRY DRUMMOND.

"To waive all considerations of personal friendship and esteem," wrote Edward Irving, in a preface to a volume of occasional discourses, "no one whom the religious stir and business of the last thirty years hath brought conspicuously before the Church, hath so strenuously served her best interests, through good and bad report, or doth so well deserve her thanks, as doth the man who brought forward, from their obcurity and persecutions, both Burckhardt and Wolff, and upheld their way against the sharp tongues of prudential and worldly-wise Christians; who laid the foundations of the Continental Society, and hath built it up in the frown and opposition of the religious world; who detected and dragged to light the false reports concerning the state of religion on the Continent, with which the Bible Society in its palmy times had closed the charitable car of the Church; who has stood forth as the friend and patron of every society which hath any show of favour for the Jews; and finally, who hath taken us, poor, despised interpreters of prophecy, under your wing, and made the walls of your house like unto the ancient schools of the prophets."

The reader will scarce guess for whom this dedication was composed. Perhaps he will think the subject of it was some wealthy clergyman or zealous bishop for a wonder trespassing beyond conventional limits, and showing himself a man earnest in matters of religion. It will save some trouble if I declare at once the eulogy was addressed to no other than the gentleman whose name heads this sketch—Henry Drummond, M.P.—a man whose plain mission seemed to be to teach that all was humbug under the sun. The

Egyptians at their feasts placed a skeleton to remind them of their mortality. We are told the Sultan Saladin had the same message proclaimed to him day by day, lest, in the flattery of courtiers, and in a career of military successes, he should forget so terrible a truth. Drummond performed a similar duty in Parliament. In his eye we were all morally dead; all virtue was gone clean out of us. Under the mask of patriotism he saw the grovelling soul of the placeman; in the love of liberty, the desire of license; in the people, an untaught mass, the prey of charlatans and quacks. Drummond reminded you of the

"Gray and tooth-gapped man as lean as death,"

whom Tennyson describes in his "Vision of Sin," and like him, he poured out a strain so sad and atheistic you would fain hope it false. Yet Drummond was an angel of the Irvingite Church, not as the result of a sudden whim, but as the proper climax to a long professional religious career.

But I beg the reader's pardon for keeping him so long out of the House of Commons. Let us suppose it is a debate on any serious subject. The abolition of death punishments, for instance—a question embracing the whole range of subjects connected, not merely with the lives of wretched criminals, but with all the defences by which society would guard itself against crime. We will take the usual debate on this subject as an illustration. Mr. Ewart has of course defended his motion with his usual ability. Mr. Hadfield, a

Manchester attorney, but representative of Sheffield, with a querulous, unpleasant voice, like that of a man who deserves to be in a minority, has seconded Mr. Ewart, and immediately there rises from the gangway—the first bench on the floor on the left—a tall, clerical-looking gentleman, who at once makes the House laugh. Listen to him:—"The proposition was for a Select Committee to inquire into the operation of the law imposing the punishment of death. Now he should have thought the operation of that law was simple enough" (hear, and a laugh). Again the hon. gentleman extracts another laugh on a subject at the first glance certainly not very facetious. The speaker continues:—"But the hon. gentleman called upon them to abolish the punishment of death on the ground of its uncertainty. Now, what punishment could be more certain than that of death he could not conceive"—(hear, and a laugh)—and thus at any rate the amusement of the evening was heightened. Now on almost all subjects this eccentric M.P. thus spoke, invariably as much as possible in opposition to every one else.

In the memoirs of the Brothers Haldane, we read, in the early part of the present century, of the arrival at Geneva of a gentleman whose "pleasing manners and aristocratic bearing, finely-chiselled features and intellectual forehead, bespoke his breeding and intelligence; whilst in his acute and penetrating glance, wit, sarcasm, and the love of drollery seemed to contend with earnestness, benevolence, and an ever-restless Athenian craving after novelty." To this young man, just entering into life, it seemed that all the world could offer was within his grasp. As the grandson of the first Lord Melville, the high offices of State were fairly within his reach. With wit and boundless wealth, what a life of pleasure, such as Alcibiades might have envied, was within his reach! yet, while other men were climbing up the steep hill of fame, or dimming their lustre in the search after gold—or following the phantom pleasure far over hill and dale, till weary and way-worn she left them in utter darkness and despair—Henry Drummond was drawing around him a select circle to study the dark sayings of the prophets, and to gather from them the weapons with which to turn to folly the wisdom of these latter days. Three curious volumes in octavo, entitled "Dialogues on Prophecy," written by the host himself, and much subsequent confusion in the Christian Church, evinced that these bewildering conferences were not altogether without influence in their day. But one can't go on studying the prophets for ever. Englishmen especially cannot get rid of their inborn propensity to break away from cloudland into practical life. Not merely do such as he of "Locksley Hall," with strong hearts torn and bleeding with the bitter agony of a manly love wantonly trifled with or basely betrayed, exclaim—

"I must nerve myself to action, lest I wither in despair;"

but all men, whatever be their inward sorrows,

recognise the truth, not merely as a universal law of humanity, but as a blessed means of escape from entanglements of the heart, or difficulties of the head. Another reason may be urged—(the mighty master dead—the eloquent tongue, that, like the voice of a trumpet, terrified our Modern Babylon with the certain coming of a millennial day, silent in the grave—the brain become dust that had to contend, not merely with the wit and wisdom of the world, which in its higher light it would see to be folly, but with the keen and cruel enmities of the Church)—silence in the halls of the prophets, and they

> "Scattered on the Alpine mountains cold,"

what was there to forbid Drummond laying down his spiritual pursuits and betaking himself to others more congenial with human weakness and the claims of actual life. Thackeray sings—

> "Ho! pretty page with the dimpled chin,
> That never has known the barber's shear,
> All your wish is woman to win,
> This is the way that boys begin,—
> Wait till you come to forty year."

By the light of years one reads things differently to what one does in one's earlier days; or if that be not the case, possession cloys the appetite, and we find in change relief. Just as the elegant *roué* subsides into fat and matrimony, or the spendthrift becomes penurious, so Henry Drummond left the fathers for the senators, and forsook the school of the prophets that he might raise in St. Stephen's a voice almost as obscure and unmeaning as those of prophecy itself. West Surrey contained the country-house of Henry Drummond; what more natural than that it should return him as its representative? West Surrey belongs to a few lords, and was not Drummond lordly by connexion with wife and mother? In West Surrey at any rate such logic was not unpalatable, and accordingly in 1847 Henry Drummond, a country gentleman of a sanctimonious turn—a theologian and a banker—a wit, yet a member of the *haut ton*—became its M.P. The man who combined all these characteristics—who could tell a scandal with a relish one moment, and the next plunge many a fathom deep into the millennial controversy; who could talk in the true bucolic vein to the Tyrrels and Newdegates, and at the same time could say a good thing worthy to be told at the clubs with the last epigram of Jerrold or the newest sarcasm of Rogers; who could uphold the sacraments and yet abhor the Pope; who would admit the existence of all the abuses complained of by reformers, and yet uphold them on the plea that it were vain to attempt to make things better—till He should come whose right it was to reign; who could abuse the Church and yet spurn Dissent—was not an ordinary man.

Austere and crotchety, elderly and cynical, Henry Drummond was an extraordinary man merely to look at. He was tall and thin, with an oval head, a calm, passionless face, and short, scant grey hair. There was an air of the recluse about him. One would expect to find him at Oxford or Cambridge rather than in the House of Commons. Yet not only did you find him there, but he was a favourite with the House. When he spoke there was always a rush from the smoking-room and the lobbies. In the first place, he was what all Englishmen like—rich; in the second place, he had the good sense never to bore you, and never to be long; in the third place, he was often witty, and invariably crotchety and odd. There are several men who attempt wit in the House. Lord Palmerston does, but his is generally sheer flippancy, and would be insufferable in a man who was not on the pedestal, but had a position to make.* Sibthorp did, but his was of an inferior character, yet an enlightened English constituency could return him, and will return his family for ever—at any rate, so long as they keep the estate. One of the Lennoxes—the stout one, not the thin one who handed glasses of water to Mr. Disraeli when he was doing the orator on an extensive scale—attempts to be jocose, but his is the tragic mirth of a gay man about town, and has the same effect on you as that of the celebrated peer of whom Tom Moore sang that when

> "The House looks unusually grave,
> You may always be sure that Lord Lauderdale's joking."

Then there is the wit of the cynic of the Dean Swift

* This, it must be remembered, was written during Lord Palmerston's first premiership.

school, but slightly altered and improved, with all the improper passages omitted, with a dash of extra bitterness gathered from the fairest regions of theological controversy—scholarly and gentlemanly. That was the wit of Drummond, uttered in the mildest manner, and with the thinnest possible of voices, almost inaudible in the gallery, so that the House was kept in a state of the utmost soul-harrowing quiet and suspense, till he got to the end of a sentence, when it occurred to every one that Mr. Drummond had been uncommonly funny, and the House relieved itself by a hearty laugh —a laugh generally heralded by a few preliminary explosions from the more impulsive members, as the orchestra tunes up previous to a grand overture, or as a few random shots may be heard ere rank and file on the battle-field may begin their murderous fire; and when you read the *Times* next morning you were not surprised to find that "laughter" was reported after most of Mr. Drummond's remarks. I cannot find that the debate gained much by Mr. Drummond's speeches. I do not imagine he intended it should. His object appeared to be simply to amuse and mystify the House. He seemed to assume that the House had made up its mind how it should vote long before the discussion commenced, and therefore in a quiet, unostentatious way Mr. Drummond merely uttered a few sentences and attained his object. I need scarcely observe then that he was an original; no other definition of him can be given. He was neither Whig, Tory, nor

Radical. I believe the author of "Who is Who" would be puzzled to describe to what class the member for West Surrey belonged. In the early part of Disraeli's career, a pamphlet was published with the title "What is He?" I could imagine a pamphlet having such a title with reference to Mr. Drummond, would have a very fair sale among his constituents. In 1847 Mr. Drummond walked over the course unopposed, yet I much question whether his constituents could have told what he was. Dod tells me Mr. Drummond was a Conservative; that he was a member of the Royal Academy of Fine Arts in Florence; that he founded the Professorship of Political Economy at Oxford—feeling, I suppose, his own deficiency in this respect; I learn also, that he was a magistrate; and as he always sneered at the present age, I am not surprised to find that he was the president of one of the literary institutions (the Western) so peculiar to the present age. He believed people cannot live without good beer, yet he only knew one house in Surrey where they could get it good. He said that the food of the people should be as free from taxation as the air they breathe, yet he derided the free traders. He was opposed to all measures for taxing one sect for the support of the clergy of another, yet he always wrote against the abolition of church rates. He believed in God's goodness, and yet rolled as a sweet morsel under his tongue—and would propound it unhesitatingly in the House of Commons, where, of all places, theological dogmas should have no room—the utter depravity of infants at their birth. He borrowed from Rome the idea of a Catholic and Universal Church, and then abused the Pope. All men are rogues, and therefore, he argued, it was folly to expect honesty in politics or in the administration of state affairs. He thought so meanly of his constituents that he told them they did every day what the Czar did when he originated the late war. He was an author, yet he abominated the press. But time fails me, and I give up the task of attempting to chronicle the opinions of the eccentric member for West Surrey. Are they not recorded for future ages in the chronicles of Hansard? Once or twice the *Times* was guilty of the folly of attempting to write him down; but in this country you cannot write down a statesman with an aristocratic connexion and a good estate. Mr. Drummond was more than the *Times* imagined, and hence its ridicule was thrown away. Mr. Drummond was not a statesman in the common acceptation of that term. You could never fancy him, with a patient air, tying up red tape, and doing the work of the Circumlocution-office. Still less was he a party man; for if he sat on one side of the House, he generally voted on the other, and his speech was no index to his vote. Nor was he a worshipper of public opinion, nor did he stand forth as its representative in the House. He was merely a country gentleman, cultivated into a paradox—at all times consistent in his aim at originality in politics and theology—with a tone of extravagance caught in the prophetic conferences of his earlier years; a man with a keen perception of the vanity of practical politics, and yet not strong enough to attain unto something purer and better.

SIR CHARLES NAPIER.

You are standing in the lobby of the House of Commons about four P.M.—just as the Speaker has passed by in all the pomp and majesty due to his awful rank, and are watching the varieties of costume and figure in which honourable M.P.'s rejoice. We will suppose it is the middle of the summer, and that the younger M.P.'s are got up in the most expensive and fashionable style. No one on the face of the earth dresses better than the English gentleman, and if you want to see the finest specimens of that splendid animal, you cannot do better than stand for an hour or two, where now, mentally, we have placed you. A very odd and curious figure approaches: it is that of an old man—short and stout, very bent, leaning heavily on a stick. Look at the man's dress. He does not ruin himself with tailors' bills. That old straw hat on his head is dear at a shilling; that tweed slop never could have cost more than a pound when new; that yellow waistcoat and those white trousers evidently have seen better days. Look at the man's face. It is broad, cheerful—like that of most sailors—almost rollicking in its expression; some old captain, you say, come to stare about him. But look! he has passed the door-keeper. Surely the latter gentleman will call him back! By no means. The rough old sailor is no other than Sir Charles Napier.

"Ben Block," says Tom Dibdin, "was a veteran of naval renown." The same might have been said of Sir Charles Napier. But Sir Charles Napier had this advantage over Ben Block—that he got into Parliament, and had a name as familiar in St. Stephen's as on the quarter-deck.

Sir Charles Napier had good blood in his veins. He was a descendant of the inventor of Logarithms; was born on the 6th of March, 1786; entered the navy at the age of thirteen; was a post-captain at twenty-three, and in 1815, when the Euryalus, which he commanded, was paid off, was made a C.B. In 1829 he went to sea again, in the command of the Galatea—of the seedy, dirty appearance of which naval men still talk. In 1830 Sir Charles took command of the fleet of Don Pedro, and captured the fleet of Don Miguel, off St. Vincent, and thus helped to establish that precious Spanish Government which was a scandal to our age. In the Syrian war, in 1840, Napier was commodore under Sir Robert Stopford, who commanded in the Mediterranean. Here he did considerable service. The landing at D'Journic, the capture of Beyrout and Sidon, and the bombardment of Acre, were all owing to his instrumentality; and at Alexandria he astonished the liberating squadron by running in under a flag of truce, and concluding a convention with Mehemet Ali, out of his own head, which, in spite of its irregularity, was confirmed by the authorities at home. He returned to England full of popularity, and was brought into Parliament as member for Marylebone. He had before that time unsuccessfully contested Portsmouth and Greenwich. He took the command of the Mediterranean fleet, and retired from Parliament. The Russian war broke out. He went up the Baltic and did nothing. The men of Southwark thought he was badly used, and sent him into Parliament.

The author of "Singleton Fontenoy" gives us a graphic sketch of Sir Charles as a sailor. Singleton is off Beyrout, and is sent on board a very dirty ship for orders. "Singleton, having copied the order, went on deck and ordered his boat to be called alongside. While waiting for it he saw a figure emerge from the cabin under the poop. There was a sensation on deck, and my hero perceived at once that the figure was that of a Great Man. He was dressed in a rather seedy uniform, and had an awkward stoop. His face was eccentric, but expressed power. He crossed his hands behind his back, and began to pace the deck with a gait that was as remarkable as everything else about him. It was Benbow with a dash of Garibaldi." Sir Charles also has painted a portrait of himself, but in a more flattering style. In 1851 he collected and republished all the letters he had sent to the *Times*, the *Sun*, and other newspapers, under the title of "The Navy, its past and present State." It is hardly possible to conceive anything more vainglorious than Sir Charles's assertions. A few paragraphs taken at random will suffice. "Had I not displayed energy and boldness, the probability is that this country would have been involved in war and our foreign policy overthrown." "I dethroned Don Miguel. Had the battle of Cape St. Vincent been lost, Don Miguel would have been on the throne of Portugal, the dynasty of Louis Philippe shaken to its centre, and most probably Lord Grey's administration." "I upset the Grand Prince of Lebanon, the ally of Mehemet Ali, defeated Mehemet's son, and drove his troops out of the mountain." "My services are unsurpassed by those of any admiral on the list—I think I may say, without fear of contradiction, that they have had more influence on the state of Europe than those of any other officer in the navy." "The battle of Cape St. Vincent changed the dynasty, as well as the whole political face of Europe." But for him, Sir Charles assures us, "the Syrian expedition would have failed, Acre would not have been attacked, war with France would have been inevitable, our policy overthrown, and with it the Melbourne Administration." Such was the gallant admiral's modest assurance!

Some people called Sir Charles the modern Bombastes. He reminded me of a humbler character, one Thomas Codd. The reader asks who was the last-named gentleman? I will endeavour to answer that question.

There lived, many years ago, in a certain city in the south of Ireland, an odd personage whose real name was a mystery, but who was popularly known by the name of Tom Codd. Now, like Sir Charles, he believed that all the great events that had taken place in Europe during his own time were owing to him. He was consulted by every statesman in Europe. From him the Duke of Wellington derived the plans of his most successful campaigns. It was his advice that prevailed in the councils of Europe. The wags of the city in question encouraged the poor man in his delusions to such a pitch that he verily believed the world could not go on without him. He preserved, says the writer from whom I take my account, his delusions to the last moment of his life, and he died in the full belief that he was the wisest and most influential man of his age. In naval matters, to compare greatt hings with small, Sir Charles was, I fear, another Tom Codd.

Sir C. Napier was a capital illustration of the truth of the old adage, "Second thoughts are best!" Southwark elected him at the bidding of the *Morning Advertiser*, and because Southwark deemed he had a grievance. It is to the credit of Southwark that it should thus sympathize with what it deems the victim of a wrong; but it would be to the credit of the Southwark collective brains if they recollected that impulse is by no means a safe rule of action. A wider knowledge of human nature should have taught Southwark that the man who is eternally boasting his own merits has but few merits; and that the man who wails his wrongs on the house-top generally has few wrongs to be redressed. On their own merits modest men are dumb. The woman who comes to you in the street, with an expression of abject misery in her face, with three children in her arms, whom she pinches all the while, and with a tale of villany on the part of a monster of a husband, who has left her all forlorn—is a female of questionable repute, and has hired the children at a moderate sum per day; if, in your morning walks, you give a cripple as you deem him something for charity, in the evening the impostor, over a jollier supper than your limited means will enable you to procure yourself, will be laughing at you as a precious flat. The public is constantly imposed on. It is often giddy and thoughtless as a child. It is the loudest rant the Marylebone householder will most rapturously endorse. It is only education and intelligence that can teach men to detect the cloven foot under the mask of the popular tribune.

What, it may be asked, had Sir Charles done that he should take the vacant place of Sir W. Molesworth? Sir W. Molesworth—no one can deny it—was a statesman; Sir Charles was nothing of the kind. He was a sailor in search of promotion. Not engaged in his profession, he had a seat in Parliament. Immediately professional advancement was offered him, his seat in Parliament was resigned. A war breaks out; amidst a wonderful flourish of trumpets Sir Charles is despatched to the Baltic; the Reform Club gives a dinner to the naval hero, who declares over his cups that he will either be at St. Petersburg, or in a place that shall be nameless, in a month. The time passes, and Sir Charles is neither in one place nor the other; the nation strains itself to listen, but no sound of victory is borne to us over the tideless waters of the Baltic, and at length Sir Charles returns home—Sir James Graham would not let him fight the Russians, and Sir Charles hauls down his flag, and tells us he is an injured man. Sir Charles is lifted into Parliament, to have his revenge and impeach Sir James; but the House listens, laughs when the old admiral begins swearing, and finally is counted out. That Sir Charles did nothing he argued was not his own fault. He tells us he had a bad crew; it is a bad workman that quarrels with his tools. I question whether the infamous press-gang gave Nelson a better lot. That fleet that lay a summer in the Baltic,

> "Idle as a painted ship,
> Upon a painted ocean,"

was got together with some difficulty, cost the nation some money, and was expected to do something. Lord John Russell, it seems, on one occasion intimated that Sir Charles evinced a want of discretion. Certainly this was not the case as regards the Baltic campaign. An excessive discretion is a little out of place in war.

An excessively discreet man would not go to war at all—would take to farming or shop-keeping rather than become a warrior, and go in for glory and cannon-balls. Sir Charles—if the Sir Charles of old—would have won in his Baltic campaign either a peerage or Westminster Abbey. Sir Charles had more valour in his youth.

We pass on to other days: to Nelson expecting every man to do his duty; to Blake leaving politics to the Parliament, and telling the seamen, "It is not our business to mind state affairs, but to keep foreigners from fooling us!" In these days of magnificent promises and puny performances—when our most formidable sea-captains are only formidable with their pens, when their greatest achievement is to keep a fleet out of harm's way, when the finest fleet the world ever saw sails upon the Baltic as if it were so many yachts on a pleasure trip—it is well to look back to the time when English ships were not afraid of stone walls; when the Dutch were driven from the sea—when Spain, and France, and Italy trembled at the sight of the red cross of the Commonwealth—when Algerine pirates, of bloody lives and natures, freely gave up Christian captives—when, as a writer of the time expresses it, "England was everywhere held in terror and honour!" The review will measure the exact difference between a Blake and a Napier; it will do more—it will indicate, in one department of public life, a falling off piteous and sad indeed!

Sir Charles's popularity, we fear, is of an evanescent character. It is true he bore a well-known name, but it was the war with Mehemet Ali that made him popular. Sir Charles came victorious out of the affair, and we welcomed home the conquering hero, forgetful all the while that we had thus destroyed what promised to have been a rising empire, one which, taking the place of Turkish weakness and venality, would have been in time a natural barrier to Russia in the East.

The old school of sailors found an admirable representative in Sir Charles. Young fellows who went to sea at an early age, from schools in which they learned nothing or next to nothing, during our fighting days were in great demand, and did the state good service. They are in these days of education and competition in the civil service very rare; but of the old school it may be remembered that the first gentleman of the age, as his toadies called him—that poor bloated, dissipated prince, at whom we all are so ready to throw stones—while deeply engaged in solving the question as to the cut and colour of the garments of naval officers, gave up the attempt in despair, exclaiming, with an oath, that dress them how you will, it is impossible to make them look like gentlemen. Well, these men never turned out great statesmen; even the gallant Nelson did not shine when he exchanged his proper business for diplomacy and considerations of national policy. Jack ashore is proverbially easily duped, and is much given to play the fool. But, unfortunately, an admiral, like a lawyer, must have a place in Parliament. Unless he has one he has little chance of promotion; and now-a-days, as the liberal is the winning side, the number of adherents to popular principles is encouraging or alarming according to the point of view.

Sir Charles was a rough, jolly, free-and-easy old gentleman. He would shake hands with his sailors; he would rush into a peace meeting, as I have seen him do at Edinburgh, and make a good fight on behalf of a standing army and navy; he would stick to his own opinion, however unpopular, and would, in very plain language, bid you be —— if you didn't like it. He was very honest, considering that he represents a popular borough. It is true, on one occasion he did preside at a Sunday School meeting (the Dissenters are strong in Southwark), but he boldly voted against the bill for the repeal of the Paper Duty, instead of, like the majority of M.P.s on that occasion, sending up the bill with a small majority as a hint to the Lords to throw it out. These are my honest opinions, said an American candidate, but if not those of my hearers they can be altered. Sir Charles Napier did not act in that way. You never caught him at anything sneaking or underhand. But, after all, honesty, and bluntness, and dash do not constitute a statesman. Other qualities are requisite. To these Sir Charles could lay no claim. I fear he was indebted, after all, for his public position, such as it was, chiefly to his own efforts to secure employment and place, by his constant attacks on Government, and by his obstinate proclamation of his merits. That he would pass away and be forgotten—that he would leave no impress on his age —that he would never rise to the rank of statesman was very clear. No one listened to his speeches; they were all on the same subject, in almost the same words, and very clear to most men, as soon as he got into Parliament, all set to the same tune. There is nothing like leather, was the one unvaried cry; and, to judge from appearance, it really mattered little to the gallant admiral whether men listened or not; whether they approved or condemned. There he stood drawling away, on the same seat in the gangway as Mr. Horsman, just below the Manchester party. M.P.s studied parliamentary reports, got up and went out, found their way into the lobby or the smoking-room, but Sir Charles was not discouraged, and would have his say—

> "He is an ancient mariner,
> And he stoppeth one of three,"

says Coleridge. The Ancient Mariner of the House of Commons was not so fortunate. I question if he gained the attention of one of thirty. Lord Clarence Paget was obliged to listen and reply, but no one else did. On the whole Sir Charles belonged to the past. He was born in fighting times, and bred to fighting. He harped on one string till he became a little behind his age. When he became an M.P. the times were altered; the old days were gone, the old ideas exploded, the old watchwords lost; and, like the bold Sir Bedivere, he might have exclaimed—

> "And I, the last, go forth companionless,
> And the days darken round me, and the years,
> Amongst new men, strange faces, other minds."

SIR CORNEWALL LEWIS.

Mr. Disraeli tells us literature and statesmanship of a high order are not incompatible. He quotes Julius Cæsar as an example in ancient times. Our parliamentary history is rich in illustrations of the same truth. There was a prophecy, when the Reform Bill was being agitated, that, in this respect, the character of the House of Commons would much deteriorate. At present such does not appear to have been the case. The subject of this sketch has written much, and has led the life of a hard student. He has published works on "The Romance Languages," on "The Use and Abuse of Political Terms," on "Local Disturbances and the Irish Church Question," on "The Government of Dependencies," on "The Influence of Authority in Matters of Opinion," on "Methods of Observation and Reasoning in Politics," on "The Credibility of Early Roman History," an edition of the fables of Babrius, an old Greek writer of whom nothing is known, and the time of whose existence is mere matter of conjecture; besides, he has edited the "Edinburgh Review." It is clear, then, Sir George Lewis was a hard student, and that he was pre-eminently a literary man; and that he was not unfitted for official life is evident from a glance at his Parliamentary career.

In 1847 he entered Parliament as M.P. for Herefordshire, having been for some time a Poor-Law Commissioner. He was Secretary to the Board of Control from November, 1847, to May, 1848, when he was appointed Under-Secretary for the Home Department. In July, 1850, he became one of the Secretaries to the Treasury, which office he held until the resignation of Lord John Russell's ministry in February, 1852. At the election of that year he was an unsuccessful candidate for Herefordshire, and at Peterborough soon afterwards; but, upon the death of his father, in February, 1855, he obtained the seat which the late baronet had occupied in Parliament, as member for the Radnor boroughs. Upon the memorable resignation of the Chancellorship of the Exchequer by Mr. Gladstone in February, 1855, Sir G. C. Lewis was appointed to that office, and then filled the important post of Home Secretary. Such a man, it was evident, must have had some sort of official aptitude; must have been something more than a respectable Whig baronet, or a decent literary man. He could not have been in office so long unless he had made his mark as an administrator. It is not mere favouritism that pitches men into foremost places in Parliament. A premier may be a nonentity, as was the Earl of Liverpool, or the Duke of Portland; but there must be merit in his officers, or he and his Cabinet would cut a sad figure. Writing in 1817, of the new ministry, Lord Ward says, "Their prodigious success, which, without at all meaning to deny their merits and abilities, must be allowed by all reasonable men to have been vastly beyond their merits, and beyond their abilities, had made their underlings insolent, and the House too obedient." Well, in these days noble lords cannot thus write. Ministers don't achieve great successes; indeed, they find it hard to hold their own; and if in talent for debate and legislation they are no match for their opponents, they may be sure that their term of office is not for long. Lord Palmerston, when Premier for the first time, tried to do all the work himself, and hence it was he broke down. In the formation of his second Cabinet he showed more sagacity. "Whenever difficult times come," writes the noble lord whom I have already quoted, "the greatest speaker in the House of Commons must have considerable weight;" and the greater the oratorical power of the Cabinet—other things being equal—the greater is the chance of its stability and success. As a debater Sir Cornewall Lewis most wonderfully improved. When he first took his place on the Treasury benches he seemed the incarnation of red tape—just the sort of man to sit in a dark, dingy closet in Downing Street, and read official reports and parliamentary blue books all day long. I could imagine he could write one with the greatest ease.

I am sure the "Edinburgh" under his management grew as dull as one—duller it could not be. The learned gentleman looked as if he had studied, and written, and read till all life had left him. "There was no speculation in his eye;" he looked brown and mouldy, as if he knew little of fresh air and the light of day. Were he ever taken poorly in the House of Commons you would have exclaimed—as was said by a wit of another inveterate parliamentarian—"Give him the journals to smell to." He spoke in a slow, solemn, uninteresting way; and even when he was Chancellor of the Exchequer, and had the mysteries of a budget to unfold, it seemed impossible for him to rouse himself into life, yet it would not have been difficult for him to have done so. Outwardly, he was tall and well formed—a man in the prime of life; nor did he hesitate, and hem, and haw, and repeat himself; nor could it be said that he was unlearned, and not a master of literary style, nor that the subject was dull and uninteresting, for, if there be one thing more than another in the course of the parliamentary session in which all Englishmen, high and low, rich and poor, take a deep interest, and are really anxious about, it is the Budget; yet, expounded by the right honourable baronet, it must frankly be confessed that it was terribly "stale, flat, and unprofitable." In the ensuing session quite a change for the better seemed to have come over Sir Cornewall Lewis. In debate he turned out to be quite smart and ready, and, on one occasion, he even achieved success as a wit. It may be remembered that on one occasion all England was excited by the great international contest between Sayers and Heenan. Whilst some joyfully looked forward to it as something grand, and worthy of a place in Homeric poems, others deprecated it as a disgrace and a shame to a country so Christian, and advanced, and enlightened as our own. In the British House of Commons both opinions were entertained, and those who maintained the latter were very anxious that the whole affair should be put an end to. Foremost among this latter class was Mr. Scully, an exemplary and well-known Irish M.P. Such a scene he considered most disgraceful, and one that would not be permitted in his country. He indignantly asked if the Home Secretary was not prepared to interfere with the strong arm of the law. Sir Cornewall Lewis's reply was a masterpiece, and his delicate allusion to the use of the shillalagh as, at any rate, quite as censurable as the English fist, was understood, and very much enjoyed by the House, and created considerable amusement. It was certainly one of the happiest repartees administered that session, and showed that if the right hon. baronet wished, he had only to shine as a ready, and accomplished, and smart debater. Practice, in his case, it was clear, makes perfect. Lord Bacon tells us, "Reading makes a full man, writing a correct man, and speaking a ready man;" and as Sir Cornewall Lewis had ample experience of the three systems, he was naturally expected to take a high position. In an eminent degree he abounded with the materials out of which good speaking might be made. His main fault was a tendency to be doctrinaire, to forget the feelings and prejudices of Englishmen, to reason too much like the philosopher in his closet, and to forget to make allowance for the infirmities of human nature. Thus, in the Census Bill he suffered a signal defeat. It was intimated that instead of getting the returns of attendants at churches and chapels of all denominations, on one particular Sunday, as the best way of arriving at the strength of the various religious denominations, the fairest plan would be to get each person to add to the particulars of his age and occupation, his religious profession, Churchman or Dissenter, as the case might be. The Church party rather supported this idea; indeed the suggestion was supposed to have emanated from them. Dissenters immediately took the alarm. Demonstrations and counter-demonstrations were made, and, at length, Sir Cornewall Lewis had to get up in his place in the House of Commons, and state that the obnoxious clause would be withdrawn, adding his surprise that it should have been so unpalatable, as such a clause was in force in other countries, and, as an illustration, he referred to Austria, as unpopular a way of supporting his favourite scheme as, perhaps, could well be imagined. This was a mistake which a man far less learned in ancient history would have avoided; but students, when they turn statesmen, are apt to commit such blunders; they are apt to get cloudy and foggy—a state of mind which the severe ordeal of a British House of Commons is, however, very inimical to, and under the salutary influence of which Sir Cornewall Lewis became more practical and ready every day.

Horatio says to Hamlet—

> "I am more an antique Roman than a Dane."

Sir Cornewall Lewis might have said the same. He reminded you much in some respects of Plutarch's heroes. His classical studies gave him a classical turn. He borrowed the indifference of the ancients to common people and common matters; he coveted not the *profanum vulgus;* he seemed to feel himself above its censure or praise. In a parliamentary crisis he was calm and unmoved. He would have explained away to Brutus the apparition of the phantom which appeared to him as he was about to cross over from Asia with his army, just as did "Cassius, who followed the doctrines of Epicurus, and was accustomed to dispute about them with Brutus." It is a grand thing to have reached that serene height where, lifted up immeasurably above your fellows, you can look down calm and unmoved on the crowd toiling and moiling in the dust and dirt below. Such a state of mind is essential to a first-class official. Sir Cornewall Lewis had reached this point, such was his rare philosophy, and he found it as a precious pearl in value in the Home Office. The minister in that department is not a little subject to popular pressure. Ruined agriculturists—manufacturers and mill-owners on the verge of bankruptcy—metropolitan grievance-mongers, and their name is Legion—all look on him as their prey. He has to tone down the popular mind; to harmonize official denials with non-official demands; in other words, in the language of the railway world, he has to act the part of buffer in the parliamentary train. For this work an antique Roman is much to be preferred to a Dane, and for this work Sir Cornewall Lewis was fitted in an eminent degree.

THE RT. HON. SIDNEY HERBERT.*

As regards ourselves, perhaps the most responsible post in the ministry is the Secretary of the War Department. No one supposes that England is in any danger of invasion—no one supposes for a moment that a successful invasion is possible; but the moral influence of a nation greatly depends upon its display of physical power. If you travel in France, or converse with Germans, or indeed, with almost any class of foreigners, they will tell you that England has seen her best days; that she does not take the high position among the nations of the earth she once assumed; that, in short, we are used up, and only fit to play second fiddle to France. If we ask for proof of this

* Subsequently raised to the Peerage as Lord Herbert.

monstrous assertion we are referred to the Crimean war, but our unfriendly critics forget that if, at the first, our official system broke down—that if our brave men were badly officered—that if we lost them by thousands—that if our stores, and plans, and generals proved old and useless—public opinion had been aroused—efforts, such as only England can make, were made, and that we were in a condition to carry on a successful struggle, just as France, exhausted and weary, was but too glad to have recourse to peace. Let Europe see that our army is in a thoroughly effective state, and Old England will be held in as much honour, and her alliance as earnestly desired, and her displeasure as deeply dreaded, as in the days of Nelson, or Wellington, or the other mighty heroes of the past. But in order that this may be the case, we need a man at the head of the War Department in the House of Commons who is above that fear of giving offence in high quarters which bringeth a snare—a man who thoroughly understands the faults of the present condition of the army—who is desirous to remove them, and who is determined that the English army shall be as effective as it is costly. When Mr. Herbert went to the War Office the public anxiously asked whether he was the man for that post? What was known of him was to his credit. In a small way he had done the State good service. He had been "faithful over a few things." For many a useful reform, for many an extra comfort, the English soldier had to thank him. When out of office he vigorously supported those who advocated a better education of officers, and especially of those for the staff. Besides, he dared to attack the purchase system—that most monstrous of all abuses. A War Minister of determined will, backed by public opinion, might make the English army the most perfect military machine in the world: but to do this he must be prepared to encounter the pains and enmities of the Upper Ten Thousand. He must be prepared to make sacrifices of the severest character: his self-reliance would be put to a very terrible trial, and in Parliament he would be worried almost to death. Even at the Horse Guards —where, from the position of the present Commander-in-Chief, he might naturally look for sympathy and aid, he would receive nothing but discouragement. In the many debates which have taken place in the House of Lords, his Royal Highness the Commander-in-Chief did not conceal his bias in favour of the present system, and indeed he has often confessed his strong reluctance to undertake the responsibility of selecting deserving officers, and promoting them over the heads of the wealthy but less deserving. In Spenser's "Fairy Queen" we read of a philosopher who argues with a giant; the giant has an iron mace and knocks him down. Will Mr. Sidney Herbert submit thus to be knocked down? Such was the question asked in many quarters when he commenced his career of army reform.

Mr. Herbert was one of the governing classes. The

right honourable gentleman, born in 1810, was son of the eleventh Earl of Pembroke by his second wife, the only daughter of Count Woronzow, and was half-brother and heir-presumptive to the present earl. I am particular in giving Mr. Herbert's genealogy, because it was a favourite cry of the beery politicians of London that Odessa was spared because Sidney Herbert's wife was a Russian princess. Small politicians made considerable capital out of the charge, and one daily paper—the intelligent reader can guess which—laid considerable stress upon the fact. The real truth is, that in 1846 Sidney Herbert married a daughter of Major-General A'Court, a lady well known for a life of untiring activity and energy in the walks of philanthropy more especially fitted for female coöperation and aid.

It is said a change of blood improves the breed. The nobles of Spain intermarry and become intellectually and physically weak. The French occupation of Hamburg is said much to have aided in the production of a better race of citizens in that pleasant and thriving town. Speaking of the celebrated Irish Brigade, Lord Cloncurry tells us in his memoirs, "There could not be a better example of crossing blood than was afforded by these gentlemen. They were generally the offspring of Irish fathers and French mothers, and were the finest models of men I ever recollect to have seen." The fact that the true-born Englishman has in his veins the blood of almost every country under heaven, may account for the beauty and energy of which we boast, and which even rival nations reluctantly confess. I believe there is nothing like the infusion into an English family of a little genuine northern blood. Sidney Herbert was emphatically a case in point. There was undoubtedly something very fine and vigorous about his personal appearance. He was the very model of the modern English gentleman;—not the port-wine drinking, anti-French, Church-and-King man of the last generation, under whom the nation was going headlong to the devil, but of a man born in affluence, whom Christianity has made decent, and whose intellectual and bodily powers have been strengthened and matured by the habits of a life. At the same time, he exhibited all the disadvantages of having been brought up in a class, and accustomed to look at everything in a distorted light. Such men are like men coming out of a cave, and it is long before they discern things as they really are. Hence, as in the case of Lord Stanley, half their time is devoted to unlearning the preposterous notions acquired at home, or at school or college. The parliamentary career of Mr. Herbert illustrated this. He began life in 1832 as a Conservative. The first occasion of his taking part in a debate in Parliament was on the 20th of June, 1834, upon a motion for the second reading of a bill for the admission of Dissenters to the Universities. Mr. Estcourt, the predecessor of Mr. Gladstone in the representation of the University of Oxford, having moved as an amendment that the bill be read a second time that day six months, he was seconded by Mr. Sidney Herbert, who opposed the measure on the ground that, in these times of dissension of every species, the admission of Dissenters to the Universities would be nothing less than opening these institutions to conflicting opinions, and making them the arena of religious animosity ! ! ! Again, up to the year 1841, Mr. Herbert's opinions on the principle which should guide us in our commercial intercourse with the nations were decidedly protectionist. He opposed the motion of the then Whig government, to substitute for the sliding scale an eight-shilling fixed duty on the imports of corn, as well as Lord John Russell's proposal for the reduction of the duties on foreign sugar; but when Peel turned round, Sidney Herbert, who had been successively Secretary to the Admiralty and Secretary at War, with a seat in the Cabinet, turned round with him; and in a debate in 1846, on the motion of Sir Robert Peel for a committee of the whole House on the customs and corn importation acts—having been taunted by the Earl of March with an abandonment of his oft-expressed convictions, the right honourable gentleman confessed that, after the most mature deliberation, he had been compelled to take the course he had. Of course Mr. Herbert's constituency was protectionist to the backbone all the same; and when a general election came in 1847, an attempt was made to displace him in the representation of the county. Mr. Herbert's influence in Wiltshire was enormous; and Wiltshire, in the person of its representative, decided in favour of Free Trade. Then came the Crimean war, when one statesman after another became bankrupt. The Duke of Newcastle became the scapegoat, and was sent forth into the desert, bearing on his shoulders the sins of the Ministry. In the unpopularity of that period Sidney Herbert had his share; nor was his unpopularity altogether undeserved. It is clear that he relied upon the misstatements of the officials, and contended that our army was in a prosperous condition, when in fact it was the reverse; that he, and those who acted with him, never thought we should have had a real war; and that, when war actually broke out, they were not prepared to carry it on with vigour, or to punish Russia. This was another disadvantage Sidney Herbert experienced on account of his birth and breeding—he had lived in an ideal world, he had never stood face to face with the English nation. Had he lived and toiled as the people live and toil, he would have had a clearer perception of the facts of the case, and of the aim of the nation. The people is not a profoundly learned or acutely logical body; but they had the idea, and in this they were right, that Turkey was wronged—that Russia was an aggressive power, and they believed that as Russia had been the mainstay of despotism on the continent, that a war that would have crippled Russia would have aided the cause of freedom and of man all over Europe. Under such an idea alone was war justifiable. Our statesmen entered on it with no such idea, and by large classes the war cry was reechoed for even still less worthy ends—as a means of plunder after inglorious years of inactivity, half-pay, and peace. The war came, and the people grew mad as the *Times* told them what Sidney Herbert and the Government denied. Mr. Roebuck's motion was carried, and down went the Aberdeen Cabinet like a ship at sea. We remember well the night of the debate. Generally, when the tellers come up to announce the result, they are cheered by the winning party as only Englishmen can cheer. For a wonder, on that occasion not a cheer was heard! There was silence, amazement, wonder everywhere; and then a short derisive laugh, as M.P.'s saw the vaunted coalition melt into thin air. They did well to be silent and amazed. Thoughtful men were already asking—of this victory who was to reap the fruits? Were the Derbyites to be placed in power; or was the Great Britain of the nineteenth century, the mother of colonies compared with which those of imperial Rome were pigmies—the asylum of liberty denied a home elsewhere, to be the appanage of the House of Bedford; or was there to be but a shuffle of the cards—Palmerston premier, in the place of Lord Aberdeen; Lord Panmure in the room of the Duke of Newcastle; Fred. Peel, *vice* Sidney Herbert? Were the old faces again to come back to us? was the old fearful system of administration again to be continued? was the old hideous weight of aristocracy again, like a nightmare, to press upon the land? was there to be no hope of a better state of things? Well, there was then silence, for who was there to cheer? Lord John Russell ignominiously escaped from the sinking ship. Sidney Herbert and his colleagues at any rate bravely stuck to their posts. Sidney Herbert was driven from office that Mr. Frederick Peel might fill his vacant place. We doubt whether the nation gained anything by the change.

A man who is born to enormous wealth, like Sidney Herbert, owes much to society. A landlord who knows nothing of his property but to draw his rents from it—who merely comes into the country to hunt, and then spends an idle and vicious career in the capitals of Europe, is the most dangerous possible character; and in times of fierce political excitement would precipitate anarchy and revolution. But the landed class have grown philanthropic. Their aim is to build churches, to form schools, to caution their labourers against beer-shops, to send out distressed needlewomen to Australia, to turn ragged boys into decent and industrious shoeblacks, and to teach St. Giles the value of a cheap bath and a clean shirt. Of this class of philanthropists Lord Shaftesbury may be placed at the head; next, perhaps, was Sidney Herbert. He did as much, possibly, as could be done, in mitigating the many hardships of the British poor, and while in office it must be remembered that he did much for the improvement of the soldier's condition, and that it was he who broke through routine, despised the clamour of the religious press as to infecting the army with Puseyism, and suffered Florence Nightingale and her noble company to proceed on their mission of mercy and love.

But I have not yet pointed him out to you. You will see him seated side by side with Palmerston and Russell and his colleagues, on the right hand of the Speaker. It is the time appointed for private business. Military men are numerous in the House, and as every man of them has his own peculiar views, which he is anxious to see put in practice, Mr. Herbert has enough to do to answer the numerous interrogatories addressed to him on all sides. Look at him on his legs. What a contrast to General Peel, or Mr. Frederick Peel, or Sir Joshua Ramsden, and other amiable mediocrities! What strength seems to lie in his well-formed and manly figure! How full is his face of power, and sharpness, and determination! How clearly and pleasantly he speaks! In debate, how ready and practical he is! What a clear ringing voice he has! He may not be a great orator, but he is certainly a useful and able man, and such was the verdict pronounced on him—when he died as it were in life's prime.

THE END.

www.ingramcontent.com/pod-product-compliance
Lightning Source LLC
Chambersburg PA
CBHW032301280326
41932CB00009B/659
* 9 7 8 3 3 3 7 1 5 6 1 0 7 *